Trafficking and Women's Rights

Women's Rights in Europe Series
Series Standing Order ISBN 1–4039–4988–3

You can receive future titles in this series as they are published by placing a standing order. Please contact your bookseller or, in case of difficulty, write to us at the address below with your name and address, the title of the series and the ISBN quoted above.

Customer Services Department, Macmillan Distribution Ltd, Houndmills, Basingstoke, Hampshire RG21 6XS, England

Trafficking and Women's Rights

Edited by

Christien L. van den Anker
Principal Lecturer in Politics
University of the West of England

and

Jeroen Doomernik
Lecturer
Institute for Migration and Ethnic Studies
University of Amsterdam

Series Foreword
Yakın Ertürk
UN Special Rapporteur on Violence against Women

First published in 2006 by
PALGRAVE MACMILLAN
Houndmills, Basingstoke, Hampshire RG21 6XS and
175 Fifth Avenue, New York, N.Y. 10010
Companies and representatives throughout the world

PALGRAVE MACMILLAN is the global academic imprint of the Palgrave
Macmillan division of St. Martin's Press, LLC and of Palgrave Macmillan Ltd.
Macmillan® is a registered trademark in the United States, United Kingdom
and other countries. Palgrave is a registered trademark in the European
Union and other countries.

ISBN-13: 978–1–4039–4995–0
ISBN-10: 1–4039–4995–6

This book is printed on paper suitable for recycling and made from fully
managed and sustained forest sources.

A catalogue record for this book is available from the British Library.

Library of Congress Cataloging-in-Publication Data

Trafficking and women's rights / edited by Christien L. van den Anker,
Jeroen Doomernik.
    p. cm.—(Women's rights in Europe)
Includes bibliographical references and index.
ISBN 1–4039–4995–6 (cloth)
    1. Human smuggling – Europe. 2. Prostitution – Europe.
3. Forced labor – Europe. 4. Women's rights – Europe.
5. Human smuggling – Europe – Prevention. I. Anker, Christien. van den,
1965– II. Doomernik, Jeroen. III. Series.

HQ281.T714 2006
306.74'2094—dc22   2006044789

10 9 8 7 6 5 4 3 2
15 14 13 12 11 10 09 08 07

Printed and bound in Great Britain by
Antony Rowe Ltd, Chippenham and Eastbourne

Contents

Foreword

This series is a timely initiative to counter the mounting opposition and challenge to the progress made thus far in transforming mainstream human rights discourse from a feminist perspective. Expansion of the concept of human rights to address violations experienced by women due specifically to their sex has considerably altered international and domestic law, and demystified the public/private distinction that justified women's subordination.

The Convention on the Elimination of All Forms of Discrimination against Women, adopted in 1979 by the UN General Assembly, was an important step in the recognition of the universality of human rights, a view that became officially endorsed at the Vienna World Conference on Human Rights in 1993. Also referred to as the International Bill of Rights of Women, the Convention enjoys the ratification of 180 member states today. Yet, after over quarter of a century since the adoption of the Convention and the numerous human rights instruments that followed, what remains universal is the gross violation of women's rights worldwide.

Notwithstanding the notable progress achieved in the advancement of women in the past decades, women in all parts of the world still face obstacles in accessing rights, such as the rights to education, health, political participation, property and to decide over matters related to their sexuality, reproduction, marriage, divorce and child custody, among others. Women's bodies are the zones of wars and the sites of politics and policies as revealed in the armed conflicts around the world, transgressions over their reproductive and sexual rights, trafficking, dress codes as well as immigration and refugee policies, etc. Even in countries where traditional patriarchy is transformed, as in the European experience, gender-based discrimination and violence against women continues to persist in modified, subtle and discrete forms.

In many of the countries in the European region, where human rights standards and institutions are in place, women's formal political participation is still extremely low, reproductive rights are an area of continuous contestation and struggle, social entitlements are at risk and single mothers and minority and immigrant women are at the highest risk of poverty. We need to learn more and understand how gender hierarchies are reproduced under diverse conditions and in different places.

The books in this series promise to do that. They illustrate the need for increased attention from researchers, NGOs and policymakers throughout Europe for these instances of violations of women's rights.

This series comes at a time when the EU enlargement process has shown that respect for women's rights within different regions in Europe is diverse. It is fascinating to see that specific rights for women are protected better in some countries than others, while it may also be the case that in the same region other rights for women are less well observed. By illustrating these trends and inconsistencies, this series allows for comparison across the region as well as for reflection on the policy gaps across Europe.

The four books cover the areas of trafficking, political participation, social entitlements and reproductive rights in detail, from a multidisciplinary perspective and with contributions from activists, professionals, academics and policymakers. State-of-the-art debates are reflected on and burning issues in women's rights are brought together in one series for the first time. The depth of the arguments, coverage of recent developments and clear focus on their implications for gender equality are most commendable aspects of the series. The books push forward the agenda for all of us and remind us that women's rights are not protected equally and intrinsically. In fact, the contributions confirm that we still have a way to go to achieve women's equality in contemporary Europe. This unique and compelling collection is a must for everyone striving for rights, equality and justice!

Yakın Ertürk
UN Special Rapporteur on Violence against Women

Acknowledgements

This series is the result of the involvement of a large number of people in the work of the Network for European Women's Rights (NEWR). We would like to thank them all for their input, although we cannot name them all here.

We want to thank especially those who spent time and energy discussing the four themes of NEWR during a series of intensive and engaging workshops across Europe and in the final conference in Birmingham.

We would also like to thank Professor Donna Dickenson for initiating the project and leading it for two years, and Christien L. van den Anker for taking over this leadership for the final year of the project, as well as the project partners Dr Itziar Alkorta Idiakez, Professor Francesca Bettio, Dr Krassimira Daskalova, Dr Jeroen Doomernik, Dr Aitziber Emaldi Cirión, Dr Anne Maria Holli, Professor Dr Maria Katsiyianni-Papakonstantinou, Dr Lukas H. Meyer and Dr Irina Novikova for their contributions.

We could not have done the project without the commitment and persistence of Audrey Guichon and the consistent support of Jose Vicente. We thank Rebecca Shah for taking over from Audrey in the final months of the NEWR project and for her thorough editing work of all four volumes in this series.

We thank the European Commission for funding the NEWR project under its 5th Framework Programme.

We hope that this series of books will contribute positively to the debate on women's rights and to improving the lives of all women in Europe.

With regard to this book, *Trafficking and Women's Rights*, we would like to thank those who participated in the workshops on this topic. Unfortunately, the participants are too numerous to name, but it is they who made this project possible. Without their input the project and this volume would have been very different. In particular we are grateful to the many activists and NGO representatives who gave up valuable time to enlighten academics about the burning issues in trafficking across Europe. These on-the-ground perspectives were invaluable in determining the content and issues which this book addresses, and it was they that ensured that the focus of the workshops and the book remained on issues which are fundamental to women in Europe today.

We would also like to thank the institutions that hosted the workshops, the University of Birmingham, the University of Amsterdam and the University of Siena.

* * *

The editors and publishers would like to thank the following for their kind permission to include copyright material:

Anna Marie Gallagher, 'Triply Exploited: Female Victims of Trafficking Networks'. Reprinted with permission of Georgetown University and *Georgetown Immigration Law Journal* © 2004.

Notes on the Contributors

Bridget Anderson is a senior research officer and research programme head at the Centre on Migration, Policy and Society at the University of Oxford. She is author of *Dirty Work, the Global Politics of Domestic Labour* (2000). She is currently working, with Julia O'Connell Davidson, on a project examining the markets for migrant sex and domestic workers.

Christien L. van den Anker taught International Relations for five years at Sussex University. From 2001 to 2006 she was Deputy Director of the Centre for the Study of Global Ethics at the University of Birmingham. She now works as a lecturer at the University of the West of England. Her research interests are global justice, human rights and the ethical implications of globalisation. Her most recent publications include: (ed. with R. K. Smith) *Essentials of Human Rights* (2005) and (ed.) *The Political Economy of New Slavery* (2004).

Julie Bindel is a freelance journalist and researcher. Most of her research focuses on local and international sex industries. She writes regularly for the *Guardian* newspaper, *La Republica* and numerous magazines. She is the co-editor of *The Map of My Life. The Story of Emma Humpreys* (2002).

Donna Dickenson is Professor of Medical Ethics and Humanities at the University of London, where she is also Executive Director of the Birkbeck Advanced Studies Centre in the Humanities. She has written extensively on women's reproductive rights, including *Property, Women and Politics* (1997) and a number of articles in international refereed journals. At present she is working on a new book and several articles concerning property in the body.

Jeroen Doomernik is lecturer in Political Science and senior researcher at the Institute for Migration and Ethnic Studies, University of Amsterdam. He has published on Turkish Islam in The Netherlands and Germany, Soviet Jewish immigrants in Berlin, and was commissioned by the Dutch government and several international organisations to evaluate in a comparative perspective immigration and integration policies. His current research is on irregular migration in general and human smuggling in particular.

Anna Marie Gallagher is an American lawyer based in Spain, who teaches refugee and migration law and procedures, access to justice, and gender and protection issues. She has practised criminal defence, human rights, and immigration and refugee law during the last two decades in the US, Central America and Europe. She is coordinator of the International Coalition on the Detention of Refugees, Asylum Seekers and Migrants.

Giulia Garofalo is writing a PhD thesis on the Political Economy of Prostitution in Europe at the School of Social Sciences, Media and Cultural Studies, University of East London. She has been involved in feminist, lesbian and sex workers' rights politics in Italy, the UK and the Netherlands.

Heleen de Jonge van Ellemeet works as researcher at the Bureau of the Dutch National Rapporteur on Trafficking in Human Being. The National Rapporteur and her bureau advise the Dutch government on the issue of human trafficking and formulate policy recommendations for the fight against trafficking. She carried out the first BNRM research in the Netherlands on exploitation in the workplace other than in the sex industry.

Helga Konrad, a former Austrian Federal Minister for Women's Issues, was appointed OSCE Special Representative on Combating Trafficking in Human Beings in May 2004. From 2000 to 2004 she chaired the Stability Pact Task Force on Trafficking in Human Beings for South-Eastern Europe. In 1996 she hosted the first EU conference on Trafficking in Women for the Purpose of Sexual Exploitation.

Ilse van Liempt is a PhD student at the Institute for Migration and Ethnic Studies, University of Amsterdam. Her research is on human smuggling towards the Netherlands and includes interviews with smuggled migrants from Iraq, the Horn of Africa and the former Soviet Union.

Julia O'Connell Davidson is Professor of Sociology at the University of Nottingham. She has been involved in research on various aspects of the sex trade for over a decade and is author of *Prostitution, Power and Freedom* (1998) and *Children in the Global Sex Trade* (2005). She is currently working on a project, with Bridget Anderson, exploring the markets for migrant sex and domestic workers in the UK and Spain.

Adrienne Reilly has worked as a research assistant and associate of Professor Fionnuala Ní Aoláin, the current Director of the newly established Transitional Justice Institute (TJI) at the University of Ulster since 2002. Her main research focus is on emergency laws and gender issues. She is currently undertaking doctoral work on female sexual slavery.

Monika Smit works as senior researcher at the Bureau of the Dutch National Rapporteur on Trafficking in Human Beings (BNRM). The task of the National Rapporteur and her bureau is to inform the Dutch government on the issue of human trafficking and to formulate policy recommendations for the fight against trafficking. Among other things Monika Smit coordinates and supervises the research activities at BNRM and gives presentations on human trafficking and related issues for national and international audiences.

Gillian Wylie is a lecturer on the MPhil in Peace Studies programme at the Irish School of Ecumenics, Trinity College Dublin, teaching international politics and gender studies. Her research on trafficking focuses on the ethics of trafficking research and counter-trafficking networks. She is a member of Ireland en Route, a network of Irish non-governmental organisations and statutory bodies responding to trafficking in Ireland.

Introduction

Christien L. van den Anker and Jeroen Doomernik

Trafficking in women and girls is an issue that affects the whole of Europe (in its widest sense) as countries of origin, transfer and destination or a combination of these. The Network for European Women's Rights (NEWR) project brought together women from across Europe to identify burning issues for research and policymaking in the area of women's rights. The themes of NEWR were political participation, social entitlements, reproductive rights and trafficking. On each theme we held two workshops: the first discussed a variety of country reports by NGO representatives and some research papers, whereas the second discussed a set of commissioned research papers on the burning issues coming out of the first workshop. For each theme, we produced a report and identified areas for research in a programme of further study (see www.NEWR.bham.ac.uk). The results of the project were presented at the final conference, where many participants gave further papers on trafficking and the other three themes of NEWR. The Palgrave series on women's rights has published volumes on each of the NEWR themes; the combined expertise from the network in the area of trafficking is collected in this volume.

The main findings on trafficking are as follows. First, the debate has moved on considerably since we first started the NEWR project. Since 2002, when the debate was largely deadlocked due to the diverging moral stances on the issue of prostitution, we have moved on to a period where we have seen the first internationally agreed definition of trafficking in the Palermo Protocol (adopted in 2000, which came into force in 2003), a European Convention on Action against Trafficking (2005) and several further initiatives to spur governments into action: the OSCE produced an action plan on trafficking (2003) and a handbook on national referral protocols (2004) in order to arrive at

1

harmonised protection measures for trafficking victims. Other relevant developments were the appointment of a UN Special Rapporteur on Trafficking in Human Beings, especially Women and Children, and the nomination of an Expert Group on Trafficking at the European level, which reported extensively and made specific recommendations to governments.

The latest research shows that trafficking occurs in industries other than the sex industry; this was known in relation to domestic workers, but is now being researched in a wider context by the ILO, Anti-Slavery International, London, and academic researchers.

Widening the applicability of law enforcement and victim support to industries other than the sex industry raises issues such as defining the contributing elements of trafficking in these other contexts and the gender distribution of the cases and provisions. NEWR found that there were wider issues around data collection and storage, from both an ethical and a comparative perspective. We further concluded that combating trafficking cannot be seen as an issue for national governments alone; instead, the processes of globalisation and regionalisation need to be studied in the context of demand for cheap, flexible and compliant labour and the supply of people who are willing to take the risk of migrating under less than ideal circumstances to fulfil these demands. The transition in Eastern Europe and the former Soviet Union is also an important part of this research.

All chapters in this book relate to subsets of these themes. In Chapter 1 Julia O'Connell Davidson and Bridget Anderson set out their objections to the use of the term trafficking. Although it may be seen to cover an aspect of human rights not otherwise considered, they argue that the fact that trafficking has become big business for middle-class professionals both reflects and reinforces very serious definitional, conceptual and political problems with the term. Their chapter therefore sets out a list of problems with the definition of trafficking in the UN Protocol to Prevent, Suppress and Punish Trafficking in Persons (the Palermo Protocol). The definition used in the Palermo Protocol describes a process including various actions and is therefore difficult to use in practice. Moreover, it does not define 'exploitation of the prostitution of others or other forms of sexual exploitation', 'other forms of coercion' or 'abuse of power or of a position of vulnerability'. Another problem is that by being attached to the Convention on Transnational Organised Crime the Palermo Protocol treats trafficking as a subset of illegal migration. This assumes a clear line between legal and illegal migration, whereas in practice this is much more fluid. Likewise, the Protocol generally lacks a definition of exploitation. This relates to the highly disputed nature of acceptable employment practices.

Another area this chapter identifies as overlooked in the debates on trafficking is the state's role in creating the conditions in which employers benefit from using trafficked or otherwise unfree labour. By not insisting on labour laws in certain areas of work, the state creates niches where formal protection of workers is not available. The chapter shows that in the context of the role of the state as controlling migration, an important distinction is the one between smuggling and trafficking. In practice, however, this distinction is more opaque than that between legal and illegal migration trajectories.

The authors then discuss whether the term trafficking adds anything to our understanding of violations of the human rights of migrants and argue that trafficking creates moral hierarchies of 'deserving' and 'less deserving' victims. Furthermore, the situating of trafficking in the context of transnational criminal networks allows for anti-migration policies to be passed as pro-human rights policies.

In Chapter 2 Ilse van Liempt analyses the attempt to define trafficking in the Palermo Protocol by giving an historical overview of the term, comparing recent definitions in international documents with the definition and usage of the term smuggling. Van Liempt starts by pointing to the difficulties in collecting and comparing data on trafficking and smuggling. With trafficking legislation lacking in some countries and without systematic collaboration between countries, illicit activities like trafficking and smuggling are very hard to track.

Over time, the definitions of trafficking have also changed. The issue of consent has entered the most recent UN definition whereas the 1949 Convention considered all persons working in prostitution to be victims. Van Liempt, like O'Connell-Davidson and Anderson, objects to the clear demarcation between voluntary and forced migration trajectories; as she shows, women working in prostitution often know they will work in the sex industry yet willingly migrate as they expect conditions to be better than in their country of origin. In reality they are shocked by the levels of violence and exploitation present. She concludes that we should avoid simplifications into dichotomies of forced or voluntary migration in the context of trafficking.

Van Liempt then discusses the issue of how to measure exploitation in order to establish that trafficking has taken place. The notion of exploitation is the distinguishing feature between trafficking and smuggling. She reiterates the point made in Chapter 1 that labour standards differ between countries and that exploitation is therefore very hard to define. Van Liempt also refers to the lack of regulation in certain sectors and in the informal economy. She further argues that barriers to legal migration routes and the resulting debt of migrating through illegal channels leave people vulnerable to exploitation.

Van Liempt shows that restrictive migration policies make women especially vulnerable to trafficking. By deporting women without giving them the opportunity to identify themselves as victims of trafficking, the police not only fail to protect them but also forgo information from women willing to act as witnesses against their traffickers.

The final section of the chapter discusses the organised crime angle of the Palermo Protocol. Van Liempt shows that the organised crime focus of anti-trafficking policies seemingly justifies anti-migration strategies whereas in practice it is not clear to what extent organised crime is involved in trafficking. In conclusion, Van Liempt argues for a broader approach to the trafficking debate by placing it in the wider context of migration. Moreover, the non-*refoulement* principle (protecting migrants from being returned to an unsafe country of origin) should be recognised in the context of trafficking and smuggling in order to protect human rights of victims of trafficking.

In Chapter 3, Donna Dickenson argues that the issue of consent in prostitution is more problematic than has been recognised in the current debate on trafficking. She addresses two core assumptions in the prostitution debate: 1) that the sale of sexual services is like the sale of any other good or service; and 2) that, by and large, women involved in trafficking for prostitution freely consent to sell such services. In respect of the first assumption, Dickenson refers to parallels in Marxist arguments on unfree labour, arguments on adaptive preferences and feminist theory on the social construction of women. In respect of the second, Dickenson further refers to legal systems making exceptions for sexual exchanges and to arguments in bioethics on property in the body. Her conclusion is that we need to break away from the tradition of seeing property in things as the model for thinking about property in the body, body parts or services like sex or surrogate motherhood.

In Chapter 4 Giulia Garafalo develops a feminist economic perspective on trafficking in the sex industry. With economic theory not making progress on the concept or practice of trafficking the question is raised of whether it should expand into this area. The author shows that some specific parts of economic reasoning, especially a political economy approach, may contribute to developing a wider perspective on trafficking without having the repressive effects of the current positions in the debate. Garafalo develops the tools of institutional and feminist economics in response to the only existing model of economic theory of prostitution: the Edlund and Kom model. This model views prostitution as complementary to marriage. In other words, every woman may either sell reproductive sex in the marriage market or non-reproductive sex in the prostitution market. This model is criticised for not recognising the considerable differences in the organisation of prostitution across space and time. The chapter develops an approach to trafficking as a pre- and post-contractual situation and critically engages with the question of the extent to which sexual services are different from other kinds of exchanges. It concludes by stating that the contribution political economy may offer to the understanding of and the fight against 'trafficking' is based on the idea that gender (or other) power asymmetry between agents takes shape in the effective contractual regimes. Therefore, in contrast to the anti-'trafficking' policies currently in force, promoting the freedom to exit from work and promoting freedom of movement should become priorities in anti-'trafficking' policies.

In Chapter 5, Gillian Wylie analyses the present methodologies in research into trafficking and identifies several dilemmas. These vary between the obvious difficulties of researching an illegal activity to the lack of agreed methods and definitions and the ideological divides within the trafficking field. The chapter engages in particular with the situation of trafficking in Ireland and develops a research methodology relevant to the Irish situation.

The recommendations Wylie makes are that a research methodology is needed which has at its foundations an initial, workable definition of trafficking. The research must be inventive, exhaustive, ethical and collaborative. The best way forward is to forge a research coalition with those agencies that need the data in order to further their own service provision and advocacy work on trafficking, as advocated by feminist researchers. Forming a research coalition requires that the researcher views the researched as her primary resource, recognising them as agents and not as hapless victims. The shared knowledge such research produces will be used by the coalition as they seek to further their other aims – for example, providing best practice in service provision to trafficked women and children and possessing sound information which can be used to lobby governments for appropriate legislative changes.

In Chapter 6, Adrienne Reilly sets out the case for making trafficking offences part of anti-slavery legislation. Her reasons are that the shift in the prosecution of slavery away from a crime under the freedom from slavery legislation has now become persecuted under the term trafficking. This has diluted the debate and provides fewer obligations to prosecute and protect women from the crime of slavery. The chapter shows how freedom from slavery has become the customary and non-derogable right it now is under international law. It then outlines how sexual slavery is still a major problem and sketches how current international law deals with the phenomenon. The chapter then goes on to criticise the persecution for sexual slavery under anti-trafficking legislation and argues for the return to anti-slavery legislation. In conclusion, Reilly proposes setting up a new slavery convention to deal explicitly with new forms of slavery currently occurring.

In Chapter 7, Helga Konrad presents a comparison between policy-making on combating trafficking in the Netherlands, Sweden, Italy and the United States. Her aim is to review the practice of the specific policies in order to overcome the emotive stand-off in the trafficking debate. Her conclusion is that for anti-trafficking measures to be effective, fighting it must not be seen primarily or exclusively from the perspective of national security, the main interest of which is to prevent illegal immigration. The emphasis on border controls, deterrence and immediate deportation or repatriation of victims of trafficking is often the beginning of a vicious circle of re-trafficking.

Konrad's in-depth research shows that efforts to control migration and emphasise criminal prosecution run counter to the needs and rights of the victims of trafficking. The construction of illegal migrants enables criminal organisations to profit due to the fear of and vulnerability to deportation. Traffickers also take advantage of the demand for cheap, unprotected labour and the promotion of sex tourism in many countries.

Konrad further argues that trafficking in human beings is both a law enforcement issue and a human rights concern. Policies must address them in conjunction in order to be successful. She recommends intensive training of law enforcement officers, both front-line police and special investigators, and of prosecutors and judges.

All countries are called upon to revise their criminal law and clarify their definitions in line with the Palermo Protocol. This also has an impact on victim/witness support programmes and protection. Central to the policy development process, according to Konrad, is assistance to and protection of victims of trafficking. In turn this will enable better law enforcement through wider availability of witnesses. These measures need to go beyond existing provision. Konrad holds that victims need comprehensive social and economic support, but also legal assistance. The legalisation of the status of a trafficked person is a crucial element in any effective victim and witness protection strategy. This also includes family reunification in order to protect close relatives from repercussions. (See also Chapter 9.)

States must also play a key role in changing the perception of victims of human trafficking. Konrad calls for a 'truly comprehensive and multi-pronged' approach addressing poverty reduction, education and human rights protection, as well as addressing issues of corruption, organised crime, immigration and legal reform. Short- and long-term measures both need to be addressed. Konrad concludes that we need fast-acting counter-measures and raise issues of the root causes: the global inequalities in the distribution of jobs, resources and wealth, despite these being 'complex, difficult and forbidding'.

In Chapter 8, Julie Bindel calls for the eradication of the false distinctions between pornography, prostitution and trafficking, while resisting any alliance with the Moral Right. She argues strongly against the trend towards the mainstreaming into everyday life of pornographic imagery, the idea that prostitution can well exist without the involvement of (organised) crime, and should never be seen separately from the exploitation of gender inequalities in our societies. She further argues that there are risks involved in a disproportionate focus on trafficking for prostitution. In doing so, researchers and policymakers abandon the non-trafficked, but nevertheless abused prostituted woman.

In Chapter 9, Anna Marie Gallagher advocates the rights of women to claim asylum after having been trafficked. Her purpose is to discuss avenues to obtain legal status in destination countries for women who fear returning to their home country or who cannot return because of economic hardship. The chapter first provides a general background to trafficking, including a discussion of the relevant legal instruments. It then discusses asylum protection for survivors of trafficking, and includes an overview of cases from several countries around the world in which such status has been considered and in some cases granted. The chapter concludes with an overview of selected countries' special trafficking visas, with an analysis of their weaknesses and strengths and suggestions for improvement consistent with human rights concerns. In cases where women can prove eligibility, asylum can and should be pursued as an avenue of relief for those who cannot comply with requirements for special trafficking visas. Asylum may be the only relief available to victims of trafficking, many of whom suffer serious violations of human rights subsequent to their arrival in the destination countries. Finally, in countries where prostitution is legal, governmental authorities should discuss the possibility of providing work permits for foreign-born women who wish to work as prostitutes. Such permits would greatly reduce the need for smugglers in this area. However, given the dangers that women are exposed to in the sex industry, creation of a permit scheme is not enough. Governments should also regularly monitor the labour and related conditions of foreign-born women working in prostitution to guarantee that all their rights are respected.

In Chapter 10, Christien L. van den Anker shows that 1) prevention is used in widely divergent interpretations, and 2) that even if organisations commit to it, they often mean short-term programmes and not long-term prevention by addressing root causes, while 3) even if they have the rhetoric of long-term prevention, their action in this direction is minimal. Van den Anker argues that in order to combat trafficking successfully, long-tem prevention needs to be taken much more seriously, and governments, international organisations and NGOs need to prioritise setting up collaborative schemes to address this issue.

For some, such a move towards looking at the big picture of injustice in the world distracts from the immediate cause in hand; the role many NGOs see for themselves initially is actively to help people in need. However, after setting up support services and successfully campaigning for changes in the national and international law, NGOs working to combat trafficking are increasingly aware of the need for prevention by addressing the root causes of trafficking. Van den Anker concludes that a cosmopolitan approach is helpful in doing this by providing a bigger picture as the context for the problem of trafficking, recommending policies to be developed and coordinated globally, setting up a set of guiding principles for national policies and in pointing out that by focusing our efforts on creating justice globally, not only trafficking but a lot of other problems caused by globalisation and gender inequality would be solved. Global justice needs to be on the agenda of NGOs working on trafficking as well as other immediate problems.

In Chapter 11, Jeroen Doomernik first explores how the globalisation process leads to greater human mobility. There is the generally officially welcomed migration of the highly skilled but at the same time an increasing emigration pressure among those who are adversely affected by economic globalisation. He goes on to show that among those people who feel compelled to leave their homes, those who find themselves in an irregular position in a more developed country are vulnerable to exploitation. Among these females are particularly vulnerable and not just when they are sex workers. Not only is there a growing supply of migrants from underdeveloped nations, the core countries in the globalisation process experience a considerable and growing demand for cheap, flexible, uncritical workers. Irregular migrants fit those demands perfectly. Doomernik shows that these demands as a rule are gender-biased and, as far as demand for female labour is concerned, this is first and foremost located in the personal service sector, be it sex work or services in and around the home. If these services cannot be provided on a legal basis, these workers run the risk of being virtually invisible and unprotected from abuse. In conclusion, the question is asked if the demand and supply sides can be meaningfully addressed. No clear-cut answer can be offered other than that, at the very minimum, the rights of migrants should be strengthened, e.g. by granting them residence and work permits, for instance through a regularisation process, something which at present is much easier to organise in some European countries than in others. As to the supply side, any recommendation easily states the obvious and they all amount to reducing the need for emigration, which even with the best of efforts is not quickly achieved.

Finally, in Chapter 12 Heleen de Jonge van Ellemeet and Monika Smit discuss the widening agenda of trafficking in industries other than the sex industry by focusing on the specific example of Dutch policymaking. The chapter examines exploitation in labour situations outside the sex industry. The authors call for attention to trafficking for 'other forms of exploitation', without slowing down our efforts to tackle exploitation in the sex industry. The cases they present illustrate that a variety of factors can lead to a situation in which a victim – male or female, adult or minor – provides work or services under the threat of some sort of penalty, be it physical harm, threats to denounce his or her illegal status to the authorities, or other forms of abuse or intimidation. In other words, it is not necessary for a victim to be held in captivity in order to speak of grossly exploitative labour situations. While extremely poor or hazardous working conditions do not constitute exploitation as such in the sense of trafficking as defined in the Palermo Protocol, in combination with restriction of the victim's personal freedom – for instance, due to debt bondage – they can represent a severe violation of human rights.

Even so, the definition of exploitation in labour situations outside the sex industry is not absolutely clear. The authors show that in the Netherlands as in many other countries the dividing line between illegal employment and trafficking for exploitation outside the sex industry is fluid. They argue that we do not need to wait for conceptual clarity before taking action. They recommend striving for agreement on the scope of the term 'other forms of exploitation' on an international, at least European, level. This will assist in building jurisprudence, as well as facilitating international cooperation in trafficking cases.

The authors conclude that in the current political climate, undocumented migrants cannot rely on much compassion in the Netherlands or elsewhere in Europe. Great efforts are made to tackle illegality and, in this repressive climate, it is crucial that the authorities recognise, regard and treat victims of trafficking first and foremost as victims of a crime, including when the exploitation takes place outside the sex industry.

*   *   *

In this book we provide an up-to-date overview of the conceptual developments in the debate on trafficking as well as a critical analysis of the policies being developed across Europe. Eventually, the task is to contribute to combating trafficking through a better understanding of the issues involved. Despite the agreed international definition and a common understanding that victim support and prevention are important in public policy, there are many differences of opinion and barriers to implementation of international agreements, so that that all the policy efforts to combat trafficking have not yet resulted in significantly reducing the numbers of people trafficked in Europe. We hope that this book contributes to the clarifications needed to move forward in this respect.

1
The Trouble with 'Trafficking'

Julia O'Connell Davidson and Bridget Anderson

Why is the need to combat 'trafficking' emphasised so much more strongly in European policy, non-governmental organisation (NGO) and academic discourse than the need to promote and protect migrants' rights? There are two rather different possible answers to this question. First, some commentators would argue that the virtue of the concept of 'trafficking' is that it helps us to identify and combat human rights abuses that would otherwise go unrecognised. The classic example would be that of a teenage girl who is 'befriended' by an older man who seduces her into believing that he can find her well-paid work in a bar or restaurant overseas, then takes her illegally across a border where he sells her to a partner in crime (a pimp or brothel owner), who confiscates her documents and uses physical force to compel her to prostitute. In this example, the concept of trafficking is considered helpful because it recognises the process to which she has been subjected as more than the sum of its parts (deception, abduction, false imprisonment, assault, rape, slavery-like employment practices, etc.), and so allows us to identify the man who befriended and betrayed the girl, and all those who colluded with him along the way, as fully implicated in her abuse. It is also sometimes asserted that women and children feel more trapped and less able to resist 'when the criminal organisations control the whole chain from recruitment, through transportation to the concrete sex exploitation' (EC Justice and Home Affairs, 2001: 3). The supposed value of the concept 'trafficking' is that it can grasp situations in which abuse and exploitation at the point of destination are linked to the use of force or deception within the migration process.

A more cynical answer would be that people are talking about 'trafficking' because it is big business. In saying this, we refer not to the money made by those involved in organising the movement and

11

exploitation of persons by means of deception or coercion, but to the financial and other rewards that trafficking brings to middle-class professionals like us: the jobs (and travel opportunities) created by the ever-growing number of national and international programmes for the recovery, repatriation and reintegration of 'victims of trafficking'; the increased resources made available for border control and other aspects of 'anti-trafficking' law enforcement; the funding for academic and NGO research and conferences and workshops on trafficking; the expanding opportunities for academics and others to secure lucrative consultancy, project/programme evaluation and training contracts; and the opportunities for politicians, bureaucrats and lobbyists to secure bigger budgets or gain prestige or publicity by claiming the issue of trafficking as their own.

Since the adage about glasshouses and stones may spring to mind, let us hasten to add that all those aboard the 'trafficking' gravy train have not joined it out of naked self-interest. Indeed, many people have climbed aboard because they believe that, at this point in time, their more general agenda on human rights may be most effectively pursued through engagement with the issue of 'trafficking'. Even the most committed, humanitarian and selfless NGOs, lobbyists and academics need funding to continue their work, and in a world of scarce resources it is unsurprising if they try to fit their preoccupations with topics that are currently viewed as politically important, 'sexy' and worthy of funding. However, the fact that trafficking has become big business for middle-class professionals both reflects and reinforces very serious definitional, conceptual and political problems with the term 'trafficking'. Indeed, it is because 'trafficking' is so poorly defined that so many individuals and interest groups – often with radically different moral and political goals – are able to claim it as their own. These definitional problems are the focus of this chapter.

Problems with the definition of 'trafficking' provided in the UN Protocol to Prevent, Suppress and Punish Trafficking in Persons (2000)

Until recently, there has been no international agreement as to the proper legal definition of trafficking. However, in November 2000, the United Nations (UN) Convention against Transnational Organised Crime was adopted by the General Assembly, and with it two new protocols – one on smuggling of migrants and one on trafficking in persons. The latter defines trafficking as:

a) The recruitment, transportation, transfer, harbouring or receipt of persons, by means of the threat or use of force or other forms of coercion, of abduction, of fraud, of deception, of the abuse of power or of a position of vulnerability or of the giving or receiving of payments or benefits to achieve the consent of a person having control over another person, for the purpose of exploitation. Exploitation shall include, at a minimum, the exploitation of the prostitution of others or other forms of sexual exploitation, forced labour or services, slavery or practices similar to slavery, servitude or the removal of organs;
b) The consent of a victim of trafficking in persons to the intended exploitation set forth in subparagraph (a) of this article shall be irrelevant where any of the means set forth in subparagraph (a) have been used.[1]

Rather than describing a single, unitary act leading to one specific outcome, 'trafficking in persons' is thus being used as an umbrella term to cover a *process* (recruitment, transportation and control) that can be organised in a variety of ways and involves a range of different actions and outcomes. This, in itself, makes any definition of 'trafficking' difficult to implement in a uniform way, since different individuals may make different decisions as to which particular actions and outcomes, and in which particular combination, should be included under its umbrella. This problem is compounded by the fact that the constituent elements of trafficking may also be deemed to constitute other separate or related phenomena (for instance, the condition of slavery is one of the outcomes included in the protocol definition, but not all enslaved persons are 'victims of trafficking'); and that some of the constituent elements identified in the protocol definition of trafficking themselves present definitional problems within international law (there is no international consensus regarding the definition of 'servitude', or of 'sexual exploitation', for example). But a number of other important issues are fudged over.

Fudge No. 1 – the relationship between trafficking and prostitution

Debate about the relationship between trafficking and prostitution reflects the deep political divisions that surround the issue of prostitution more generally, which is to say divisions on the question of whether prostitution always and necessarily violates women's fundamental human rights to dignity, or whether prostitution can represent a mutual, voluntary contractual exchange between adults, and should therefore be considered as a form of paid work. Because the protocol makes particular and special reference to prostitution and sexual exploitation, but simultaneously places a responsibility on governments to protect the human rights of persons trafficked in sectors other than the sex industry, it can be read as taking a neutral stand on 'the prostitution debate'. Yet this semblance of neutrality is achieved at the expense of precision. For instance, the protocol does not define the phrase 'exploitation of the prostitution of others or other forms of sexual exploitation' because 'government delegates to the negotiations could not agree on a common meaning' (GAATW, 2001: 31). Nor does the protocol specify precisely what is meant by 'other forms of coercion' or 'abuse of power or of a position of vulnerability', although in the *travaux préparatoires* a note states that the 'abuse of a position of vulnerability is understood to refer to any situation in which the person involved has no real and acceptable alternative but to submit to the abuse involved' (Raymond, 2001: 5).

The lack of clarity on these issues may be pragmatic in the sense that it means the trafficking protocol can be adopted 'without prejudice to how States Parties address prostitution in their respective domestic laws' (Interpretative note 64 to the protocol), but it also allows space for conflicting interpretations of what does and does not constitute trafficking for prostitution. This in turn means that diametrically opposing proposals for the reform of prostitution laws can each be presented as contributing to the struggle against 'trafficking'. Thus, feminist abolitionist groups such as the Coalition against Trafficking in Women are lobbying hard for measures to suppress the general market for prostitution (for example, for legal penalties against clients as well as third party beneficiaries) on the grounds that demand for prostitution stimulates trafficking. Meanwhile, sex workers' rights activists, among others, argue that as long as prostitution is criminalised and stigmatised, it is impossible to establish and monitor labour standards in the sex sector, and it is the absence of such standards that encourages the use of trafficked and other forms of unfree labour in the sex industry.

The protocol's failure to define explicitly difficult terms such as 'exploitation', 'coercion', 'vulnerability', and so on is equally problematic for those who are concerned with persons trafficked into sectors other than the sex industry.

Fudge No. 2 – the relationship between trafficking and legally sanctioned systems of immigration

Framed by concerns about transnational organised crime, the UN protocol appears to approach trafficking as a subset of illegal migration. Yet this assumes a neat distinction between 'legal' and 'illegal' migration, when in practice legal migratory processes often have illegal elements (illegal payments for facilitation of valid passports for example), and persons who have been trafficked according to the protocol definition may have entered a state legally. For example, women may enter legally as 'wives' and then be exploited in slavery-like conditions and/or forced into various forms of unpaid work; children may enter a country legally with kin who then subject them to slavery or servitude. But it is also vitally important to recognise that the actions and outcomes taken to constitute 'trafficking' by the UN protocol (violence, confinement, coercion, deception and exploitation) can and do also occur within legally regulated systems of migration and employment, and within legal systems of migration into private households.

Migrant workers' rights organisations have recently reported a 'rise in the incidence of unpaid wages, confiscated passports, confinement, lack of job training and even violence' against migrant workers who are legally present in a number of countries under various work permit schemes (AMC, 2000). In many cases, their abuse and exploitation at the point of destination are linked to deception or the abuse of a position of vulnerability at the recruitment stage. Moreover, debt can be and often is a feature of legal as well as illegal immigration. The fees of legal recruitment agencies are often so high that would-be migrants have to borrow in order to pay them, and in some cases, loans are offered by the recruitment agencies themselves. This effectively constructs a type and degree of dependency between migrants and third parties that would almost certainly be regarded as coercive if arranged within the informal economy and/or by criminal organisations. It also restricts workers' freedom to retract from exploitative employment contracts – to quit is to be left facing demands to repay recruitment and travel costs without the means of so doing.

Let us illustrate with just one example, taken from recent research on forced labour in the UK (Anderson and Rogaly, 2005), a case in which 32 highly qualified nurses in Asia were recruited by a UK-based company with offices in an Asian city to work for an NHS Trust. The 'selection' process ended up costing each nurse a total of £700 – for which no receipts were given – after which they were informed that they needed to raise one month's deposit and one month's rent for their accommodation on arrival in the UK. Not wishing to lose the money they had already spent on attempting to secure legal employment in the NHS, the nurses took out loans to raise the deposit and advance rent, loans that were provided by a British-based finance company, affiliated to the original recruitment agency and specifically set up to provide loans to professionals. The loans required monthly repayments of £302. When the nurses arrived in the UK, the NHS hospital held a welcoming tea party, at which they were given tenancy agreements to sign. They had not yet seen their accommodation, but signed, thereby contracting themselves to pay £305 a month for what turned out to be hugely sub-standard accommodation.

When they later attempted to retract from this contract, their manager told them that if they did not pay the full house rental they would have proved themselves 'not trustworthy' and that the NHS Trust therefore would not support their application to register to practise in the UK. Forms had been prepared authorising the deduction of their rent from their salaries, and they were told that if they did not sign, they would not be registered. 'We were caught between the fear of being sent home and the fear of not paying back the debt, when the interest is getting higher all the time', one of them explained. The nurses signed. This money, together with the recruiter's loan, was deducted at source by the NHS Trust. After deductions of £305 for rent and £302 for loan repayment, they were receiving £46 a week as pay for full-time employment in the NHS, from which they also had to repay the loans incurred during the initial selection process (Anderson and Rogaly, 2005). They could not afford to eat, but neither could they afford to quit and return home. If the manager concerned had been operating a brothel rather than working for an NHS Trust, there is little doubt but that she would be viewed as part of a 'trafficking' chain.

This should alert us to a more general problem with regard to distinguishing trafficking from legally tolerated employment contracts (also from legally tolerated forms of exploitation of women and children within families). The protocol attempts to mark off trafficking from other forms of migration by employing concepts such as 'exploitation', 'deception' and 'consent'. And yet questions about what constitutes an exploitative employment practice are much disputed – indeed, they have historically been, and remain, a central focus of the organised labour movement's struggle to protect workers. There is variation between countries and variation between economic sectors in the same country in terms of what is socially and legally constructed as acceptable employment practice. For example, in India, an employer who expects her live-in domestic worker to sleep in a cupboard or on the kitchen floor, and to get up in the middle of the night to serve guests should the employer decide to return late with friends, may not be regarded as transgressing legal or social norms regarding terms and conditions of domestic work. An employer who did the same thing in Britain would, by contrast, be widely regarded as behaving in an exploitative fashion towards her domestic worker. Meanwhile, in India, a university vice-chancellor who required a professor, under threat of dismissal, to sleep on his kitchen floor and provide tutorials at any hour of the day or night would doubtless be considered an abusive and exploitative employer.

In the absence of a global political consensus on minimum employ-ment rights, and of cross-national and cross-sector norms regarding employment relations, it is extremely difficult to come up with a neu-tral, universal yardstick against which 'exploitation' can be measured. The protocol definition of trafficking thus leaves open questions about precisely how exploitative an employment relation has to be before we can say that a person has been recruited and transported 'for purposes of exploitation'. Likewise, we need to ask just how deceived a worker has to be about the nature and terms of the employment prior to migrating before s/he can properly be described as a 'victim of trafficking'. There are numerous different elements to the employment relation: hours of work, rates of pay, job content, work rate, working practices, living con-ditions, length of the contract, and so on. Is it enough for a worker to be deceived about just one of these elements by a recruiter, or must s/he be entirely duped about every aspect of the work in order to qualify as a trafficked person?

Without a neutral measure of 'exploitation', it is also unclear how 'trafficking' is to be distinguished from the legal movement of women and children into households, for instance, through marriage, adoption or fostering. Expectations regarding the amount of unpaid labour that women and children will provide within households vary cross-nationally and within nations, as do social norms regarding the powers that men can properly exercise over women and that adults can properly exercise over children. How bad does a woman's or child's experience need to be in order for the agents who facilitated her movement to be viewed as 'traffickers'? Must she be imprisoned in the household, starved, beaten, raped and forced to work all hours in order to qualify as a 'victim of traf-ficking'? Or should a 'mail order bride' or adopted child who does not enjoy all the freedoms and privileges that would normally be enjoyed by a middle-class, ethnic majority wife or child in the host country qualify? Or is it somewhere between the two? (O'Connell Davidson, 2005).

It is naïve to imagine that migrants can be divided into two entirely separate and distinct groups – those who are trafficked involuntarily into miserable, slavery-like conditions in an illegal or unregulated economic sector or illegally moved into abusive households, and those who voluntarily and legally migrate into the happy and protected world of the formal economy or 'good' families and marriages. Violence, confinement, coercion, deception and exploitation can and do occur within both legally regulated and irregular systems of migration and employment. Moreover, these abuses can vary in severity, which means they generate a continuum of experience rather than a simple either/or dichotomy. At one pole of the continuum, we can find people who have been transported at gunpoint, then forced to labour through the use of physical and sexual violence and death threats against them or their loved ones back home. At the other pole, we can find people who have not been charged exorbitant rates by recruiting agencies or deceived in any way about the employment for which they were recruited, and who are well-paid and work in good conditions in an environment protective of their human and labour rights. But between the two lies a range of experience. Ideas about the precise point on this continuum at which tolerable forms of labour migration end and trafficking begins will vary according to our political and moral values.

Because 'trafficking' has been framed as a problem of transnational organised crime, the fate of those who are deceived or coerced and abused within legal systems of labour migration is largely overlooked. So too is the state's role in constructing conditions under which the use of trafficked or otherwise unfree labour becomes a realistic and profitable option for employers. And yet because trafficking and other forms of unfree labour are closely associated with what is sometimes termed 'poor work', states do certainly play an important role (through both action and inaction) in shaping the demand for the labour/services of 'exploited persons'. National governments are heavily implicated in the construction of both 'poor work' and 'vulnerable workers' through their policies on immigration, employment, economic development, welfare, education, and so on. For instance, by failing to ensure gender equality in education, and/or failing to enforce legislation against gender discriminatory social practices, the state can be said to construct female workers as more vulnerable to 'poor work', and as more vulnerable within it, than their male counterparts. Also, by excluding particular sectors of employment (such as that in private households, or in small firms) from legislation on employment rights, the state can be said to create pockets within which some workers lack the formal protections accorded to others, and are therefore more vulnerable to abuse and exploitation. Indeed, the ILO has commented that:

> A major incentive for trafficking in labour is the lack of application and enforcement of labour standards in countries of destination as well as origin ... Tolerance of restrictions on freedom of movement, long working hours, poor or non-existent health and safety protections, non-payment of wages, substandard housing, etc. all contribute to expanding a market for trafficked migrants who have no choice but to labour in conditions simply intolerable and unacceptable for legal employment. (ILO, 2002: 8)

State policies with regard to immigration and asylum also help to construct situations within which certain groups of migrants are especially vulnerable to extremes of exploitation. The tension between states' spoken aim of combating trafficking and their desire to restrict immigration becomes especially clear when we look at the supposed distinction between 'trafficking' and 'smuggling'.

Fudge No. 3 – the relationship between trafficking and smuggling

If the boundary between trafficking and some migrants' experiences of legal migration is indistinct, that between smuggling and trafficking is yet more clouded and ambiguous, although it is one on which policy-makers are increasingly dependent. This distinction centres on questions about whether the migrant consented to irregular entry; and the relation of the trafficker/smuggler to subsequent exploitative working conditions. Trafficking requires the continued exercise of control over migrants once they have moved, while the role of the smuggler is simply to facilitate border crossing. The two protocols (The Palermo Protocol and its twin on human smuggling) assume that smuggling and trafficking can be distinguished through reference to where and how profit is extracted by third parties, and through reference to the specific intentions of the third parties who recruit and transport them. Thus, profits from the process of smuggling are said to come merely from the movement itself, whereas profits from the movement of 'trafficked' persons are held to be inextricably linked to the end purpose of exploitation.

This implies some kind of active conspiracy between the third parties who profit from recruitment and transportation, and those who exploit the trafficked person's services/labour at the point of destination, and so reflects a particular concern with trafficking as the outcome of organised and purposive action on the part of third parties. Certainly there are cases that conform to this narrow definition, including cases in which criminals cooperate with one another in, and jointly profit from, a process that involves recruitment, transportation and exploitation, and cases in which employers send agents to 'recruit' people from other regions or countries for purposes of exploitation. But there are many other cases in which the agents who recruit and transport people into forced labour or slavery-like conditions have no established relationship with the third parties who ultimately orchestrate and profit from the labour/services of the people so transported. Instead, they use deception or other means of coercion to entice or pressure women, men and/or children to accompany them to places where there is a demand for labour, and then collect a fee from any employer who happens to be looking for 'workers'. Since the subsequent condition of those persons is a matter of indifference to the recruiting agents (they get paid regardless of whether the people they move are abused and exploited, or free and well paid), they cannot be described as having an intent to subject the victim of the coerced transport to additional violations in the form of forced labour or slavery-like practices.

Likewise, there are those who offer to facilitate migration, but encourage migrants to consent to indebt themselves massively by deceiving them about earning opportunities and working conditions in the point of destination. Once transported, the migrant finds it impossible to repay the debt except by selling themselves into slavery-like conditions or by working in prostitution, even though they initially consented to take on the debt because they had been led to believe that they could earn enough to repay it from some other occupation. Again, the person who facilitates migration profits from the movement, but does not directly organise or control the exploitation of the migrant's services/ labour at the point of destination. S/he is, presumably, a 'smuggler' rather than a 'trafficker' according to the UN protocols.

Taken together, the trafficking and smuggling protocols assume a neat line of demarcation between voluntary and consensual, and involuntary and non-consensual processes of migration. And yet there is an extensive research literature showing that these assumptions vastly oversimplify the systems and processes that facilitate irregular migration in the real world, and fail to recognise the complexity and variety of social relations between irregular migrants and those who benefit directly or indirectly from their exploitation (for instance, Agustín, 2005; Andrijasevic, 2003; Lutz, 2004; Parrenas, 2001; see also King, 2002). But perhaps the most urgent and troubling problem with the two protocols is the fact that they 'provide no guidance on how trafficked persons and smuggled migrants are to be identified as belonging to either of these categories' (Gallagher, 2002: 27). In effect, the two protocols allow states to divide deserving 'victims of trafficking' from undeserving 'partners in smuggling' without actually providing 'any guidance on how trafficked persons and smuggled migrants are to be identified as belonging to either of these categories' (Gallagher, 2002: 27).

Two further comments. First, given this volume's focus on women's rights, it is important to note that the trafficking/smuggling distinction rests on a model of gender difference that many feminists would regard as problematic. It is frequently asserted that most smuggled persons are men, while most trafficked persons are women and children, and yet this claim is not and cannot be supported by empirical evidence for there are no reliable empirical data on the numbers of trafficked and smuggled persons.[2] Instead, it seemingly rests on a gender essentialist model of social relations, within which only men are imagined to be capable of making an independent and voluntary decision to migrate or enter into the commercial 'partnerships' that facilitate migration. Women, by contrast, are lumped together with children as categories of person requiring special protection, and constructed as the passive victims and objects of third parties within the migration process (see Agustín, 2002; Doezema, 1999; Murray, 1998).

Second, because the UN protocols start from a concern with questions about transnational crime control and prevention, and assume that migrants can be neatly divided into moral categories such as 'adult men' (strong, active, agent) and 'women and children' (weak, passive, victim), and smuggled (complicit in a crime against the state) and trafficked (victim of a crime against the person), they obscure the fact that irregular migration can actually represent a means through which people access their fundamental rights. It may, for example, be the only possible way for a child to join parents who are undocumented workers in another country, or for a woman to escape domestic violence, or for a gay youth to escape a homophobic family and society, or for a person – man, woman or child – to stand any chance of securing 'a standard of living adequate for the health and well-being of himself [sic] and of his family, including food, clothing, housing and medical care' (UN Universal Declaration of Human Rights, 1948, Article 25).

The trouble with trafficking

In light of the conceptual, definitional and methodological problems associated with the term 'trafficking', it is important to ask whether this concept adds anything to our understanding of the processes and practices that constitute or contribute to human rights violations against migrant persons. It was noted at the start of this chapter that 'trafficking' is valued by some commentators because it supposedly captures the full and cumulative horror of the sequence of events to which the classic 'trafficking victim' is subject. And yet the stories of many migrants who find themselves confined or trapped and abused and exploited at the point of destination (whether in prostitution or any other sector) do not entirely match the classic model of 'trafficking', and it is therefore dangerous to attach special significance to abuse arising from a process that is more than the sum of its parts. This is because what happens within the migratory process and what happens at the point of destination represent two different, though sometimes overlapping, continua of experience. Though a range of different forms of deception, force and exploitation can occur in either or both these fields of experience, the concept of trafficking focuses our attention on situations in which abuses at the point of destination are linked to the use of force or deception within the migration process. This may sometimes be important from a crime control perspective, but from the viewpoint of the individual who is subject to exploitative and slavery-like practices, it makes precious little difference whether her exploiter is in cahoots with the person who recruited her or not, or whether she entered the country through legal or illegal channels, or indeed whether she is being abused in a distant region or land or in her own home town. The point for her is that she cannot quit or escape, is denied basic freedoms, is not getting paid, is forced to live and work in bad conditions, has no control over her work pace, hours of work or job content, and/or is subjected to physical violence or its threat.

Our concern with regard to policymaking in this field is that the increasing centrality of the concept of trafficking deflects attention from this point and encourages the construction of moral hierarchies as well as practical and legal barriers between 'deserving', 'less deserving' and 'undeserving' causes and victims. How, for example, does the concept of trafficking speak to the experience of those who make their own way across a border to seek work and subsequently find themselves subject to slavery-like practices by an abusive employer? What happens to those who agree to work out a period of indenture in another country because even an extremely exploitative labour contract represents an improvement to their current living and working conditions? Where does a woman who is cheated, exploited and/or raped by a smuggler turn for justice or support?

Because international debates on 'trafficking' have been so firmly situated in the context of concerns about organised criminal involvement in international and internal migration, and because they have conflated two fields of experience that are not always or necessarily conjoined (exploitation and abuse within irregular migration and exploitation and abuse at the point of destination), the dominant discourse on 'trafficking' allows both national and international policymakers and agencies much room for doublespeak. When asked whether their primary concern is the breaching of immigration controls or the breach of migrants' human rights in transit and at the point of destination; or whether they seek to combat the illegal movement of people, or traffickers, or the exploitative and abusive practices to which trafficked persons (among others) are subject; it is possible for them to answer that they are equally concerned with all of these alternatives. So, for example, the Italian Foreign Minister told a press conference during the Central European Initiative meeting in Trieste in November 2001 that 'Cracking down on illegal immigration is one of our goals. Strengthening our efforts against human trafficking is essential in the fight for fundamental human rights.' This conflation of anti-immigration and anti-trafficking measures obscures the fact that policies designed to control irregular forms of migration are known to encourage, permit or exacerbate violations of migrants' human rights, and policies that focus on the prevention of illegal movements of people do nothing to address the factors that make it possible for employers and others to engage in exploitative and slavery-like practices at the point of destination.

In short, it is the woolly and imprecise nature of the term 'trafficking' that allows EU governments to state a commitment to combating the abuse and exploitation of migrant women and children while simultaneously setting in place an immigration system that can actually create opportunities for employers legally to subject migrant workers to conditions that, if imposed by 'criminal gangs', would often be deemed a form of 'trafficking' (see, for example, Anderson and Rogaly, 2005), and that is widely regarded as threatening fundamental human rights such as the right to asylum (Morrison, 2000) and that even threatens the right to life itself – it is estimated that more than 2,000 deaths result annually from border policing, detention and deportation policies and carrier sanctions in Europe (Andrijasevic, 2003; McGill, 2003: 73).

It is also the woolly and imprecise nature of the term 'trafficking' that makes it possible for so many people to clamber aboard the trafficking gravy train. And – to extend the metaphor – few of them agree on where the train is or should be heading. This is what makes debates on 'trafficking' so confused, confusing and frustrating. In one carriage we find feminist abolitionists who recognise no distinction between forced and free choice prostitution, and who have leapt aboard in the hope of advancing a struggle against the commercial sex trade in general, not the abuse and exploitation of migrant sex workers in particular. They have no wish to extend the concept of 'trafficking' to sectors other than the sex trade, and are joined by various likeminded women's lobby groups keen to ensure that 'trafficking' is understood as a *women's* issue rather than a migration or labour issue that can affect both sexes. In another carriage we may find human rights NGOs that have joined the train out of a desire to combat a rights violation that they deem to constitute a form of 'modern slavery'. For these NGOs, it is not important whether the victims end up in the sex industry or another sector, or whether they are female or male, adult or child, but it *is* important that their suffering can be clearly distinguished from other forms of exploitation to which migrant workers may be subject. Milling around in the corridors, often wondering whether and how to disembark, are assorted others – including trades unionists, migrants' rights NGOs, sex workers' rights activists and academics like ourselves who do not believe that the concept of 'trafficking' actually helps us to grasp, analyse or counteract the array of serious, but different, human rights violations to which migrant women, children and men may be subject in the European Union.

Though networking among these various groups could certainly contribute to the development of more sophisticated and nuanced understandings and policy responses in relation to human rights violations in Europe, we would argue that greater conceptual clarity, and a greater willingness to recognise and discuss the political differences amongst those currently involved in debates on 'trafficking' are necessary preconditions for this positive outcome.

Acknowledgements

This chapter draws on on-going research funded by the Economic and Social Research Council (Award No. R000239794) and builds on a report on 'trafficking' commissioned by the Swedish Ministry of Foreign Affairs, SIDA and Save the Children Sweden (Anderson and O'Connell Davidson, 2002).

Notes

1. It continues: 'c) The recruitment, transportation, transfer, harbouring or receipt of a child for the purpose of exploitation shall be considered "trafficking in persons" even if this does not involve any of the means set forth in sub-paragraph (a) of this article; d) "Child" shall mean any person under eighteen years of age.'
2. The gender of victims of trafficking is only systematically recorded by a minority of EU governments that contribute data on trafficking to the Inter-Governmental Consultations, and trafficking statistics are rarely disaggregated by age (Morrison, 2000: 35; Boonpala and Kane, 2002). Furthermore, the most commonly cited statistics on trafficking have not been gathered using the definition of trafficking provided in the UN protocol, and are in any case crude estimates based upon a series of extrapolations and assumptions, rather than 'hard' facts about the numbers of people involved (Salt and Hogarth, 2000).

References

Agustín, L. (2002) 'Challenging "Place", Leaving Home for Sex', *Development*, 1 (45): 110–16.

Agustín, L. (2005) 'Migrants in the Mistress's House: Other Voices in the "Trafficking" Debate', *Social Politics*, 12 (1): 96–117.

AMC (2000) *Asian Migrant Yearbook 2000: Migration Facts, Analysis and Issues in 1999*, Hong Kong: Asian Migrant Centre.

Anderson, B. and O'Connell Davidson, J. (2002) *Trafficking – A Demand-Led Problem?* Stockholm: Save the Children Sweden.

Anderson, B. and Rogaly, B. (2005) *Free Market, Forced Labour?* London: TUC.

Andrijasevic, R. (2003) 'The Difference Borders Make: (Il)legality, Migration and "Trafficking" in Italy among "Eastern" European Women in Prostitution', in S. Ahmed, C. Castaneda, A. Fortier and M. Sheller (eds) *Uprootings/Regroundings: Questions of Home and Migration*. Oxford: Berg.

Baro, D. (2001) 'Trafficking of Children: International Legal Framework' (n.d.).

Boonpala, P. and Kane, J. (2002) *Child Trafficking and Action to Eliminate It*, Geneva: ILO.

Doezema, J. (1999) 'Loose Women or Lost Women? The Re-emergence of the Myth of "White slavery" in Contemporary Discourses of Trafficking in Women', *Gender Issues*, 18 (1): 23–50.

EC Justice and Home Affairs (2001) 'Trafficking in Women: The Misery behind the Fantasy: From Poverty to Sex Slavery', The European Commission. Available at: http://europa.eu.int/comm/justice_home/news/8mars_en.htm [Accessed 17 May 2005].

GAATW (2001) *Human Rights and Trafficking in Persons: A Handbook*, Bangkok: GAATW.

Gallagher, A. (2002) 'Trafficking, Smuggling and Human Rights: Tricks and Treaties', *Forced Migration Review*, 12: 25–8.

ILO (International Labour Office) (2002) 'Getting at the Roots: Stopping Exploitation of Migrant Workers by Organized Crime', International Labour Office, Paper presented to *International Symposium on the UN Convention Against*

Transnational Organized Crime: Requirements for Effective Implementation, Turin, 22–23 February.

King, R. (2002) 'Towards a New Map of European Migration', *International Journal of Population Geography*, 8: 89–106.

Lutz, H. (2004) 'Life in the Twilight Zone: Migration, Transnationality and Gender in the Private Household', *Journal of Contemporary European Studies*, 1(12): 47–55.

McGill, C. (2003) *Human Traffic: Sex, Slaves and Immigration*. London: Vision.

Morrison, J. (2000) 'The Policy Implications Arising from the Trafficking and Smuggling of Refugees into Europe', Documentation of the European Conference *Children First and Foremost – Policies towards Separated Children in Europe*, Stockholm: Save the Children Sweden.

Murray, A. (1998) 'Debt-bondage and Trafficking: Don't Believe the Hype', in K. Kempadoo and J. Doezema (eds.), *Global Sex Workers: Rights, Resistance, and Redefinition*, London: Routledge.

O'Connell Davidson, J. (2005) *Children in the Global Sex Trade*, Cambridge: Polity.

Parrenas, R. (2001) *Servants of Globalisation: Women, Migration and Domestic Work*, Stanford, CA: Stanford University Press.

Raymond, J. (2001) *Guide to the New UN Trafficking Protocol*, North Amherst, MA: CATW.

Salt, J. and Hogarth, J. (2000) *Migrant Trafficking and Human Smuggling in Europe: A Review of the Evidence with Case Studies from Hungary, Poland and Ukraine*, Geneva: IOM.

2
Trafficking in Human Beings: Conceptual Dilemmas

Ilse van Liempt

Introduction

Each year many people are smuggled or trafficked across international borders. Exact numbers are hard to come by. The International Organisation for Migration (IOM), which received European Union (EU) STOP funds to produce accurate estimates for trafficking in women across Europe, came to the conclusion that it was not possible to give estimates with any level of accuracy. Several factors explain the poor data availability. In the first place trafficking is a covert activity and as such may be hard to recognise. Second, trafficking is a relatively new phenomenon (on this scale) and data systems have not yet caught up (see also Chapter 8). Methods of data collection in individual countries are ad hoc rather than systematic. Besides, individual authorities collect statistics using their own definitions. In most countries no single agency acts as a focal point for collection, collation or harmonisation of such statistics and the sharing of information between states is done on an ad hoc basis, particularly with migrants' countries of origin (Salt and Hogarth, 2000: 35). In addition, there are still countries lacking trafficking legislation, which makes collecting data more difficult and illustrates that the priority placed on the need to combat the phenomenon is not the same everywhere.

Smuggling and trafficking are often mentioned in one breath, and in the past the terms trafficking and smuggling have frequently been used more or less synonymously, even though there are huge differences between the two, especially in terms of the impact on the individual entering the destination country. Smuggling and trafficking are mostly separated by the fact that trafficking implies that there are victims and smuggling does not. The focus of smuggling usually is on the illegal movements of migrants across international borders and is defined as a voluntary, consensual form of migration (which does not necessarily refer to the reasons for leaving someone's home country or the abuse or exploitation that can result from travelling with a smuggler). For trafficking the focus is on coercion and exploitation. The profit in this case comes not from the movement itself, a border does not even necessarily have to be crossed, but from the migrant's labour in the country of destination. In this chapter I will give an overview of changes and differences in the trafficking definition over time to see how the Palermo Protocol came about, and will compare trafficking with other issues like smuggling and migration to give an insight of what the problems linked to the practical implementation of the Palermo Protocol can be.

Different trafficking definitions over time

Trafficking in human beings is not a new phenomenon. What is new is the transnational character of the phenomenon and the scale on which it is taking place. For trafficking no international borders have to be crossed *per se*, but recently more international migration has been involved. Besides the phenomenon could not have grown if powerful market forces did not support it. The increased demand for cheap labour and sex, coupled with restrictions on legal migration possibilities, have clearly opened a niche for traffickers (see Chapter 1).

In 1949 the UN Convention on the Suppression of Trafficking in Women and the exploitation of prostitution of others was the first UN Convention dealing with trafficking. This treaty was, however, not widely ratified and has been criticised for its lack of definition and of enforcement mechanisms and for addressing it as solely the cross-border movement of persons into prostitution (Pearson, 2002). The Netherlands did not sign the Convention because trafficking was considered the same as exploitation of prostitution and that vision did not go along with the Dutch 'toleration policy' (*gedoogbeleid*) for prostitution (Leun and Vervoorn, 2004). After a period of silence, trafficking became an issue at the UN level again as well as at the European level during the 1980s and the beginning of the 1990s. In April 1989 the European Parliament adopted its first resolution on the exploitation of prostitution and the traffic in human beings. In this resolution both prostitution as such and trafficking for prostitution were condemned. In September 1993 the resolution called for international cooperation to combat trafficking in women and to improve the situation of victims. One of the reasons for the revival of the trafficking issue was that the women's movement was strong (feminists had a concern with exploitation of women); another was the global concern at that time with HIV/AIDS (Wijers and Lap-Chew, 1997).

In the 1990s, under the influence of increasingly restrictive immigration policies especially of the wealthy countries, trafficking became increasingly an issue of illegal or irregular movement (Wijers and Lap-Chew, 1997: 27). A shift took place in the discussion from violence against women to the illegal mode of entry into a country. In 1996 the European Parliament adopted a second resolution on trafficking and in this resolution migration was central. Trafficked persons entering the European Union, whether legally or illegally, could now be considered to have been trafficked. For a long time it was not taken into account that entry into a country might be legal, but temporary. This would, for example, be the case when a visa for artists or dancers is used for the purpose of overstaying. The new resolution, therefore, became more realistic so to speak, and trafficking was brought into line with migration laws (Pearson, 2002). For the first time the European Parliament also went beyond the traditional female-oriented concept of trafficking and adopted the term 'trafficking in human beings'. Children and men have been included in the trafficking definition ever since.

In December 1998 the European Commission proposed that the definition be made broader still, this time by including not only men, but also women who are trafficked for purposes other than prostitution – for example, the trade in domestic workers or women who are forced into marriage. But the lack of a clear definition led various organisations to adopt their own definition before the UN Protocol came into being. IOM, for example, did not wait for the official extension of the definition to other sectors. They adopted their own definition in 1999 in which they talked about profit-making in general without referring to a specific working field. They considered that trafficking occurs when:

> A migrant is illicitly engaged (recruited, kidnapped, sold, etc.) and/or moved, either within national or across international borders; [and] intermediaries (traffickers) during any part of this process obtain economic or other profit by means of deception, coercion, and/or other forms of exploitation under conditions that violate the fundamental rights of migrants. (Pearson, 2002: 3–4)

These debates paved the way for the Palermo Protocol of 2000 which no longer focuses solely on prostitution, but includes other sectors and refers to human beings rather than just women. But at the heart of the discussions on coming to terms with the definition of trafficking stood the traditional debate on sexual exploitation. A key controversy concerned the question of whether or not all forms of prostitution constitute exploitation – is there such a thing as a *willing* prostitute? In other words, can prostitution represent a mutual, voluntarily contractual exchange between adults, or does it always violate human rights and/or at what stage do we stop accepting a person's free choice? (For an in-depth discussion, see Chapter 3.) The lobbying that took place can be split into two camps. Those who see prostitution as labour are in the first camp; they are also called 'regulationists'. 'Regulationism' refers to the state system of licensed brothels, in which prostitutes are subjected to various forms of regulation. The ideology behind regulation is that 'prostitution is a necessary evil'. Regulationists hold that regulation is better than trying to abolish prostitution, since they believe that prostitution has always existed and will always exist. In the other camp are the 'abolitionists', founded in feminist movements, who place the blame for prostitution on the shoulders of men. Prostitutes are seen as victims who should be rescued or rehabilitated. The image sent out by 'abolitionists' for many is an ideal construct to elicit public sympathy to combat trafficking.

In December 2000, after two years' negotiations at the UN Centre for International Crime Prevention in Vienna, over 80 countries signed the Trafficking Protocol in Palermo (Raymond, 2001). There is now a standard against which laws, policies and practices relating to trafficking can be judged. The definition everybody agreed on is:

> Trafficking in persons means the recruitment, transportation, transfer, harbouring or receipt of persons, either by the threat or use of abduction, force, fraud, deception or coercion, or by the giving or receiving of unlawful payments or benefits to achieve the consent of a person having the control over another person, for the purpose of exploitation. Exploitation shall include, at a minimum, the exploitation of prostitution of others or other forms of sexual exploitation, forced labour or services, slavery or practices similar to slavery, servitude or the removal of organs. (UN Protocol to Prevent, Suppress and Punish Trafficking in Persons, Especially Women and Children, Article 3(a))

The trafficking definition contains three separate elements. The first is *the criminal act*: recruitment, transportation, transfer, harbouring or reception of persons. The second is *the means used* to commit these acts, threat or use of force, coercion, abduction, fraud, deception, abuse of power or vulnerability or giving payments or benefits to a person in control of the victim. The third is *the goals* for which one traffics, sexual exploitation, forced labour, slavery or similar practices and even the removal of organs (Aronowitz, 2001).[1]

Even though the definition in itself is an achievement to be proud of there are some important concerns. The first relates to the traditional debate on the issue of consent. The second has to do with the goals for which one is trafficked and touches on the issue of exploitation – it is not clear, for example, on what scale the elements of the definition must be present in order to speak about trafficking. The third relates to the question of how to protect a victim of trafficking in a context of restrictive immigration policies. I will now discuss these issues in turn.

The notion of consent

I will not go into the moral/philosophical debate on the issue of consent (for a discussion on this debate, see Chapter 3), but what is important here is that the different standpoints on prostitution within the European Union have made it difficult to arrive at a universal definition of what trafficking is. A group of NGOs supporting prostitution as work lobbied to limit the definition of trafficking to forced or coerced trafficking and to delete the term 'victims' from the text. The countries that supported this 'regulationist' stance were mostly Western, receiving countries; some have legalised prostitution or taxed the profitable sex industry. Those that supported the 'abolitionist' stance were mostly non-Western countries which were often sending countries. They wanted a definition that protected *all* victims of trafficking and that was not limited to force or coercion.

After long debates, the issue of achieving someone's consent emerged as the international standard for determining trafficking, even though there were still many lobby groups arguing that trafficking should include *all* forms of recruitment and transportation for prostitution, regardless of whether any deception took place. This recognition of the element of choice is crucially different from the 1949 Convention in which all persons working in prostitution were considered a victim of trafficking. Persons who were aware of the kind of job they were going to fulfil, but then were exploited, are also covered by the most recent UN trafficking definition by the fact that even those who initially signed the contract voluntarily are protected when it turns out that they are exploited. Article 3b of the UN Protocol on Trafficking states:

> The consent of a victim of trafficking in persons to the intended exploitation shall be irrelevant where any of the means set forth in article 3a have been used.

The new trafficking definition, however, still leaves states free to recognise sex as labour or not. The danger is that the choice/no choice divide may lead to a separation between two categories of trafficked women: the 'victims' who were lured into it, and the 'criminals' who actively choose to become a prostitute.

There is a strong tendency to simplify matters when it comes to trafficking. The media want a simple story, one that readers and viewers can connect with. NGOs sometimes also simplify because it eases their work. Rescuing women from the hands of criminals is, of course, a good thing to do. The same applies to the police, who would like to track down the major criminals behind the trafficking and have an interest in victimising the women involved. Vocks and Nyboer (1999) in this respect concludes that social workers and the police are less willing to help prostitutes who were working as prostitutes in their own country and who do not want to quit the business. These women diffuse the issue of victimisation.

It is, of course, important to protect *all* exploited migrants, but in the meantime it is dangerous to qualify *all* migrant prostitutes as victims of trafficking. In fact, the protocol does not take a clear stance for or against the possibility of prostitution to be seen as work (Doezema, 2002). A narrow focus on whether or not people consent to prostitution blurs our understanding of the whole process. To identify a victim of trafficking we have to understand more about those involved, their realities and the decisions they have made.

From previous research we know that most prostitutes willingly leave their country and enter sex work because they have no alternative. Some even start to work in prostitution in their country of origin. In the Netherlands an empirical study was conducted on trafficked women from Central and Eastern Europe forced to work in prostitution. In this study a useful typology was presented of different types of victim (Vocks, 1999). The first is the kidnapped woman; complete coercion exists when victims have been kidnapped or sold. This type rarely occurs. The second is the misled woman: deception occurs when individuals have been promised jobs in the legitimate economy but upon arrival are forced into sexual slavery. Sometimes women are deceived through half-truths – for example, when they are told they will be working in the entertainment industry as strippers but are forced to have sex with customers. The third type is the exploited woman. This type occurred most among the researched women from Central and Eastern Europe. Most women interviewed knew beforehand that they were going to work as prostitutes in the Netherlands, but did expect better working conditions than in their own country. A later study among Eastern European trafficked migrants confirmed this by concluding that the use of force to persuade women to migrate was an exception rather than a rule (Andrijasevic, 2004).

A narrow focus on whether or not women consent to prostitution hinders our understanding of the whole process. Besides, the concept of deception as put forth by the trafficking definition leaves open questions about the extent of deception needed in terms of job content, rates of pay, working practices, work rate and length of the contract, among others, in order to qualify as a victim of trafficking (Anderson and O'Connell Davidson, 2003). The vagueness of this notion establishes an oversimplified demarcation between voluntary and forced processes of migration, while in reality there are more distinctions at play.

How to measure exploitation?

According to the protocol, trafficking is defined in relation to *the intent of exploitation*. Being a prostitute, or having been lured into prostitution by false promises or deceived about the destination or the type of work, is theoretically not enough for a person to qualify as a trafficked person. The presence of exploitation is what makes the difference. This is also the demarcation between smuggling and trafficking. The definition says that exploitation shall include, at a minimum, 'the exploitation of prostitution of others or other forms of sexual exploitation, forced labour or services, slavery or practices similar to slavery, servitude or the removal of organs' (Article 3(a)). But what is meant by sexual exploitation, forced labour or slavery is not made clear. The problem is that it is extremely difficult to come up with neutral universal criteria against which exploitation can be measured. The protocol is not clear on precisely how exploitative a relation must be before we can speak about trafficking. Victims may be kept under control by violence or by placing the victim in a situation of dependency, for example by taking the income generated or the women's passports, or by limiting their freedom of movement. These criteria should be worked out more consistently so that the definition will be of more practical use.

Another difficulty with defining when someone is exploited is that there are migrants willing to accept lower working standards, simply because their earnings, compared to where they come from, are considered good or even high. The only question to ask is, therefore, when is exploitation severe enough to speak about trafficking? There is a need for state action when migrants lack the freedom to break certain contracts or when serious violations of human rights take place. Two major problems set the scene when we want to define more broadly what exploitation is. The first is that there are many variations between countries as to what are the socially and legally accepted working conditions in different sectors. The definition of exploitation should in this case be linked to *national* labour standards, even though the aim of the UN definition is *international*. The second problem is the informal economy. The informal economy provides many opportunities for power imbalances and for exploitation. In addition, there is a specific demand for cheap labour stemming from the informal economy as Anderson and O'Connell Davidson show in their report on needs and desires (Anderson and O'Connell Davidson, 2003; see also Chapter 1). For prostitution they show that third parties do not make use of migrant women in prostitution simply because they are women, but because their status as undocumented migrants makes them a cheap and vulnerable labour force. By excluding particular sectors of employment from legislation, as prostitution is excluded from the formal labour market in most countries, the state creates niches within which workers lack protection. In that case it is very hard to impose legal standards concerning exploitation.

Related to the irregular status of most trafficking victims is the pressure exercised by their traffickers concerning their (sometimes enormous) debts. Not being in debt may take away the vulnerability to being exploited. The size of the debts and the method of reimbursement can also help determine the degree of exploitation. To understand this debt bondage it is important to look at the broader picture of migration. For many it is impossible to migrate legally and the services provided by traffickers may be the only way to leave their miserable situation and seek a better future elsewhere.

Restrictive migration policy and trafficking

Doezema compared the campaigns against 'white slavery' at the beginning of the nineteenth century with current campaigns against trafficking. She comes to the conclusion that there are many similarities between the two. One could even say that trafficking is a retelling of the myth of white slavery in modern form. The reason she calls it a myth is that many researchers have shown that trafficking in so-called 'white slaves' occurred on a very small scale. At that time, however, a massive female labour migration from Europe to the United States was taking place. When this migration decreased after the First World War concerns about 'white slaves' also disappeared (Doezema, 2000). Trafficking is often studied as a subject on its own, but the link between trafficking and migration is a crucial one. The gendered power relations in the field can be seen as a starting point from which to study trafficking (Kofman *et al.*, 2000). A migration perspective allows seeing trafficked persons as migrants[2] and not only as victims. Prostitution is often considered an activity that young women are lured into under false pretences. Nevertheless the sale of sexual labour abroad can also be an integral part of women's lives and strategies, and travelling with a trafficker may be the only way out of a country.

When we look at the UN protocol from a gender perspective the distinction between trafficking and smuggling is certainly gender-biased. Women are more often conceived as objects of traffickers. In the Trafficking Protocol women and children are even explicitly mentioned as a special category. Men, on the other hand, are more often conceived as agents, capable of making decisions to migrate and enter a smuggling contract. It is therefore frequently asserted that most smuggled are men whilst most trafficked are women, yet this claim cannot be supported by the evidence for there are no reliable data on the numbers of smuggled and/or trafficked persons (see also Anderson and O'Connell Davidson, 2003; and Chapter 1 above). A clear problem with this static gendered division is that a person can be smuggled one day, but become a trafficked migrant the next. There is considerable movement and overlap between the two terms, but so far little or no discussion has taken place on the dynamic character of smuggling and trafficking.

When it comes to combating trafficking the difference with smuggling does not seem big. All attempts to combat trafficking or smuggling seem to be motivated by a growing intolerance of *all* forms of illegal migration. Controls increase and trafficked victims are often treated as illegal migrants. A report by Coomaraswamy (2000), the UN Special Rapporteur on Violence against Women, underlines how a policy preventing immigration will have the principal consequence that women (or migrants in general) will fall more readily into the hands of criminal organisations and that their debts will increase. Having or not having a visa is linked to the way in which women cross borders, with whom they cross and the degree of risk faced. All these obstacles mean higher prices paid to traffickers or other providers of illegal services.

Deportations of trafficked women and the principle of non-*refoulement*

Of special concern related to a restrictive migration policy to combat trafficking are the forced deportations of trafficked migrants. If someone is identified as a victim of trafficking, immediate expulsion against the will of the victim should not occur and the victim should be given the option of asking for protection. In practice, however, this is not always the case. The police more often arrest people and deport them to their country of origin without identifying possible victims of trafficking and therefore without offering them protection. This is when the anti-migration aspect of the anti-trafficking strategy becomes dominant. On 13 January 2003, for instance, more than 60 women were arrested by the police at the Theemsweg (a red light district in Amsterdam). A charter plane was waiting to fly the prostitutes, together with other illegal migrants from these countries, back to their countries of origin (Bulgaria and Romania). The consequence of this 'clean-up operation' was that possible victims of trafficking did not have the opportunity to give a witness statement against their traffickers as they were simply perceived as illegal migrants. Not only did the police miss potentially important witnesses for their criminal investigation, but the potential victim also lacked protection. The fact that none of these women was offered a period of reflection to consider the option of reporting to the police, the fact that they were deported together with males and females who operated as pimps and possible traffickers in the street prostitution district, and the fact that there was no form of assistance offered during or after the flight to Bulgaria or Romania, support the view that the women were very vulnerable.

In the Netherlands the B9 regulation set out in the Immigration Law Circular protects victims of trafficking. Witnesses can, when they report trafficking, enjoy temporary residence in the Netherlands, reception and shelter, medical assistance and legal aid (National Rapporteur Mensenhandel, 2002). Those who report to the police are offered a period of reflection (a maximum of three months) in which he or she must make a decision whether or not (s)he wishes to report. The police must bring the rights set out in B9 to their attention, even if there is only a slight sign of trafficking. The main interest of the B9 however is a judicial interest, namely collecting evidence to prosecute traffickers. If the criminals have been prosecuted, the victims should return home. Only a small percentage of victims therefore report their trafficker to the police. Besides, many women are badly informed or do not realise the risk they take when reporting to the police and later regret it. One Nigerian woman interviewed for research on possible return migration explains how the police misinformed her on the procedure:

> When I went to the police they didn't explain the real situation to me. They didn't say to me, 'Look you are now in this situation, maybe in two or three years you will be in even more shit. We, here in the Netherlands, we don't give papers to foreigners'. But no, they never told me. They said; 'Oh we, or the judge, will give you papers, no problem'. They said very nice things to me just to let me talk and I did. But now they refuse to help me. I have a child, but they don't care. But this is not the deal we made. They never really explained to me how it worked. Just because I don't know the law of this country ... they just said if I would bring them to these people [the traffickers] then I wouldn't have to go back to Nigeria. I took a real risk, you know, with telling them and now they are looking for me as if I am a criminal. (Eimeren, 2004: 35–6; author's translation)

The repatriation of trafficked persons is limiting the protection of victims, not only here, but also in the country of origin. Forced deportations can be seen as a failure to include the provision of a safe, voluntary return. Especially when trafficking occurs in the context of organised crime, this presents an unacceptable safety risk to victims. Their traffickers, who often come from the same village, may threaten to kill the victims or their families. The world has become smaller, not only for those migrating, but also for those who return. Most of the time strong connections exist between traffickers in countries of destination and countries of origin. This means that victims who are sent back run a real risk of encountering their former trafficker again. The principle of non-*refoulement* is the core of international refugee protection and is recognised as a norm of international law and should not be undermined (see also Hopkins and Nijboer, 2003). Non-*refoulement* refers to a prohibition on sending an individual back to a country where (s)he will be persecuted or will suffer ill treatment, for example torture, inhuman or degrading treatment, or punishment.

Organised crime and the Palermo Protocol as a law enforcement tool

The UN Protocol on Trafficking and the Protocol on Smuggling are both linked to the Convention against Transnational Organised Crime.

This Convention is the first UN instrument in the field of international organised crime. The underlying assumption is that trafficking in human beings is not only a serious violation of human rights, but must also be regarded as an area in which international organised crime is active. The UN Protocol situates trafficking firmly in the context of organised crime. The tools for law enforcement are described as: exchange of information, training in prevention, investigation, cooperation with civil society, border measures and better quality of travel documents.

A number of organisations/researchers have documented the involvement of organised criminal gangs in the trafficking in human beings (Aronowitz, 2001; 2003; Dijk, 2002; Kleemans *et al.*, 1998; Salt and Hogarth, 2000). They come to the conclusion that numerous actors are involved in trafficking. Generally speaking the criminals fit on a continuum ranging from individuals working on the side, to loose, flexible networks and ending with professional, highly structured criminal organisations controlling the trafficking process from start to finish.

On closer inspection, the trafficking business is sometimes hard to distinguish from smuggling. People with whom women establish the initial contact are not always those who await them on arrival. Studies on trafficking, however, rarely pay attention to the links among traffickers. Andrijasevic comes to the conclusion in her study of Eastern Europeans that in cases where a woman has no money of her own but incurs a debt to those who provide her with a visa (or a passport) and/or organise transport, there is some kind of collaboration between the parties in countries of origin and countries of destination. In cases when a woman has enough money to pay an agency which secures her a visa and the transportation to Europe there is usually no contact between the links in the trafficking chain (Andrijasevic, 2004: 35). So even though there are cases in which the trafficker is involved in the whole process, there are also cases in which the agents who recruit or transport the migrant have no relation to those who profit from the labour. In that case a mix of smuggling and trafficking is present. However, the trafficking definition is often used as an umbrella term to cover the whole process which can be organised in various ways and involves a range of different actors and outcomes. This in itself makes the definition of trafficking very difficult to put into practice in a uniform way (O'Connell Davidson, 2003).

Some involved profit from the transport only, others from forging documents, yet others from the labour and again others profit from all aspects involved. So when various actors are involved in the trafficking process, why is the link with organised crime so often made? The most important reason probably is that the link with organised crime justifies measurements to *combat* trafficking. Attention is diverted from protecting the victims and towards detecting the criminals. Focusing on the criminals also justifies the emphasis in the West on creating barriers to migration. Dangerously enough migrants are, in this line of reasoning, not protected from trafficking; rather, it is states that are protected from traffickers and from migration. The Trafficking Protocol offers very little in terms of human rights protections for trafficking victims.[3] Concrete measures mainly have to do with the privacy of trafficking victims and the access to information on legal proceedings. But other forms of protection, such as physical, psychological and social recovery, are formulated without any obligations:

> each State Party shall consider implementing measures to provide for the physical, psychological and social recovery of victims of trafficking in persons. (UN Protocol to Prevent, Suppress and Punish Trafficking in Persons, Especially Women and Children, Article 6 (3))

More binding measures on protection should be included in the trafficking definition. At the least a clear description has to be made of the minimum core rights to which all trafficked persons are entitled. Here again the Trafficking Protocol leaves too much leeway for states' own interpretations. Most states are reluctant to implement extensive protection measures because they fear possible abuse of the protection system and of restrictions on state capacity to control migration.

Conclusion

Most of the studies done on trafficking have been articulated from the perspective of violence against women and assume or produce the image of trafficked women as victims. By approaching trafficking from the perspective of migration, a more neutral and a broader framework is offered in which trafficking can be understood from a more dynamic perspective. Neutral here should be understood in the sense of shifting away from the traditional debate between 'abolitionists' and 'regulationists' over the definition of trafficking. When it comes to the specific relation between prostitution and trafficking a few moral dilemmas remain that lead to diverse national explanations and/or implementations of the trafficking law. The broadening of the Trafficking Protocol to other sectors also makes a more neutral approach possible. With a broader and more dynamic framework I mean taking smuggling and more generally irregular migration into account when studying trafficking. Apart from moral standpoints on prostitution there is also a static division created between smuggling and trafficking that classifies smuggling on the one hand as a victimless crime and trafficking on the other as only brought in relation with victims. This makes it hard to identify those involved in either one of the two and ignores the dynamic character of the process. Smuggling one day can turn into trafficking the next day.

Concrete problems that stand in the current trafficking definition have to do with the terms *exploitation* and *protection*. What is meant by these terms is completely vague and the compromised definition is woolly enough to allow each country to reach its own interpretation. The question remains how to measure exploitation and therefore to identify a real victim of trafficking. It would be very helpful to identify step-by-step, beginning in the country of origin, where irregular migrants are confronted with exploitative conditions. Then, of course, national standards differ and most of the work done by smuggled/trafficked persons takes place in the informal economy, which makes combating exploitation more difficult. The same is true of protection; more binding measurements should be included in the trafficking definition. At the least a clear description has to be given of the minimum core rights to which all trafficked persons are entitled.

Finally, the repressive potential of the protocol will probably prevail. Anti-trafficking measures have led to restrictions for would-be migrants and has increased the number of deportations of migrants who did manage to arrive. The principle of non-*refoulement* should therefore be included in the Trafficking as well as in the Smuggling Protocol. The UN Special Reporter on Violence against Women came to the conclusion that many governments have responded to trafficking fears with legislation to restrict women's freedom of movement. The conflation of anti-immigration and anti-trafficking measures obscures the fact that policies designed to control irregular forms of migration encourage violation of human rights. This connection with the anti-immigration policies has made it difficult to place individuals and their rights at the centre of the debate and to have a more realistic debate about what trafficking actually is.

Notes

1. The EU Council Framework Decision from 2002 on Combating Trafficking in Human Beings obliged all EU member states to harmonise their domestic

criminal legislation on trafficking by 2004, including the broadening of the definition of trafficking to sectors other than prostitution.

2. It must be said that migration is not necessarily part of trafficking; a person can also be trafficked within one country, but here international trafficking is referred to.

3. Europe-wide there is a discussion now on putting more emphasis on victim protection. The European Convention on Action against Trafficking was adopted in May 2005. In this Convention more attention is paid to protecting victims of trafficking in Europe. It offers a framework to support, assist and protect such victims. At the time of writing the Convention remains open for signature and has not come into force.

References

Anderson, B. and O'Connell Davidson, J. (2003) *Needs and Desires: Is There a Demand for 'Trafficked' Persons?* Geneva: IOM.

Andrijasevic, R. (2004) 'Trafficking in Women and the Politics of Mobility in Europe', PhD Thesis, University of Utrecht.

Aronowitz, A. A. (2001) 'Smuggling and Trafficking in Human Beings: The Phenomenon, the Markets that Drive it and the Organisations that Promote it', *European Journal on Criminal Policy and Research* 2 (9): 163–95.

Aronowitz, A. A. (2003) 'Trafficking in Human Beings: An International Perspective', in D. Siegel, H. van de Bunt and D. Zaitch (eds.), *Global Organized Crime: Trends and Developments*, Dordrecht: Kluwer.

Coomaraswamy, R. (2000) *Trafficking in Women, Women's Migration and Violence against Women*, submitted in accordance with Commission on Human Rights resolution 1997/44 (E/CN.4/2000/68, 29 February 2000).

Dijk, E van (2002) *Mensenhandel in Nederland 1997–2000*, Zoetermeer: KLPD.

Doezema, J. (2000) 'Loose Women or Lost Women? The Re-emergence of "White Slavery" in Contemporary Discourses on "Trafficking in Women"', *Gender Issues*, 18 (1): 23–50.

Doezema, J. (2002) 'Who Gets to Choose? Coercion, Consent and the UN Trafficking Protocol', *Gender and Development*, 10 (1): 20–8.

Eimeren, E van. (2004) *Een weg terug? Slachtoffers van vrouwenhandel over terugkeer naar land van herkomst*, Blinn.

Hopkins, R. and Nijboer, J. (2003) 'Trafficking in Human Beings and Human Rights: Research, Policy and Practice in the Dutch Approach', Paper presented at the *Trafficking in Persons* conference, Nottingham, 27–28 June.

Kleemans, E. R., van den Berg, A. E. I. M. and van de Bunt, H. G. (1998) *Monitor Georganiseerde Criminaliteit*, Den Haag: WODC.

Kofman, E. *et al.* (2000) *Gender and International Migration in Europe*, London and New York: Routledge.

Leun, J. van der and Vervoorn, L. (2004) *Slavernij-achtige uitbuiting in Nederland. Een inventariserende literatuurstudie in het kader van de uitbreiding van de strafbaarstelling van mensenhandell*, Den Haag: Boom Juridische Uitgevers.

Nationaal Rapporteur Mensenhandel (2002) *Trafficking in Human Beings: The First Report*, Nijmegen: Wolf Legal Productions.

O'Connell Davidson, J. (2003) 'The Trouble with Trafficking', Unpublished paper presented at the Launch Workshop of the Network for European Women's

Rights, Centre for the Study of Global Ethics, University of Birmingham, 29 January.

Pearson, E. (2002) *Human Traffic, Human Rights, Redefining Victim Protection,* London: Anti-Slavery International.

Raymond, J. (2001) *The Guide to the New UN Trafficking Protocol,* North Amherst, MA: Coalition Against Trafficking in Women.

Salt, J. and Hogarth, J. (2000) 'Migrant Trafficking and Human Smuggling in Europe: A Review of the Evidence', in F. Laczko and D. Thompson (eds.), *Migrant Trafficking and Human Smuggling in Europe, a Review of the Evidence with Case Studies from Hungary, Poland and Ukaine,* Geneva: IOM, pp. 11–64.

Vocks, J. and Nijboer, J. (1999) *Land van belofte. Een onderzoek naar slachtoffers van vrouwenhandel uit Centraal- en Oost Europa.* Groningen: Vakgroep Strafrecht en Criminologie.

Wijers, M. and Lap-Chew, L. (1997) *Trafficking in Women, Forced Labour and Slavery-like practices in Marriage, Domestic Labour and Prostitution,* Utrecht: Stichting Tegen Vrouwenhandel.

3
Philosophical Assumptions and Presumptions about Trafficking for Prostitution

Donna Dickenson

Introduction

Trafficking in women generates about $12 billion a year, making it the third largest profit industry in the world after trafficking in weapons and drugs (Bindel, 2003). The public health dimensions of trafficking involve sexually transmitted diseases, HIV/AIDS and the impact on the health of adolescent girls, since many of the women are in fact adolescents. One might assume that this obvious hazard to public health and women's rights would generate universal condemnation, but, with one or two notable exceptions,[1] the trafficking debate is dominated by those who argue against abolitionism as a hopelessly patronising and moralistic approach.

On the dominant flank of the trafficking debate are ranged the somewhat rag-tail armies of neo-liberals and neo-feminists, both of which view sex work as work like any other, more or less freely chosen by the women involved. In the Czech Republic, for example, a draft law specifically treats prostitution as a normal job, subject to the usual forms of contract and employment protection. This position takes male sexuality to be inherently promiscuous and incapable of reform, if it considers male sexuality at all. It tends to focus on the women involved, and not on their clients or traffickers; to take prostitution likewise as a given; and to reject the notion that women are exploited in prostitution.[2]

On the other side of the battle-lines stands an equally ill-matched alliance of law-and-order advocates and old-style feminists, who view sex work as inherently wrong or exploitative. This approach does examine the motives of the clients, rather than simply taking male sexuality as a given. For example, the French association Le Nid has recently published the results of interviews by the sociologist Said Bouamama with 95 clients, of whom the dominant type were classified as 'nostalgics' – men who regret the supposed emancipation of women and look back to the good old days when all women were as 'biddable' as they assume prostitutes to be (Bouamama, 2004). In Sweden, to take another practical example, criminalisation of the buyer rather than the prostitute is the model for social policy.

In my recent experience of leading a European Commission project, the Network for European Women's Rights, voices from the first position were much more vociferous and quite intolerant of the second view – to the extent that Swedish speakers gave up attending workshops discussing prostitution, because they feared being subjected to verbal abuse. There may be political reasons why the neo-liberal camp is so vituperative: many of the organisations that work with prostitutes claim exclusive knowledge of the motivations behind prostitution, and also exclusive rights to funding for working with trafficking 'victims'. In this chapter, however, I make no assumptions about the organisations' motives; rather, I examine both positions on their own merits. I want to argue that the debate is polarised largely because of a failure to examine the underpinning philosophical assumptions critically. To a philosopher it is an offensive *presumption* to make such uncritical *assumptions*.

In particular I want to take issue with two central assumptions:

1. that the sale of sexual services is like the sale of any other good or service;
2. that, by and large, women involved in trafficking for prostitution freely consent to sell such services. (A weaker form of this assumption might be that we are wrong to simply assume that their consent is not free.)

Both assumptions are too often used as a 'knock-down argument', one that closes down further debate because it is widely assumed to be palpably obvious. Philosophers are generally suspicious of knock-down arguments, although cynics might say that is because they put philosophers out of work. This pair of presumptions, however, is particularly suspect because both rely on the libertarian rhetoric which pushes all the right buttons in our psyches, the buttons marked 'choice' and 'freedom'.

However, the opposite pair of presumptions is not necessarily true either: that women never choose prostitution freely, and that prostitution has nothing in common with economic transactions. The Swedish criminalisation model seems to assume that only the clients of prostitutes exercise sufficiently free choice to be held criminally responsible for their actions, and/or that the sale of sexual services is in fact exploitation rather than free trade. Although the Swedish model has been accused of being puritanical, clearly it is somewhat more sophisticated than simple condemnation of prostitution as a sin. Otherwise the law in Sweden would penalise both the prostitute *and* the client. It seems, however, to be making both assumptions: that women do not choose prostitution voluntarily, and/or that those who buy prostitutes' services are engaging in something other than a normal economic transaction. Normal economic transactions are not criminal offences.

However, although the Swedish position makes certain philosophical assumptions about responsibility and choice, it does constitute an improvement on the blatantly false assumption that whatever one does, one has chosen to do. It implies, rightly, that we can distinguish between actions plain and simple, and actions for which we can be held responsible. Without that distinction, the criminal law would founder. For example, we would always prosecute offences committed by children or by mentally disordered offenders even if they were not old or sane enough to be held responsible for their actions. By judging clients' choice to buy sexual services as freer than prostitutes' choice to sell them, and thus as involving greater responsibility for actions, Swedish policy has gone one step further down the road to critical analysis than the view that all actions should be assumed to be freely chosen. It implies that we can distinguish different degrees of freedom in agents' actions. This is a good start, leading us into an examination of choice and responsibility.

Choice and responsibility

A choice to sell sexual services in the neo-liberal or neo-feminist view should be presumed to be freely chosen, and free choices must be accepted out of respect for the individual's autonomy. Whether or not this is really true is, of course, not self-evident at all, but is central to one of the oldest debates in moral and political philosophy. In comparatively recent times it was strongly contested by Marx, who did not question the second half of the statement – that we must respect free choices because we respect individual autonomy – but who did scrutinise the conditions in which choice is made, interrogating the notion of 'free' much more closely. Marx does this when he portrays the (male) worker as alienated, robbed of the right to control his own labour, because he lacks the power to control the conditions in which he works. The alienated worker's labour is in fact the symbol of his oppression not of his freedom – although under capitalism he is not a slave, any more than prostitutes are necessarily always sex slaves even if they have been trafficked (Marx, 1973).

At its simplest, if no work other than prostitution is available, and if I must work or starve, then there is just as much doubt about whether my choice is free as if there is no other work but coalmining, or any of the other masculine icons of the traditional labour movement – where it has been comparatively easy for onlookers to accept that the worker's choice is constrained and not free. The situation is not all that different for women in some parts of Eastern Europe, where only extreme free marketeers would claim that women's choice to sell their sexual services is entirely unconstrained. It is in relation to these women, and to under-age girls, that doubt is most often voiced about using freedom of choice and responsibility for one's actions to argue against the non-prosecution of traffickers, the legalisation of prostitution or the treatment of trafficked women as economic migrants. These are comparatively easy cases.

Feminist theory, however, takes these doubts further. In one form, it has questioned whether the choice to remain in the home is entirely unconstrained, or whether it is socially determined by lack of other choices.[3] In another, more sophisticated form, feminist theory has done more than show how the *conditions* under which women make choices about employment are socially determined and limited. Rather, the most novel insights of feminist theory concern the way in which the supposedly free subject is herself socially constructed (Hirschmann, 2003).

This is a risky move because what we are meant to respect in free choices is the notion of the autonomous individual: that is what deserves respect, embodied in her choices – even if the choices seem irrational or ill-advised, undeserving of respect in themselves. But if the individual is not autonomous and free, exactly what is it that we are respecting when we respect her supposedly free and autonomous choice? Might we then be merely colluding in a woman's oppression by respecting her choice to remain with an abusive husband, for example? Or to enter prostitution? It would be ironic if, by respecting liberty of choice, we were in fact diminishing freedom.

Feminist theory has developed a novel take on responsibility and choice out of precisely this tension. On the one hand, feminism has long had to contend with the assumption that women are incapable of real choice: that political decisions, for example, should be made for them by their husbands and fathers, so that they do not require the vote, in James Mill's argument. On the other hand, feminism has also had to deal with the equally sexist assumption that even if women say no, they mean yes: that when they do make an apparent choice, it does not reflect their true wishes – the basis of many a defence against an allegation of rape.

At its most fundamental, feminist theory transcends Marxist-style analysis, by going beyond the limitations imposed by conditions of choice – such as the lack of jobs other than prostitution – to the way in which the subject's own sense of selfhood and choice is insidiously undermined by the absence of choice – so that such a woman might come to view herself as undeserving of, or uninterested in, any job other than prostitution. She is not forced into prostitution, but the underpinning self that chooses is none the less constrained and limited, in such a way that her choice cannot simply be called free. As Nancy Hirschmann writes:

> Many theorists of freedom recognise that desires and preferences are always limited by contexts that determine the parameters of choice: if chocolate and vanilla are the only flavours available, I am not free to choose strawberry, but that does not alter the fact that I would have preferred strawberry if it were available. What is not addressed by most freedom theorists, however, is the deeper, more important issue of how the choosing subject is herself constrained by such contexts: could the repeated absence of strawberry eventually change my tastes so that I lose my desire for it? (Hirschmann, 2003: ix–x)

This is a contrast between the objective definition of freedom, in terms of available options, and the subjective expression of desire, in terms of self-limitation. Arguably, the second is the more dangerous and profound limitation on freedom: if slaves, trafficked women or any other agents do not want to be free, they are much easier to control than if they want to be free but are deterred by beatings or threats. Internalised 'unfreedom' is much more 'unfree' than the externally imposed variant.

However, the obvious problem with this argument again relates to Marxist thought and its difficulties with false consciousness. The trafficked woman who says she chooses freely to remain with her trafficker may be like the worker who votes for a conservative party: both can be seen as displaying false consciousness, a lack of insight into their true interests, an inability to understand the objective reality of their unfree situation. But false consciousness is a patronising notion, and one that leads us into infinite regress. Yet taking people's evaluation of their preferences at face value also leads to major paradoxes.

Isaiah Berlin insisted that freedom demands 'a range of objectively open possibilities, whether these are desired or not ... it is the actual doors that are open that determine the extent of someone's freedom, and not his own preferences' (Berlin, 1979, cited in Herschman, 2003: 5). Perhaps we can understand this point more clearly by looking at the opposite sort of case, what I shall call the Woody Allen syndrome. It is entirely possible – indeed, very common – to lack for nothing in the way of open doors, to enjoy money, status, fame and a much younger girlfriend, but still to feel dissatisfied, restless and miserable. Are we willing to say that someone like this, who defines himself as unfree and hampered by circumstances, is *less* free than the trafficked woman who says she wants to stay with her pimp? Surely there are fewer actual doors open for her – often quite literally.

What distinguishes the two camps in the trafficking debate is not only their view of the parameters of choice, but whether they tacitly accept what Carole Pateman calls 'male sex-right' (Pateman, 1988). On this understanding, trafficking merely represents the last stage of men's rights over female bodies, its globalisation. I now want to move on to examine this viewpoint in the context of the other unexamined assumption in the trafficking discourse: that buying and selling sexual services is the same as any other economic transaction.

Property in women's bodies and sexual services

Let me begin this section by distinguishing between physical property rights in women's bodies – which is atypical of modern economic and legal systems, although it persists in slavery and some forms of customary law – and rights to women's sexual services. It might be objected that a woman's body is not literally sold in prostitution, so long as she is not a slave. There may be distinctions to be drawn here between 'purchase' of a trafficked woman by a pimp, who then controls all her exchanges with clients – which does look much more like sale of the woman's body – and the self-employed prostitute who does not hand over any proportion of her earnings to a pimp. These two ends of the spectrum are very different and we ought to be wary of saying that the self-employed prostitute is selling her body as such. Rather, this argument runs, a service is being exchanged for money in the normal contractual manner.

Where women's bodies are concerned, however, the 'normal contractual manner' does not necessarily apply. I am not referring to the non-enforceability of contracts for prostitution in many jurisdictions, although that ought to alert us to practical problems about claiming that this is a contract like any other (Radin, 1996: 135). There are profounder reasons why transactions concerning the use of women's bodies, even if distinguished from the sale of women's bodies, cannot simply be assumed to be the same as any other economic transaction.[4]

In Pateman's 'sexual contract', which can take many forms – prostitution, pornography, surrogate motherhood and marriage among them – the two parties start from and end on very different footings: the rights of the woman are not protected to the same extent as the rights of the man. The marriage 'contract', for example, has traditionally established men's legitimate access at all times to women's physical persons, so that the offence of marital rape has been recognised only very recently in common law jurisdictions,[5] and is still not recognised in some countries.[6] Similarly, the right to exit from the marriage 'contract', if it exists, is often limited more strictly for women than for men: Islamic law is often interpreted as allowing a man unilaterally to pronounce himself divorced from his wife, but not the reverse. All these barriers are typical of the unequal ways in which rights are frequently apportioned between men and women in 'contracts' concerning the use of women's bodies for sexual services.[7] They would also help to explain the concept I introduced earlier, that of 'adaptive preferences'. Where men's rights over women's bodies are systematically privileged, women must adapt: even if they exercise what appears to be free choice, they exercise it under systematic limitations. As I have written elsewhere:

> Other contracts view all parties as possessing equal property rights. This may be a fiction in actuality, as Marxist critics would maintain of employment contracts, but it is a truth in law. Equal rights between men and women in property in the person do not exist in either life or law, Pateman asserts. (Dickenson, 1997: 68)

Pateman warns us to think twice before assuming that a transaction involving the sexual use of a woman's body is no different from any other contract. Rather than being an emblem of modernity or a value-neutral commercial transaction, it is simply one more manifestation of an archaic patriarchal system establishing men's rights of access to women's bodies. Thus viewing prostitution as a sale of services like any other exchange merely allows patriarchy to flourish. (Even if we expand our concerns to consider male prostitutes, male sex-right can still be seen to be at work, in so far as it is predominantly men who are the buyers.)

One could argue, however, that those who want to treat prostitution under the general rubric of services like any other are in fact undermining patriarchy. Because women have widely lacked property in their own reproductive services and sexual labour, it may seem progressive to credit them with having such property. I think this is what convinces many 'neo-feminists' that they must be critical of the entire notion of women as passive victims of trafficking. Selling sexual services seems to such commentators a liberating notion because at least it recognises women 'sex workers' as (free) agents with a property in their own labour.

Now I am quite sympathetic to the attempt to regard women as subjects rather than mere objects of property-holding, as I have frequently stated in *Property, Women and Politics*, and in the sequel I am writing on the way in which commodification of human tissue has turned all bodies, both male and female, into female bodies in so far as all bodies are objectified to a lesser or greater extent. Some earlier feminists wrongly assumed that women's only relation to property could be as its objects, I argued, although they made good polemical use of the notion of women as objects (Dickenson, 1997: 2). But in so doing they risked viewing women as eternal victims, as well as depriving feminism of other useful weapons: property rights and contract. In their justifiable distrust of the liberal discourse of individualism, rights and contract as masculinist, some feminist theorists went too far in rejecting any notion that women could be subjects of property rights.

Saying that such prostitutes sell sexual services seems to assume that they sell them freely, on equal terms, and to enhance women's status as subjects. Yet we do not make any such assumptions about other workers' sale of their time and labour. We cannot assume that these things are sold freely and on equal terms merely because they are sold. We do not assume that the factory worker sells his labour freely, on equal terms, from the brute fact that he sells it. Why should we do so with the prostitute?

This line of reasoning tends to shade over into the freedom argument, but it is also about something more than just the freedom question: property in the body and female sexuality. As Catharine MacKinnon has written, 'Sexuality is to feminism what work is to Marxism: that which is most one's own, yet most taken away' (MacKinnon, 1987: 3). Because women are so frequently reduced to mere sexual beings in patriarchal thought (and in the relentless rise of globalised pornography) sexual labour can never be unambiguous. It is not a matter of simply ensuring that women sex workers do control the conditions of their own labour, however: there the parallel with male proletarian workers' conditions breaks down. Whereas in Marxist thought collective workers' ownership of the means of production would transform workers' oppressive circumstances into life-enhancing labour, even sex workers' collectives or legalisation of prostitution would be insufficient, in my feminist analysis, to transform prostitutes' alienation into freedom.

One reason why this is so is because both the means of production and the object of the transaction in prostitution are women's bodies themselves. This is different from any other form of 'production': although labourers contract out their bodies, what employers buy is the worker's ability to labour hard, long or skilfully. They are indifferent to the shape and size of the workers' bodies in a way that prostitutes' clients presumably are not. (If they were indifferent, the objects of trafficking for prostitution would not normally be nubile young girls.) So even though women's bodies are not literally sold in prostitution, unless in conditions of slavery, women's bodies are also never merely the means by which the labour of sexual services is performed; they are also the object of the service. This puts the prostitute in the ambivalent position of being both an agent, like the male factory worker, and a thing, like the machine part the worker makes. To see oneself as a thing is profoundly alienating. Yet the neo-liberal and neo-feminist view – that prostitution is like any other exchange – assumes that a woman can stand in just such an external relation to her own sexual labour and to her physical person.

Conclusion

As a final reflection, thinking about other 'transactions' involving women's sexual and reproductive organs may also be instructive. In the debate over legalisation of 'surrogate' motherhood we frequently hear it said that women are merely renting out their wombs. Apart from the fact that they are also undergoing the risks and pain of childbirth, this is a strange, objectifying discourse. It seems to lead us down the route of selling kidneys, or even selling one's entire body for the organ trade. What's wrong with that? It's an economic transaction like any other.

The Italian political theorist Daniela Gobetti (1992) argues that we are constrained in our thinking about trade in sex, body parts and similar dilemmas by the way in which seventeenth-century natural law thinkers based the modern theory of subjective rights in Roman law tradition, which sees property in things as the blueprint for all rights-based social phenomena. Our legal and philosophical history creates habits of mind that make it hard to analyse relations among persons concerning resources which are not separable from the body of the possessor, e.g. sexual acts or 'surrogate' motherhood. Only recently have feminists, bioethicists and legal theorists begun to move beyond these restrictions. We need to break away from these habits of thought if we are to find accurate ways of characterising trade in sexual services – and not remain entrenched in presumptions and assumptions.

Notes

1. For example, Malarek (2003).
2. This is a very rough, common denominator summary of a large literature which includes J. O'Connell Davidson (1999), the country reports of the La Strada organisation, e.g. on the Ukraine and Poland; and Daniela Danna, *Donne di Mondo: commercio del sesso e controle statale.*
3. In a large literature, see, for example, Basch (1982), Davidoff (1995), Delphy (1984), Dwyer and Bryce (1988), Hartsock (1983) and Moller Okin (1989).
4. See, for example, Satz (1995), and, in the nineteenth century, Flora Tristan's ground-breaking and powerful analysis in her study of English prostitutes, *Promenades dans Londres* (1842).
5. The offence has only been recognised since 1991 in the UK, in the case of *Regina v R* (Court of Appeal, 14 March).
6. Including Albania, Bosnia-Herzegovina, Bulgaria, Macedonia, Turkey and Romania, among south-east European countries. See UNDP (2003: 19).
7. I use the term 'contract' advisedly; the marriage 'contract', although a popularly used term, is not actually a contract in English law.

References

Basch, N. (1982) *In the Eyes of the Law*, New York: Cornell University Press.
Berlin, I. (1979) 'From Hope and Fear Set Free', in *Concepts and Categories: Philosophical Essays*, New York: Viking Press.
Bindel, J. (2003) 'Tackling the Traffickers', *Guardian*, 12 August.
Bouamama, S. (2004) 'L'homme en question: le processus du devenir-client de la prostitution', summarised in M. J. Gros, 'Prostitution: les cinq client types', *Liberation*, 10 October.
Davidoff, L. (1995) *Worlds Between: Historical Perspectives on Gender and Class*, Cambridge: Polity Press.
Delphy, C. (1984) *Close to Home* (trans. and ed. Diana Leonard), London: Hutchinson.
Dickenson, D. (1997), *Property, Women and Politics*, Cambridge: Polity Press.
Dwyer, D. and Bryce, J. (eds.) (1988) *A Home Divided*, Palo Alto, CA: Stanford University Press
Gobetti, D. (1992), 'Goods of the Mind, Goods of the Body and External Goods', *History of Political Thought*, 13: 31–49.

Hartsock, N. C. M. (1983) *Money, Sex and Power*, Boston, MA: Northeastern University Press.

Hirschmann, N. J. (2003) *The Subject of Liberty: Toward a Feminist Theory of Freedom*, Princeton, NJ and Toronto: Princeton University Press.

MacKinnon, C. A. (1987) *Toward a Feminist Theory of the State*, Cambridge, MA: Harvard University Press.

Malarek, V. (2003) *The Natashas: The Global Sex Trade*, London: Vision.

Marx, K. (1973) *Grundrisse: Foundations of the Critique of Political Economy* (trans. with a foreword by Martin Nicolas), New York: Vintage Books.

Moller Okin, S. (1989) *Justice, Gender and the Family*, New York: Basic Books.

O'Connell Davidson, J. (1999) *Prostitution, Power and Freedom*, Chicago: University of Michigan Press.

Pateman, C. (1988) *The Sexual Contract*, Cambridge: Polity Press.

Radin, M. J. (1996) *Contested Commodities: The Trouble with Trade in Sex, Children, Body Parts and Other Things*, Cambridge, MA: Harvard University Press.

Satz, D. (1995) 'Markets in Women's Sexual Labour', *Ethics*, 106: 63–85.

Tristan, F. ([1842] 1980) *Promenades dans Londres* (trans D. Palmer and G. Pincetl), London: George Prior.

UN Development Programme, Regional Bureau for Europe and the CIS (2003) *Drafting Gender-Aware Legislation: How to promote and protect gender equality in Central and Eastern Europe and in the Commonwealth of Independent States*, Bratislava: UNDP.

4
Towards a Political Economy of 'Trafficking'

Giulia Garofalo

Introduction

At present economic theory has made no headway on 'trafficking'.[1] Given the expansionist lines taken by mainstream economic theory it is legitimate to ask whether it is in any case desirable for economic analysis to be developed on this subject. Yet, I shall show how certain economic tools can be useful for a much needed opening up of the debate on 'trafficking'.

The necessity is to reconcile radical critiques of society with positions that are not simply repressive in their effects – abolitionist and prohibitionist positions, which easily become neo-colonialist, nationalist and anti-feminist positions. An important step in such an opening up is to recognise that, to some extent, practices of power show a general functioning in their economic aspect, whatever the group whose resources are employed is, or the specificity of these resources. This general functioning can be subjected to study and to modification, and this is the object of political economy.

My attempt to place 'trafficking' as an object of political economy is limited to the contemporary context of Europe and is based on a project on the economic analysis of prostitution. I have developed the tools of institutional and feminist economics[2] in reaction to the only model in economic theory of prostitution – a mainstream theory model by Edlund and Kom (2002).

Edlund and Kom argue that prostitution is complementary to marriage, and that every woman may sell either reproductive sex in the marriage market or non-reproductive sex in the prostitution market. The model explains the relatively high price of prostitution as compared with other low-skill jobs performed by women;[3] the price would include

54

compensation for the prostitute's lost marriage opportunities. Edlund and Kom's model includes a few interesting aspects that will appear below. However, it is fundamentally limited since it is based on the claim that 'prostitution has been organized according to similar principles across different times and cultures' (Edlund and Kom, 2002: 187). On the contrary, the available evidence is one of marked organisational difference and of remarkably rapid change in this market (Bindman, 1997; Danna, 2004; O'Connell Davidson, 1998; Torbeik and Pattanaik, 2000). The same conceptual limit is common to analyses of other activities connected with 'trafficking', such as domestic work or simply migration, as well as from traditions of thought such as the feminist ones that one would expect to be radically different from neoclassical economics.[4]

The present work will develop a critical analysis of two assertions current in the debate on 'trafficking'. The first and rarely discussed one is that 'trafficking' situations are pre- or post-contractual situations. The second and over-discussed assertion is that sexual services are somehow different from other services.

Before introducing these points, I will situate my project within the general debate on 'trafficking' *vis-à-vis* the two issues that appear to define it. These are 1) the relationship between prostitution and 'trafficking', and 2) the possibility or necessity of a distinction between choice and non choice in practising prostitution (or other activities connected with 'trafficking').

The relationship between 'trafficking' and prostitution: memory and long-term strategy

Within the general debate on 'trafficking', prostitution is *de facto* a subject that clouds the issue. It is neither politically nor scientifically easy to be clear on prostitution. By being simultaneously a catalyst and a taboo, prostitution seems to prevent political and economic critical thought from developing within the 'trafficking' debate.

This can indeed be a reason for strategies aimed at limiting what is seen as a contaminating impact of prostitution. Take, for instance, the practice of deliberately ignoring prostitution when discussing 'trafficking', adopted (among others) by Anti-Slavery International (Pearson, 2002). Implicitly holding that the exploitation of prostitution is like other forms of exploitation – a position not to be rejected – Anti-Slavery glosses over any specificity of prostitution and in a sense even its very existence. In terms of policies, the utility of these strategies needs to be recognised. They may favour the extension of good policies, such as granting residence status to victims of 'trafficking'. In some European contexts[5] female and male migrant workers in domestic services, agriculture and factory work have recently started to access forms of protection from 'trafficking' previously available only to sex industry workers and that in some cases may be useful for those workers to exit exploitation.

Also, to separate 'trafficking' from prostitution may prevent repressive state action on migration from being enforced on the entire sex industry. This is the reason why it is a strategy largely used by pro-sex workers' rights groups (see International Union of Sex Workers at www.iusw.org [accessed March 2005]).

However, my interpretation is that isolating prostitution issues from the 'trafficking' debate, or dissimulating them within it, can work only as a short-term resistance tactic. Indeed, the intersection between these two spheres carries an important stratified history that should not be overlooked, and a theoretical and policy analysis of 'trafficking' always at least (if not only) implies one of prostitution.

The notion of 'trafficking' has been developed in direct continuity with the old idea of 'white slavery' as used from the end of the nineteenth century to describe prostitution, or, to be more precise, the movements of working-class women from Europe to the colonies through opportunities in sex work. The debate on 'trafficking' still makes use of the political and legal categories and imagery linked to the world of mobile prostitution as it was described and policed at that time (Doezema, 2000). Typically, the central interpretation was one of victimisation of innocent women by evil foreign men and the alleged solution was to impose restrictions on (working-class) female migration (see Doezema, 2000). Both have been extended today to all 'trafficking' activities. When this continuity is overlooked the exposition of such an old understanding of mobile prostitution based on colonialist, classist and anti-feminist arguments is easily forgotten (Augustin, 2003; Pheterson, 1996; Tabet, 1991).

In addition, 'trafficking' obviously has a renewed impact on the debate on prostitution and sex work which cannot be avoided by the decision formally to separate the two. The recent propagation of the 'trafficking' framework may indeed be seen as responsible for the marginalisation of labour and women's emancipation issues as raised since the 1970s (Pheterson, 1989), specifically by politicised sex workers. What is currently put at the centre of discussions on prostitution is instead the need to protect women and states from what is seen above all as a criminal phenomenon (Associazione 'On the Road', 2002; Pearson, 2002; Wijers, 2001).

In the context of such a twist, far from clouding the issue, an analysis of prostitution from perspectives of political economy may actually offer 'trafficking' debates an opportunity to reconnect to the larger economic and political institutions, in particular issues of gender, labour and migration.

Choice/no choice: contesting substantial distinctions

Much of the energy in the 'trafficking' and prostitution debate is invested in the question of the extent to which it is a free choice to work as a prostitute, to work in other sectors at risk of 'trafficking', or simply to migrate. Whatever the answer, this question's frame implicitly and explicitly assumes a separation between 'voluntary prostitution', 'free labour' and 'voluntary migration' on the one hand, and 'forced prostitution', 'slavery' or 'trafficking' on the other (Doezema, 1998).

From the knowledge produced by projects that directly intervene against 'slavery' and 'trafficking' it clearly emerges that the difference between slavery-like cases and labour cases is not attributable to an *a priori* intention to engage in a certain practice (typically prostitution) (Carchedi *et al.*, 2003; Wijers and Lap-Chew, 1997). Instead, it is discernible in the conditions in which the work (or the migration project) is effectively performed. Rather than focusing on matters like deceit or violence at the origin, it is useful to:

> concentrate on the place where it is practiced, on relations of dependence or exploitation undermining decisional autonomy of movement, on working conditions [for example the impossibility to refuse clients or sex acts, or of leaving prostitution, given constraints exerted mostly with debt systems] and, above all, on profits: dominance is exerted by the pimps imposing work in certain places with a certain timetable, direct or indirect control being achieved with the supply of money and unused prophylactics. (Virgilio, 2000: 50. Author's translation)

A first-level critique of the choice/no choice frame is offered by what may be called a pragmatic approach. From perspectives of political economy this may represent the most interesting line. What matters in terms of concrete social and legal action is the definition of a series of devising criteria corresponding to a sort of 'tolerable exploitation', a culturally acceptable limit that would distinguish 'trafficking' from acceptable migration and labour. This would include measures such as the minimum wage, maximum working hours, maximum and defined interest rates, protection of workers' freedom to break the contract, security at work, right to access translation, unionisation, housing, and many others.

Significantly, this implies the correct recognition that there are no good reasons to treat the worst forms of exploitation with tools other than those applied to the rest of the labour market, since it is in the market that they prosper, responding to similar incentives, and so forth (Bales, 2000).

However, such a pragmatic approach developed from the experience of social and legal work over the last 20 years has been unable to form an alternative position in a debate on 'trafficking' which remains firmly articulated in the choice/no choice trap. This may be partly due to the tendency among 'pragmatic' activists, social workers and policymakers (strategically?) to accept the mainstream dualistic conception that sees trafficking as radically different from cases of exploitation, whether in the field of prostitution or domestic work, or other industries. For instance, emphasis is often placed on the capacity of 'trafficking' to camouflage within the world of prostitution or domestic work or migration. Attention is given by many (see Carchedi, 2003; Giammarinaro, 2003) to ways of unmasking the forms of slavery or forced migration which are 'hiding' among the forms of free labour or migration. Such an approach assumes that the core problem is our access to information, while the agents – for instance, the woman who works as a prostitute, her 'employer' and perhaps also her client – are assumed to be fully aware of being in a forced situation. As most people working in the field know by direct experience, this view is contestable on the grounds of the accounts of 'trafficked' people who typically see themselves as migrant workers and their 'traffickers' as employers, helpers, friends or lovers (see Andrijasevic, 2003; Augustín, 2003; Corso and Trifirò, 2002).

My suggestion is that the concrete fights against 'trafficking' need to develop a more robust theoretical framework. This should be able to address the two key weaknesses of the 'trafficking' framework consisting of the 'white slavery' interpretation of sex work and the choice/no choice trap. One possible way is the consideration of the relations experienced by trafficked persons as economic transactions, not constituting exceptions in the wage labour market but rather representing different answers to similar problems.

Every economic exchange has a history of emancipations and regressions in terms of social justice (Nussbaum, 1999). To look at the continuities between the more and the less contractual forms of a particular exchange instead of considering the former or the latter as a deviation from the others can account for and promote change.

In the case of sexual and domestic services in contemporary Europe such an analysis necessarily also implies the exploration of sectors of labour that are not waged but exchanged in informal ways within families or other 'private' relationships. Feminists, in particular materialist feminists, have shown how exchanges which are considered 'cultural' or 'private' have indeed an economic content that needs political scrutiny.

For instance, the exchange of sexual services is one of the ways in which women and men access material advantages not only within paid regimes called prostitution, in an explicit monetary bargaining of time and sexual acts, or according to other rules established by a control structure such as a brothel, but also in other contexts such as marriage or loving relationships. To enlarge labour analyses to these spheres and to look at what has been called the *sexual-economic exchange* (Tabet, 1991), whether in the market or not, does not mean overlooking the differences in social or political meanings that each singular transaction may have within a particular family or within a particular club. On the contrary, it means taking into account how specific allocative practices can produce opposite political meanings, whether within a particular family or within a particular club. Whether paid or unpaid a sexual-economic transaction reproduces, gives access to, the same social hierarchies, but can do so in linear or, on the contrary, in modified ways, according to how it is specifically organised.

Extending the notion of contract

One point of my critique is the understanding of 'trafficking' situations as pre- or post-contractual. In this largely shared discourse reference is implicitly made to a notion of contract supposedly existing elsewhere, which economists should study.

Now, contract studies in economic sciences suggest that a contract is never comprehensible in itself; in other words, it is not a good unit of analysis. The idea of a clear-cut separation between what is 'contract' and what is 'extra' has been largely contested. Some use the term *transaction* to speak of economic exchange in a different way (Commons, 1931). The transaction indicates the set of conditions making the exchange not only possible and sustainable at a level of *a priori* efficiency, but also *enforceable* (Bowles and Gintis, 1993). In practice, the contrasting interests of the parties – their opportunism – come into play not only in defining the contract *a priori* but also *a posteriori*, when the concrete exchange of the good or service is performed. For this reason there is always some extra-contractual room that has to be included in the study of a transaction where what counts is the degree of power the parties enjoy due to their role in institutions or conventions which may have no part in the 'internal logic' of the exchange but are fundamental to its very existence, belonging to the economy as a whole.

This extra-contractual effect is especially remarkable in the case of exchange of labour services, and even more so for personal services, such as sexual or care services, which are often even less definable *a priori* and where a broad margin of conflict remains open between the two parties (see Hochschild, 1983 for an analysis of emotional labour).

As a further complication, the appropriate reference framework for personal services involves the combined bargaining of at least three parties. Looking at prostitution, these are the sex worker, the client (often disregarded in institutionalist analyses, see Ramseyer, 1991)[6] and the 'third party' (often ignored in feminist analyses; see Pateman, 1988), in the context of which account may be taken of the alliances that may arise in real situations. The 'third party' is, first and typically, the 'employer', the 'organiser', but it could be one among a plurality of subjects emerging in real situations as having a share of control on the transaction, including the landlord, the tax official or the police.

Among the mechanisms that the client and/or employer can impose on the sex worker in order to make the exchange enforceable, the mechanism acting upon price is of particular interest. We may interpret low prices – common in Europe in the sphere of workers coming from Eastern Europe, Latin America and Africa[7] – as an economic instrument applied by the two parties, client and employer, in practice allied to control the sex worker's work. The sex worker's poverty and debts reduce her bargaining capacity *vis-à-vis* both client and third party. This interpretation tallies with that of the Committee for the Civil Rights of Prostitutes in Italy. The element of control over the actual work of the sex worker is clearly identifiable in the low market segments, and particularly in the area of street prostitution:

> Our hypothesis, rather than making reference to causes that might be defined as exogenous (the large number of girls on the streets, the range of performance supplied, problems of illegal status, etc.), begins ... with the factors determining the terms of employment as

such. What is in the pimp's interests? Firstly that the girls work, and work hard: it is essential to increase the nightly number of clients, if necessary reducing the quality and cost of performance; secondly, that the girls be left with little or nothing in return, since this makes it easier to compel them to work ...

Supply devaluation restores to the client positions of force and shares of power over the bodies of the new prostitutes: lacking union support and political strength, confined to the damned conditions of their illegal status, at the mercy of pimps and police, street girls pay in the first place for their relations with pimps. (*Comitato per i Diritti Civili delle Prostitute*, 1999: 3; author's translation)

Within this kind of enlarged contractual analysis, the relations experienced by 'trafficked' persons are considered economic transactions, not constituting exceptions in the wage labour market but rather representing different answers to similar problems. It becomes possible to study other interesting aspects of 'trafficking' applying some tools for economic analysis of transactions (Williamson, 1980).

Let me take another example. A woman working as a sex worker in a particular club or for a particular agency will in practice be forced to supply a certain sexual service to certain clients in a certain way under the plausible threat of being fired by the owner. The power of dismissal – of exit (Hirschman, 1970) – held by the employer, clearly carries great weight in guaranteeing the enforcement of a contract that the worker wishes to see prolonged in time. This power works because of the availability of new workers, guaranteed by larger processes of proletarianisation and migration. But what about her power over the owner's (and the client's) enforcement of the contract? Somehow less obvious is the impact on organisation exerted by the worker's power to exit from the transaction, i.e. of the woman to leave the brothel or the agency (or the client). This action may not have such a direct effect, nor is it symmetrical to the power of dismissal held by the brothel owner (or in a different way by the client). Yet it certainly is one of the fundamental modifying forces in workers' hands, since the employer too has an interest in maintaining continuity in the transaction. Indeed, according to Yann Moulier Boutang (1998), the difference between free wage labour, 'bridled' wage labour and slave labour depends on the way the employer ensures continuity in the workforce. Control of this continuity within the contract entails considerable costs for them. It is, for instance, necessary to raise wages and improve working conditions, or alternatively to administer a strong and constant level of violence.

It is in fact mainly elements of broader social-juridical institutions that block workers' exit mobility. One of these elements is to be found in the state or local community (legal or illegal) social protection systems serving the worker and his/her family. Other examples relevant in contemporary European contexts are the laws regulating immigration. These are often perceived in the function of limiting the entry or welfare of foreign workers, but actually can be seen as serving to limit workers' exit mobility. These laws impose various bureaucratic restrictions on 'legal' migrants which keep them in one particular region and, with the new 'residence contract' model (see the Bossi-Fini immigration law in Italy l.189/30.07.2002), with one specific employer. And of course the scarcity of accommodation for migrants also means a further tie to one single landlord, who, for many workers, is often also the employer. Moreover, in indirect ways restrictive migration laws increase the dependency of migrants on those who help them to enter the destination country and in their migration project generally (Andrijasevic, 2003; Augustin, 2003; Torbeik and Pattanaik, 2002). An additional anti-exit tie then appears to be the debt migrants get into with these 'helpers', which has been produced by restrictive migration laws in the first place.

In the case of prostitution this sort of exit bar is historically of great importance. The state brothels of Napoleonic origin, known as *maisons closes* (closed houses), were closed in two senses. Not only was entry barred to respectable women, but also exit was barred to the women working as prostitutes, who could not change work or even employer in some cases (for a similar organisation in Imperial Japan, see Ramseyer, 1991). Similar 'confinements' within a place where workers' rights are systematically violated are still common for prostitution in today's Europe (Expert Group on Trafficking in Human Beings at the European Commission, 2004).

Indeed, the stigma people working as prostitutes suffer from in most communities may also be seen as having a similar economic meaning. On the one hand, it means lack of information, and thus barriers to entry to people engaged in other types of work, and on the other difficulty for the sex workers in changing work, or even employer. The stigmatisation of people working as prostitutes often also makes it impossible for them to live in certain communities – typically those of their family of origin.

The questions that can be addressed to 'trafficking' along this line of analysis are linked to how it develops within the same structure as the rest of labour and migration transactions. However, it does remain relevant to address the political meanings produced by the different organisations of specific labour sectors.

The specificity of sexual services

This brings me to the second assertion I wish to consider, which holds that prostitution is not a service like any other.

The debate on this issue is well known in political and feminist philosophy. Important contributions have been developed, for instance, by Carol Pateman (1988) who describes male clients' power as a special one, since to them it is an end rather than an instrument. On the opposite side Martha Nussbaum (1999) demonstrates the logical-political poverty of arguments that there is any substantial difference between prostitutional service and other services, such as massage or colonoscopy.

My approach is not to deny that there is something particular about exchanging sex for money. On the contrary, theoretical space should be given to the fact that prostitution is not a 'normal job'. I will do this with reference to its gender dimension in its internal relation to sexuality,[8] while the issues related to 'race', nationality and migration, and class of origin, which are also often central in the prostitution market (and to sexuality more generally), remain to be analysed. Hopefully this selection will not constitute a closure to the consideration of these dimensions, which are at least partially distinct from the gender one.

Two types of evidence show the role of gender in prostitution. The first is of an organisational nature. What seem at first sight to be the specific characteristics of the prostitution transaction completely change when the genders of the parties change, namely, it emerges that with female clients and male sex workers:

1 the risk of aggression, among the greatest risks faced by female sex workers, does not affect male sex workers performing with women; in this case the risk is on the client's side;
2 the sex worker often pays no price of social stigma, and often no law establishes the legality or illegality of the activity;
3 often male sex workers for women require payment after service (Roberta Tatafiore refers to 'post-coital bargaining'), which is a rare exception for female sex workers;
4 the price formation mechanisms include criteria such as the age and the attractiveness of the client, concerning the (presumed) desire of the sex worker;
5 the market organisation tends to be autonomous;
6 the prices are relatively high. (Phillips, 2002; Tatafiore, 1998)

This evidence suggests that in prostitution gender is a dominant institution in comparison to other market institutions.

The second piece of evidence emerges by taking the viewpoint of consumption study. Interviews with clients show their direct interest in the gender of the person who is performing the sexual service[9] (see Leonini, 1999). Whether the sex worker is a woman, a man or a trans-gender person, her/his gender in relation to the client is a central element of the client's desire for commercial sexual services. 'Buying gender' is understandable at the level of subjectivity within a frame that sees gender identity as dependent on a repetitive set of practices rather than as a given naturally producing these very practices (Butler, 1990).

Accounting for both pieces of evidence means taking seriously that the exchange of sexual services not only depends on an exchange of reciprocal social positions (typically gendered), but is also a vehicle for it. In a performative ring sexual practices give access to existent hierarchical identities in terms of gender (and 'race' and nationality) and simultaneously reproduce them in *linear* or, on the contrary, in *modified ways*.

The clients' peculiar interest in positioning themselves in terms of gender makes clear the political and not exclusively allocative function of the prostitutional exchange.

Gender power is mobilised at both an individual and group level. Following Hirsch's (1976) idea of *positional goods*, it is possible to conceive of prostitution as a 'group pan-positional good' (Pagano, 1999). A positional good is, for instance, a luxury car, desirable as such if and only if there are people without it, so that by buying such a car one can position oneself in relation to them. Now, what happens in prostitution between the sex worker and the client in terms of sexual-economic practices will produce an impact on both their reciprocal positions as individuals (bi-positional dimension) and, automatically, due to the particular gender dimension, on all males as males, on all females as females, on all trans-gender people as trans-gender people (pan-positional dimension).

When, for instance, a woman working as a prostitute holds more power than her male client in negotiating prices and sex acts, succeeding in giving the 'least possible' in exchange for the highest possible earnings, and she works autonomously, then it is possible to say that the pan-positional effect will be a sort of public good for all women and a sort of 'public evil' for all men.

Of course, this is only a partial analysis, since each member of the gender group will simultaneously be impacted by and have an impact on other effects of the same transaction, such as 'race', nationality and class of origin effects. The relevant point of the analysis though is the idea of working on the links between the practices of power 'as a means' ('neutral', 'economic' power) and the practices of power 'as an end in itself', whether bi-positional (such as the pleasure of ordering acts from anyone) or group pan-positional (gendered, 'raced', classist, nationality-related power).

What happens in the terms of the details of prostitution transactions makes the difference for the political meaning of prostitution which is so important to feminist, homosexual, anti-nationalist and anti-racist perspectives.

Conclusion

The contribution political economy may offer the understanding of and the fights against 'trafficking' is based on the idea that gender (or other) power asymmetry between agents takes shape in the effective *contractual regimes* (Pantaleoni, 1963), and assumes that in most cases those regimes are characterised by indeterminacy.

A gender analysis of prostitution, domestic work or migration does not exclude that 'trafficking' be recognised as a contractual regime, of prostitution, domestic work or migration. I have shown that once we fully theoretically recognise it as a contractual regime of unacceptable exploitation – especially from a gender-sensitive perspective – it becomes possible to see which institutional elements prevent 'trafficked' people from improving their rent[10] while leaving ample margins to organisers and clients.

With reference to prostitution I have indicated a few of these elements. I have suggested how prices can work as a mechanism used by the 'organiser' and the client in practice allied to control and exploit the worker. Also, all elements that reduce workers' mobility, including stigma, have been shown to produce the contractual regime called 'trafficking'.

With regard to commercial sex, legalising and normalising agreements in the sex industry and recognising as legitimate the work of migrant workers emerges as a necessary step. Indeed at present most European countries do not recognise a contract that safeguards and regulates prostitution (Danna, 2004; Outshoorn, 2004). Central to these policies is not only the reduction of workers' power position generally, but also in particular the non-recognition of incomes earned through sex work for the purposes of foreigners' residence permits (see Andrijasevic, 2003). Even in the Netherlands, where prostitution is in principle equal in law to any other job, as a general rule it is not possible to obtain a work permit for prostitution (see, www.femmigration.net). If, on the one hand, the irregularity of the sex industry is an attractive avenue for people, especially women and trans-gender people, who do not have the legal right to work in formal sectors, on the other, their illegal position traps them in a particular job so contributing to the production of precisely the contractual regime called 'trafficking'.

More generally according to the proposed analysis and in contrast to the anti-trafficking policies in force, promoting the freedom to exit from work and promoting freedom of movement should become priorities in anti-trafficking policies.

Notes

1. Trafficking is a major issue in contemporary political debates. However, the empirical referent of trafficking is at best unclear, lost in a mixture of migration, prostitution and labour realities. What constitutes trafficking appears upon scrutiny as being selected on highly problematic assumptions, namely on the idea of a specificity of the activities performed by or involving a Third World Woman (Doezema, 2000). The inverted commas indicate this fundamental problem of scientific inquiry.
2. See Hodgson (2004) and Barker and Kuiper (2003) for overviews and for a feminist economic work on prostitution, van der Veen (2001).
3. The assumption that prostitution is a low-skill job is itself contestable. See Brewis and Linstead (2000).
4. For critiques see Kempadoo and Doezema (1998), Doezema (2001) and Wijers and Lap-Chew (1997).
5. For instance in Italy (private conversation with Gruppo Abele, Torino, March 2005).
6. In his analysis of the *indentured prostitution* contract between brothel and prostitute in Imperial Japan, Ramseyer totally disregards the possible role of the client.
7. In the streets in Italy prices are as low as 15 euros (£10) for a 'basic service'.
8. For an understanding of gender, sex and sexuality as internally interdependent, see Wittig (1981) and Butler (1990). Here gender is in particular a heteronormative coherence.
9. Similar observations may also be valid in respect of the worker's 'race' and nationality.
10. Technically, in economics the sex worker's rent is created when the (equilibrium) price is above the supply price, i.e. the minimum price at which the sex worker is prepared to supply her/his services.

References

Andrijasevic, R. (2003) 'The Difference Borders Make: (Il)legality, Migration and Trafficking in Italy among "Eastern" European Women in Prostitution', in Sara Ahmed *et al.* (eds.) *Uprootings/Regroundings: Questions of Home and Migration*, Oxford: Berg.

Augustín, L. (2003) 'A Migrant World of Services', *Social Politics*, 10(3): 377–96.

Associazione 'On the Road' (2002) *Article 18: Protection of Victims of Trafficking and Fight against Crime (Italy and the European Scenarios)* Martinsicuro: On the Road Edizioni.
Bales, K. (2000) *Disposable People, New Slavery in the Global Economy*, Berkeley: University of California Press.
Barker, D. and E. Kuiper (eds.) (2003) *Toward a Feminist Philosophy of Economics*, London: Routledge.
Becker, G. (1991) *A Treatise on the Family*. Cambridge, MA: Harvard University Press.
Bindman, J. (1997) *Redefining Prostitution as Sex Work on the International Agenda*, London: Anti-Slavery International.
Bowles, S. and H. Gintis (1993) 'The Revenge of *Homo Economicus*: Contested Exchange and the Revival of Political Economy', *Journal of Economic Perspectives*, 1(7): 83–102.
Brewis, J. and S. Linstead (2000) *Sex, Work and Sex Work*, London: Routledge.
Butler, J. (1990) *Gender Trouble*, London: Routledge.
Cairnes, J. E. (ed.) (1968) *The Slave Power*, New York: Kelley.
Carchedi, F. (2003) 'Le modalita di sfruttamento coatto e la prostituzione mascherata', in Carchedi *et al.* (eds.), *Lavore servile nuove schiavitù*, Milano: Franco Angeli, pp. 125–46.
Carchedi, F. *et al.* (2003) *Lavoro servile nuove schiavitù*, Milano: Franco Angeli
Comitato per i diritti civili delle prostitute (1999) *Sesso comprato e venduto: considerazioni economiche e sociosanitarie* available at www.luccioleonline.org.
Commons, J. (1931) 'Institutional Economics', *American Economic Review*, 4(21): 648–57.
Corso, C. and A. Trifirò (2002) *... e siamo partite. Migrazione, tratta e prostituzione straniera in Italia*, Firenze: Giunti.
Danna, D. (2004) *Donne di mondo. Costruzione sociale e realta' della prostituzione in Italia e nell' Unione Europea*, Milano: Eleuthera.
Doezema, J. (1998) 'Forced to Choose: Beyond the Voluntary v. Forced Prostitution Dichotomy', in K. Kempadoo and J. Doezema (eds.), *Global Sex Workers: Rights, Resistance and Redefinition*, New York: Routledge.
Doezema, J. (2000) 'Loose Women or Lost Women? The Re-emergence of the Myth of "White Slavery" in Contemporary Discourses of Trafficking in Women', in *Gender Issues*, 11(18): 23–50.
Doezema, J. (2001) 'Ouch! Western Feminists' "Wounded Attachment" to the "Third World Prostitute" ', *Feminist Review*, 1(67): 16–38.
Doezema, J. (2002) 'Who Gets to Choose? Coercion, Consent and the UN Trafficking Protocol', *Gender and Development*, 1(10): 20–8.
Edlund, L. and E. Kom (2002) 'A Theory of Prostitution', *Journal of Political Economy*, 1(110): 181–214.
Expert Group on Trafficking in Human Beings (2004) *Report*, Brussels: European Commission Directorate-General Justice, Freedom and Security.
Giammarinaro, M. G. (2003) 'La servitu' domestica. Spunti per una definizione giuridica', in Carchedi *et al.* (eds.), *Lavoro servile nuove schiavitù*, Milano: Franco Angeli, pp. 147–67.
Hirsch, F. (1976) *Social Limits to Growth*, Cambridge, MA: Harvard University Press.
Hirschman, A. O. (1970) *Exit, Voice and Loyalty* Cambridge, MA: Harvard University Press.

Hochschild, A. (1983) *The Managed Heart. Commercialization of Human Feelings*, Berkeley: University of California Press.

Hodgson, G. (2004) *The Evolution of Institutional Economics*, London: Routledge.

Jeffrey, S. (1997) *The Idea of Prostitution*, Melbourne: Spinifex.

Kempadoo, K. and. J. Doezema (eds.) (1998) *Global Sex Workers. Rights, Resistance, and Redefinition*, London: Routledge.

Leonini, L. (1999) *Sesso in acquisto. Una ricerca sui clienti della prostituzione*, Milano: Unicopli.

Lim, L. L. (1998) *The Sex Sector. The Economic and Social Bases of Prostitution in Southeast Asia*, Geneva: ILO.

Moulier Boutang, Y. (1998) *De l'esclavage au salariat*, Paris: PUF.

Nussbaum, M. C. (1999) *Sex and Social Justice*, Oxford: Oxford University Press.

O'Connell Davidson, J. (1998) *Prostitution, Power, and Freedom*, Cambridge: Polity Press.

Outshoorn, J. (ed.) (2004) *The Politics of Prostitution. Women's Movements, Democratic States and the Globalisation of Sex Commerce*, Cambridge: Cambridge University Press.

Pagano, U. (1999) 'Is Power an Economic Good? Notes on Social Scarcity and the Economics of Positional Goods', in S. Bowles, M. Franzini and U. Pagano (eds.), *The Politics and Economics of Power*, London: Routledge, pp. 63–89.

Pantaleoni, M. (ed.) (1963) 'Tentativo di analisi del concetto di "forte e debole" in economia', in M. Pantaleoni, *Erotemi di economia*, Padova: CEDAM, pp. 319–47.

Pateman, C. (1988) *The Sexual Contract*, Cambridge: Polity Press

Pearson, E. (2002) *Human Trafficking, Human Rights: Redefining Victim Protection*, London: Anti-Slavery International.

Pheterson, G. (ed.) (1989) *A Vindication of the Rights of Whores: The International Movement for Prostitutes' Rights*, Seattle: Seal.

Pheterson, G. (1996) 'The Category of Prostitute in Scientific Inquiry', in G. Pheterson, *The Prostitution Prism*, Amsterdam: Amsterdam University Press, pp. 30–6.

Phillips, J. (2002) 'The Beach Boys of Barbados: Post-colonial Entrepreneurs', in S. Torbeik and B. Pattanaik, *Transnational Prostitution: Changing Global Patterns*, London: Zed Books, pp. 42–56.

Posner, R. (1992) *Sex and Reason*, Cambridge, MA: Harvard University Press.

Ramseyer, J. M. (1991) 'Indentured Prostitution in Imperial Japan', *The Journal of Law, Economics and Organization*, 1(7): 89–116.

Reynolds, H. (1986) *The Economics of Prostitution*, Springfield, IL: C. C. Thomas.

Tabet, P. (1991) 'Les dents de la prostituée: échange, négociation, choix dans les rapports économico-sexuels'. in P. Tabet, *Sexe et Genre. De la hiérarchie entre les sexes*, Paris: CNRS, pp. 227–44.

Tatafiore, R. (1998) *Uomini di piacere*, Milano: Frontiera Editore.

Torbeik, S. and B. Pattanaik (2002) *Transnational Prostitution. Changing Global Patterns*, London: Zed Books

Truong, T. D. (1990) *Sex, Money and Morality: The Political Economy of Prostitution and Tourism in South East Asia*, London: Zed Books.

Virgilio, M. (2000) 'Le nuove schiavitu' e le prostituzioni', in Diritto, *Immmigrazione e Cittadinanza*, 3: 39–52.

van der Veen, M. (2001) 'Rethinking Commodification and Prostitution: An Effort at Peacemaking in the Battles over Prostitution', *Rethinking Marxism*, 2(13): 30–51.

Wijers, M. and Lap-Chew, L. (1997) *Trafficking in Women, Forced Labour and Slavery-like Practices in Marriage, Domestic Labour and Prostitution*, Utrecht: Foundation against Trafficking in Women.

Wijers, M. (2001) 'Keep your Women Home: European Union Policies on Trafficking in Women and Strategies for Support', in G. M. Rossilli (ed.), *Gender Policies in the European Union*, London: Peter Lang.

Williamson, O. (1980) 'Transaction Costs Economics: the Governance of Contractual Relations', *Journal of Law and Economics*, 2(22): 233–61.

Wittig, M. (1981) 'One is not Born a Woman', *Feminist Issues*, 1(2): 47-54.

Zatz, N. D. (1997) 'Sex Work/Sex Act: Law, Labor, and Desire in Constructions of Prostitution', *Signs: Journal of Women in Culture and Society*, 2(22): 277–308.

5
Doing the Impossible? Collecting Data on the Extent of Trafficking
Gillian Wylie

Introduction

In Anti-Slavery International's frank admission, 'it is impossible to know how many victims of trafficking there are' (2004). Yet apparently impossibility is no deterrent to governments, international organisations and non-governmental organisations (NGOs), which all offer estimates. Although these published figures invariably carry the proviso that solid data on the extent of trafficking are virtually unobtainable, these figures do tend to take on a life of their own and come to play an important role in determining policy formation in respect of combating trafficking. Yet even a cursory comparison of some of the most commonly cited estimates from influential governmental or inter-governmental sources reveals that the figures vary wildly. And what remains obscure is how these figures were calculated, leaving one to surmise that some estimates achieve acceptance perhaps more through political clout and frequent citation (e.g. those of the US State Department in its annual Trafficking in Persons Report) than through a strong sense of the basis on which they rest and their accuracy. Undoubtedly, the problems facing data collection are numerous. They range from the obvious difficulties, even dangers, of trying to chart a practice which is by its nature clandestine and may involve organised crime, through the lack of agreed international methods and definitions, to the ideological divides and ethical constraints which face researchers working in this field. In this chapter the interplay and consequences of these factors will be illustrated by detailing how they have impinged on academic research into the extent of trafficking in the particular country context of Ireland. Thereafter, admitting that the problems associated with gaining knowledge about trafficking in Ireland are experienced universally, the chapter closes by considering whether there are ways to design future research in order to mitigate the inherent difficulties in data collection.

Influential estimates and glaring anomalies

As noted above, there are several frequently quoted estimates for the numbers of trafficked people (and it is worth stressing that they are always premised as estimates). In this section just two of these will be presented in order to contrast them and raise questions about the provenance of the data they contain. While other sources could be added to illustrate further variations, these two are chosen because both come from politically powerful bodies with well-resourced research capabilities. The first is a report produced in 2000 by the European Parliament's Directorate-General (DG) for Research; the second the now annual US State Department's Trafficking in Persons (TiP) Report.

Concern about an apparently rising incidence in the trafficking of women for sexual exploitation from Eastern to Western Europe prompted the European Parliament's DG for Research to undertake a study of trafficking in 2000. The report evinces a conviction that pan-European trafficking is growing phenomenally. The first key figure it relies on to make this case is the global figure of four million people trafficked annually, which is derived from UN and International Organisation for Migration (IOM) reports. Of these four million, the European Union (EU) report then cites the IOM's estimate that 500,000 enter Western Europe (European Parliament DG for Research, 2000: 5). The research processes which lie behind the production of these large, bald numbers remain, however, mysterious. The report concedes that the basic difficulty of gathering data on a practice as murky as trafficking is compounded by the fact that 'no comprehensive database exists on trafficking in women', with many states not even collecting statistics about suspect trafficking cases because it was not considered to be a political priority (European Parliament DG for Research, 2000: iii). Although it records the methodological difficulties the researchers encountered, the EU's report makes no clear statement about its own research methodology or that of its sources. Rather, it simply records a reliance on information from a number of police, judicial and NGO sources, as well as the international reports cited above. This is despite the fact that one of the key agencies which the report relies on for statistics, the IOM, had already been forced to conclude in 1998 that accurate statistics for the numbers of trafficked women could not at the time be known (Kelly and Regan, 2000: 8).[1]

Further prodding of these figures throws up more problems concerning their reliability. On further definition it seems that the four million figure refers to 'persons [who] fall into the clutches of criminal organisations from which, with the idea of seeking their fortune abroad, they have purchased certain services – a travel ticket, entry documents, false identity papers' (European Parliament DG for Research, 2000: 3). According to a definitional division made in international law this would suggest that these four million are not necessarily all trafficked, but rather an unknown proportion of them are smuggled. Smuggling is usually differentiated from trafficking by the fact that smuggled people knowingly consent and pay to be moved illegally over borders and are not exploited at the end of their journey.[2] Thus the EU report includes as trafficked those who may not be. Moreover, the EU report does not specify whether the 500,000 moved into Western Europe are solely women trafficked for sexual exploitation or encompass adults and children trafficked for any exploitative purpose. However, this is how the figure has been read, appearing in a number of NGO publications as referring to the trafficking of women alone.[3] Finally, the only 'hard' figures presented in the report – 108 cases encountered by one Dutch NGO and 155 by another – are minuscule in contrast to the alleged 500,000.

Already we see some of the difficulties inherent in collecting data. These include the obvious problems surrounding gaining insight into criminal acts but also the fact that systematic data collection is not practised EU-wide for political reasons and definitional confusion surrounds determining who has been trafficked and for what purposes. Yet it is also clear that some numbers 'grow legs' as they are circulated, picked up and reiterated by actors and agencies seeking to influence policy. Through repetition they become accepted wisdom.

The four million mark seems to be at odds with the global estimate of trafficking that features in the second example, the US Trafficking in Persons report. Since its inception in 2001 this annual report has regularly cited a figure of around 700,000 persons trafficked each year across international borders for all kinds of exploitative purposes. The current report is no exception, offering an estimate of between 600,000 and 800,000. Of these, 80 per cent were women of whom 70 per cent were trafficked for commercial sexual exploitation (US State Department, 2004: 23). Despite presenting these figures baldly the report is again upfront about the difficulty in establishing numbers, for reasons such as the different counting regimes employed by the countries surveyed, but says next to nothing about its own methodology. In fact, the TiP presents very few specific numbers in its country case studies and has consequently been criticised for its patchy presentation of statistical data. Although 'some chapters provide basic data on the numbers of trafficking victims, arrests, prosecutions and convictions, many more do not' (Human Rights Watch, 2003[r1]). Just how the figure of 700,000 is arrived at is thus unclear.

Despite these anomalies, the US figure is perhaps the one that has gained the most weight internationally, at least if frequency of citation is taken as evidence of influence. Yet, the question must be asked whether this is because of the accuracy of the data reporting in the TiP or the political punch this report carries. The TiP report does not simply enumerate cases, it also leads to a political judgement being made as to whether individual nations are doing enough to combat trafficking (US State Department, 2004: 29–30). On the basis of the report all states are categorised in tiers and those deemed not to be doing enough are placed in tier 3. The consequences of tier 3 assignment are threatened aid cutbacks and black marks at the IMF where the US wields disproportionate power. In another line of criticism Human Rights Watch has taken issue with the report's lack of explanation as to why some states have moved around tiers over the years, allowing suspicion to grow that there are political considerations behind certain countries' gradings. For example, despite a widespread belief that Pakistan is a country of origin, transit and destination for very many trafficked people, the country moved up the grades concurrent with its offer of support to the US War on Terror in 2002 (Human Rights Watch, 2002).

700,000 globally; 500,000 pan-Europe. These figures have become commonplace citations. Yet, even at face value, they seem to be at odds with one another, the European figure disproportionately high in comparison to the American. More numbers from other seemingly reputable sources could have been added to the mix to demonstrate the variations and anomalies. For instance, one year after the European Parliament's report came a contradictory document from the EU Commission, indicating that 120,000 women and children were being trafficked annually into Western Europe, although 'again it is unclear how these figures were reached' (Laczko, 2002: 2). Contrasting with the US numbers for all cases (adult and child) is the International Labour Organisation's estimate of 1.2 million children trafficked in 2000 (Kaye, 2003: 4) or UNICEF's figure of 200,000 in Central Africa alone (UNODC, 2004). Admittedly, these figures do refer to different contexts and years (although all within the last four). They differ too in whether they are primarily concerned with women, children or men and what exploitative ends the victims are subjected to. But taking all these variations into account what is clear is that these estimates do not concur. What this section has shown is that behind the production of these highly variable estimates lie practical problems, mysterious methodologies, definitional disputes and political manoeuvrings. This is all suggestive of the need for further, more careful research that is sensitive to all these pitfalls. Perhaps, rather than trying to take a global sweep at estimation, more useful and reliable information could be gleaned by paying attention to detail and accumulating smaller-scale country case studies. Yet, as the next section will show by reflecting on two academic research attempts to date in Ireland – one by myself and one under the auspices of the IOM – even less grandiose studies will almost inevitably encounter similar, if not yet more, problems.

Trying to discover the extent of trafficking into Ireland

In March 2003 a conference on 'Migrant Women Transforming Ireland' was held in Dublin (Lentin and Luibheid, 2003). I was already interested in and concerned about human trafficking, but this conference provided the context which finally prompted me to try to determine the scale of the trafficking of women for sexual exploitation into Ireland, with a particular focus on the Eastern Europe–Western Europe trafficking route. The obvious initial lines of enquiry were to approach the Gardai (police), the NGO community and to use the Internet as a supplementary research tool. It is important to stress here that that this was an extremely preliminary enquiry and by no means exhaustive. However, the problems encountered in trying to gather information, even on this small scale, are indicative of the general problems which dog all attempts to quantify human trafficking for any exploitative end.

In dealing with the Gardai, one anonymous interview was secured with an officer working in the field of sexual violence. What became clear in talking to this detective was that he felt constrained about saying anything on the record concerning the scale of trafficking to Ireland because officially the evidence did not exist. As he stressed, employing the strict Garda usage of the term 'evidence', there was no evidence of trafficking for sexual exploitation into Ireland (up to March 2003) because there were no official complaints made to the police and no cases taken which could lead to even a potential, let alone a successful, prosecution. It is worth noting that this lack of legal proceedings is partly reflective of the fact that existing Irish law which purports to cover trafficking (The Illegal Immigrants (Trafficking) Act of 2000), is in fact geared to the prosecution of smuggling (Conroy, 2004: 14). Moreover, the Gardai source indicated that during the one raid made by them through the brothels of Dublin in 2002 (the oddly named 'Operation Gladiator'), the Gardai found no Eastern European women working as prostitutes in any circumstances. Since my initial research, the Gardai have made one further raid, this time on the city's lap-dancing clubs. Acting on the suspicion that such clubs might be involved in the exploitation of 'non-national women', the Gardai mounted 'Operation Quest' in the summer of 2003. As a consequence of this raid, 101 people were arrested and at least ten prosecutions resulted. However it is notable that these prosecutions were all related to breaches of visa regulations or work permits and were not prosecuted as trafficking cases (Ward, 2004: 7). By identifying these women primarily as violators of visa regulations, they became categorised instantly as illegal migrants and liable to be deported. The question of whether they had been trafficked therefore receded from sight, although suspicion remains that this was the case, particularly in the media and in the NGO community (Ward, 2004).

Turning to that community, I interviewed two key workers in the Dublin-based NGO Ruhama, which exists to work with women involved in prostitution.[4] In Ruhama's experience the vast majority of the women with whom they have contact and work continue to be local, yet they have met a number of women whose stories follow the classic pattern of transnational trafficking. Indeed the (then) director of Ruhama had published the (anonymised) story of the organisation's encounter with one such woman in the newsletter of Ireland's National Women's Council (Connolly, 2001: 13–15). And in one annual report (from 1999) the organisation recorded having direct contact with 25 women whom they suspected had been trafficked (O'Connor, 2004: 11). Moreover, Ruhama have been most prominent in raising public concern about lap-dancing and the employment status of women in the clubs.

Although very open to being interviewed, for the understandable reason of wishing to protect their clients, the workers at Ruhama were reticent about discussing actual cases or even numbers. The idea of allowing a researcher direct access to their clients (although not requested) was clearly anathema to them. Without this concrete information, in the course of the interview Ruhama's suspicion of a link between lap-dancing, trafficking and prostitution became a focus for discussion. This was indicative of the fact that this particular organisation takes the view that these practices, particularly prostitution and trafficking, are inseparable. In effect, this means that Ruhama are working out of a broad definition of trafficking, which defines any woman travelling for prostitution as trafficked. Yet, this is not an understanding which would be shared by all NGOs in the field. There are others in the anti-trafficking community who would not necessarily see all movement across borders for 'sex work' as trafficking.[5]

The third strand in the initial research used the Internet to see if there were any further reports of trafficking into Ireland. This produced mainly press stories, and again the conflation of lap-dancing and trafficking was evident. Press reports on the clubs stressed the constrained lives women lead as they are escorted to and from the clubs, forbidden wider social interaction and live in crowded accommodation controlled by their employers. Further speculation was reported as to whether the women are able to control the money they earn or whether it is extorted from them by criminals (Guerin, 2002a; 2002b). Beyond these reports there was one extended piece of investigative journalism which raised the possibility that Ireland is being used as a transit state for women being trafficked to the UK. Membership of the EU, the Common Travel Agreement with Britain and the Irish state's need for low-wage labour make it a convenient context from which to advertise bogus jobs and through which to move people. Thus Sue Lloyd Roberts' investigation documented how legitimate Irish job adverts posted on the Web were redirected by organised criminals to put women seeking employment into contact with traffickers. When the women believing they were to be waitresses were asked about the size of their breasts and HIV tests they grew suspicious, while the bemused legitimate employer, tracked down in Galway, could not fathom how his advert had become a front for traffickers (Lloyd Roberts, 2002).

This then was the meagre evidence I had to present at the conference. Obviously, I had not at this stage pursued enough contacts to get anywhere close to a comprehensive picture, but I had already learned much about the difficulties that beset researching this field, which will be dwelt on below. However, before going further, it is worth noting that at the conference a further complication arose which affects any attempt to compile and present data about trafficking. My paper was subject to rigorous criticism from those who feared any attempt to quantify trafficking from Eastern Europe to the West had undesirable political and social consequences. In particular, a concern was voiced that my research was feeding negative public perceptions about Eastern European women in Ireland as undesirable, illegal immigrants.

All the above are indicative of the multiple difficulties that data collection on trafficking encounters. Beside the obvious practical problem of trying to gather information on an activity which is often organised by criminals, and thus secretive and dangerous, there is a range of problems which are legal, definitional, ethical and political.

Since human trafficking is a criminal offence, law enforcement officials are a natural constituency to turn to as a source of information. Yet, as shown here, police information is constrained by their conceptualisations of evidence. What must also be borne in mind is that police evidence alone cannot be relied on as the only source of revelation about trafficking, for the obvious reasons that traffickers are determined to avoid them and trafficked women are either unable to reach them or would fear to do so. It is widely acknowledged that a key factor in enabling trafficking from countries of origin is corruption within police forces, giving trafficked women little reason to trust law officers anywhere (Connolly, 2001: 14). In addition, these women's position in their states of transit or destination is illegal and they are aware that they would be on 'the wrong side of the law' should they manage to access it.

At each point in the research the relationship between lap-dancing and trafficking casts a confusing shadow. Despite their continual conflation, there is a complication in defining all lap-dancers as 'trafficked' because, until recently, 'non-national' women were able to gain short-term 'entertainment visas' in order to be employed legally as lap-dancers in Ireland. This visa regime has now been suspended, yet the question remains that if these women were here legally and knew they would be lap-dancers, can they be said to have been trafficked? When a similar controversy blew up in Northern Ireland, one member of the Women's Coalition opposed the majority opinion in her party by querying, 'What is wrong with lap-dancing? ... I know people who work in what might be called the sex trade: they are there freely' (McAdam, 2002).

The lap-dancing controversy therefore illustrates vividly the divides among the non-governmental anti-trafficking community in its understandings of trafficking. For some, like Ruhama, prostitution and trafficking are inseparable. The sex trade is always about the commodification of women's bodies and their sexual exploitation by those more powerful. Lap-dancing, prostitution, trafficking are all manifestations of this trade in women's bodies. For those of an opposing view however, there is a belief that some adult women choose sex work (e.g. in legal lap-dancing) and therefore it is essential to see trafficking for sexual purposes as a distinct process involving 'forced prostitution'. Thus data collection on trafficking is problematised by the need to decide (or even take sides) between these opposing understandings and definitions.

Obviously what is needed most of all in relation to sorting out this definitional muddle is more research. It would be important to know, for instance, how women working in lap-dancing or those who more readily fit the definition of trafficking perceive themselves. Yet, for a researcher this is far from an easy task, either practically or in terms of conducting research ethically.

According to the Sociological Research Association of the UK, not all research projects can be justified. Researchers must weigh up the value of acquiring particular knowledge against considerations of the potentially harmful consequences of their work on the lives of those studied (Ethical Guidelines, 2003). As Lee argues, research can pose various levels of threat, ranging from harm to the individual through to the social and political implications of work undertaken (Lee, 1993: 4).

Research on trafficking could incorporate all these potential threats. Trafficked people have inevitably suffered much in their lives, having been deceived, threatened, coerced and exploited. They have much to fear from those who trafficked them, as well as from their new foreign context. They are likely to be illegal immigrants liable for deportation, as well as bearing the social stigma of prostitution. In such a situation, why reveal anything to anyone – particularly researchers who publish? Furthermore, there is the danger that doing such research plays into the stigmatising of groups of people. Maybe trafficking research feeds public mythology about Eastern European men as dangerous Mafiosi or colours views of all women migrants from that region. Or, if it does not stigmatise, research might sensationalise and compound someone's exploitation. A recent edition of the *Observer Magazine* seemed to encapsulate this problem. While trying to raise the issue of Moldovan women trafficked to the UK, the accompanying photos, showing naked or partially dressed women with their gazes only slightly averted, could be construed as further sexual exploitation of them (Gibb, 2003: 24–9). The potential political consequences of trafficking research also need to be considered. As Lee points out, research can be harmful politically if it enters the public domain and is used in policymaking which may have detrimental effects on the researched community (Lee, 1993: 4). How policy should be shaped around trafficking and related issues like prostitution and migration are sharply contested questions in most European states. Any research on the topic could be used in these debates but not always with the readings or consequences intended by the researcher.

These then are some of the lessons learned from my experiences with the difficulties of collecting data and measuring trafficking. Obviously, there are practical challenges to be overcome, but the chief lesson seems to be that collecting data is not a neutral process. It requires taking a stance on a definition of trafficking; it involves building a trustworthy relationship with 'gate-keeping' NGOs, which rightly protect their clients; it brings up inescapable issues about whether and how to speak for or about women whose experience is very different from one's own; it requires sensitivity to the political consequences of putting data into the public domain. Academics researching trafficking have to realise that the research act itself – and its consequences – are by definition political and ethical. All these difficulties are reiterated in the second example from Ireland, the Dublin Mission of the IOM's commissioned research on *Trafficking in Unaccompanied Minors in Ireland* (Conroy, 2004).

Trafficking in Unaccompanied Minors: An IOM report on Ireland

Published in the summer of 2004, this report is part of a wider European project of the IOM trying to determine the extent of trafficking in unaccompanied minors. The Irish report usefully sets out the existing legal framework in Ireland for prosecuting child traffickers, examines the services which exist to protect unaccompanied minors and looks at Ireland's existing and future necessary policy responses. What becomes clear from reading the report, however, is that the author, Pauline Conroy, encountered great difficulty in trying to measure the scale of the trafficking of unaccompanied minors.

In the first instance, Conroy discovered that it was only just about possible to work out the number of unaccompanied minors in Ireland. At state level there is a 'no stock of data on ethnicity, asylum seeking and immigration' including unaccompanied minors (Conroy, 2004: 20). Some data could be generated through the Office of the Refugee Applications Commissioner (ORAC) with regard to those minors officially in the asylum process. However, this picture remained incomplete because not all children are entered by Health Boards into the asylum process, there are many incomplete case files for others and some unaccompanied children simply 'disappear' after being collected at hostels by relatives. In addition, a certain percentage of the children will be ageing out of the unaccompanied minor category at any one time. Yet, even if it were possible to know roughly the number of unaccompanied minors, this is not in itself revealing about the numbers within this group who are trafficked. In the case of unaccompanied minors, many it would seem are smuggled for the purposes of family reunification, rather than trafficked for any exploitative purpose. And since there are 'no public data reported specifically on child smuggling or trafficking' (Conroy, 2004: 25) or any way of disaggregating these categories and disentangling the trafficked from the smuggled, the report has no way of determining how many children should be classified in either category. Thus while the author can state that there were 23 investigations or preparations to bring prosecution in child smuggling and trafficking cases between January 2002 and May 2003, whether the victims were suspected of being smuggled or trafficked remains obscure. Of these cases none had reached a legal conclusion, harking back to the ongoing problem of a lack of 'hard' evidence.

A second aspect of this research involved interviews with professionals providing services to unaccompanied minors. These discussions yielded valuable anecdotal evidence of encounters with children who could well have been trafficked, thus corroborating the suspicion of bodies like the IOM that child trafficking does happen in Ireland (Conroy, 2004: 9). Yet the author made no attempt to interview those children directly, for good practical and ethical reasons. As she records, trafficked children may well be in shock, even unaware of their own identity or have been coached in what to say. Building trust with such children is of necessity the long, hard work of trained social work or psychological professionals and the sudden appearance of a transient academic researcher in their lives is definitely undesirable.

The IOM report reinforces the problems noted in the section above: the definitional troubles (between smuggling and trafficking rather than prostitution and trafficking); the lack of a clear mandate to any public body to develop a system for collecting information; the ethical difficulties in approaching trafficked people for research purposes. In addition, there are political issues shadowing the research, with at least one NGO activist expressing the reservation that as IOM is an inter-state body and this research was co-sponsored by the Irish Department of Justice, Equality and Law Reform, in whose interest would its data ultimately be used?[6]

Universal problems

Thus far this chapter has surveyed efforts to collect data and measure trafficking which have been done on widely differing scales. These included data collection which attempts to capture a global picture done at the US governmental level with all the might of presidential endorsement behind it, statistical estimates from the EU and IOM that are pan-European, right down to attempts by individual academic researchers trying to learn what is going on around them in their local context. While it is important to recognise the different agendas and motivations behind these research projects (with the US data being used for overtly political ends through the classification of states into tiers, for example), whatever level of research is under consideration it seems that there are universal challenges being faced in the endeavour. Mention and illustration of these difficulties have been scattered throughout the preceding pages, but they have been usefully brought together in one article by Frank Laczko of the IOM (2002). As Laczko summarises, data collection is fraught because trafficking is a clandestine activity, a straightforward definition of which has not been universally agreed. Although he finds hope in the recent consensus gathering around the definition developed by the UN in the Palermo Protocol (Laczko, 2002: 2), definitional disputes remain. One factor hampering an agreed definition is ideological argument about the relationship between trafficking and prostitution. Another lies in the grey area which exists between smuggling and trafficking, and while data may be collected for (detected) illegal migration, this does not necessarily reveal who has been trafficked. Then, states have different counting methods or poorer states do not have the resources to engage in the exercise at all. The different legal approaches to trafficking which exist globally mean that prosecutions are patchy and victims often unwilling to testify for fear of reprisal, leading to a lack of proven cases. While numerous victims are aided by NGOs, these organisations are usually reluctant to share knowledge, determined as they are to protect the confidentiality of their clients. Despite taking cognisance of all these factors, Laczko remains convinced of the necessity of collecting data on the grounds that the appropriate policy response can only be shaped on the basis of reliable knowledge, 'going forward all depends on sound policies based on good data' (Laczko, 2002: 6). This is a widely shared sentiment, with, for example, Anti-Slavery International deeming data collection 'essential' if trafficking is to be thoroughly understood and opposed effectively (Kaye, 2003: 4). For Laczko the future of better data collection lies with the development of more systematic international, inter-organisational systems, modelled perhaps on the 'regional clearing point' in Belgrade which centralises trafficking information on the Balkans (Laczko, 2002: 5). Such systemisation of data collection would undoubtedly be helpful for all concerned, yet it does not necessarily overcome some of the thornier ethical and political problems associated with collecting trafficking data which occur well before and continue after the point at which data can be fed into a clearing house. Overcoming these problems requires careful thinking through of research methodology on the ground at the initial point of data collection. It is with this in mind that I have been revisiting the issue of how to establish the extent of trafficking for sexual exploitation in Ireland and trying to develop a methodology which will (hopefully) enable a future research process which will be less naive, more sensitive and more comprehensive than my earlier attempt described above.

Developing a future research methodology for Ireland

Thinking through the experience of trying to do research in Ireland, in the aftermath of recognising the many problems which beset data collection on this theme, it has become clearer to me that a research methodology is needed which has at its foundations an initial, workable definition of trafficking. Then the research must be inventive, exhaustive, ethical and collaborative. By inventive and exhaustive I mean that all kinds of potential sources of information need to be pursued. But crucially, any pursuit of data must be hedged in by a commitment to ethical research practices and an awareness of the potential political consequences of the data. In order to meet these latter criteria, the best way forward is to forge a research coalition with those agencies that have need of the data in order to further their own service provision and advocacy work around trafficking, as will be explained further below.

Defining who has been trafficked has become slightly less problematic in recent years as the UN's Palermo definition has acquired a greater acceptance (van den Anker, 2004: 5). In its attempt to be comprehensive, it is undoubtedly a wordy and cumbersome definition. Yet, it is partly thanks to its wordiness that it has achieved consensus. Unusually, for example, feminists on both sides of the prostitution/sex work debate find it useful (Gallagher, 2001). Moreover, the definition carves out a distinct difference between the trafficked and the smuggled by making coercion, deception and exploitation central to trafficking. Although the UN definition can never resolve all disputes – the crossover between smuggling and trafficking will remain a grey area and anti-traffickers will interpret its clauses somewhat differently – this definition does help us know what we are looking for when trying to measure the extent of trafficking. This is particularly helpful in the Irish context where the domestic legislation which purports to deal with trafficking (of adults) is actually about smuggling and no trafficking definition is enacted. Perhaps employing the UN definition would help to dispel some of the fog that surrounds an issue like the relationship between lap-dancing and trafficking in Ireland, or at least form the basis for an informed discussion.

Using this definitional guideline, research needs to be based on contact with a wide range of relevant agencies. Again, the Gardai remain an important repository of information on trafficking. My initial contact with them has been minimal, but this can obviously be developed. Here an approach pioneered by Liz Kelly and Linda Regan in their Home Office-sponsored work on the nature and extent of trafficking in the UK is adaptable to the Irish context (Kelly and Regan, 2000). Their approach was to survey the existing British legal framework and then contact police forces throughout the UK, using questionnaires and follow-up interviews to track the incidence of trafficking. The information they gathered went further than just getting the 'hard evidence' of prosecutions and allowed for discussion of suspected cases. Suspicions aside, the hard evidence produced what they deemed to be the known minimum number of cases (71). To garner additional information Kelly and Regan used media and Internet searches, known numbers of visas for 'mail order brides', informed speculation about the probable scale of trafficking in provincial towns and interviews with topic experts to move from the 'known minimum' to the establishment of a 'probable maximum' number of cases. In the end they could say that there must have been between 142 and 1,420 cases of trafficking for sexual exploitation to the UK in 1998 (Kelly and Regan, 2000: 22). Their research was thus imaginative in its use and range of sources, but apparently sober and realistic in its eventual configuration of numbers. Research in Ireland could mirror this methodology. The Irish police are not organised regionally as in the UK but rather in specialist units and so intensified contact with relevant sections of An Garda Siochana, including the Garda National Immigration Bureau (GNIB) and the Garda Unit on Sexual Violence could reveal the extent of trafficking as it has become known to the police.

Yet, it is always important to bear in mind that, for various reasons, many cases of trafficking for sexual exploitation do not come to the attention of state authorities. Therefore it is vital to engage with other sources of knowledge. Ruhama was mentioned earlier as a key NGO responding to the trafficking issue in Ireland, yet it is only one of several NGOs, including others working with women in prostitution and with unaccompanied minors, who have recently encountered trafficked women and children. Concerned by this new experience, in 2002 the network *Ireland en Route* was formed to respond in a coordinated manner to this growing problem.[7] The network involves NGOs but also certain statutory agencies (Health Boards and the Garda National Immigration Bureau) and some academics (including myself). While each agency has its particular experiences of meeting trafficked women and children, the network acknowledges that the lack of an overall picture of the nature and extent of trafficking has problematised its work to date. It is therefore a stated aim of *Ireland en Route* to encourage research on trafficking in Ireland. Yet, while there is a mutual interest in research there is also a mutual fear of it, spawned by the types of political and ethical concerns acknowledged above. For these reasons, it seems that the best way forward is to try to work research coalition methodology amongst this group, as advocated by feminist researchers.

Feminists concerned with research methodology, worried by the power differentials between researchers and researched or the ends to which knowledge is put in traditional research, have advocated research methodologies involving the creation of partnerships and/or coalitions between researchers and the researched (Lynch, 2004: chapter 9). In this way 'outsiders with professional credentials [can] enable those whose voices are ignored to be heard' (Jaggar, 2000: 16). Forming a research coalition requires that the researcher looks to the experiences of the researched as her primary resource material, recognising them as agents and not hapless victims (Lentin, 1993: 124). Effective research coalitions operate by ensuring that the interests of the researched will be met through the work. This implies establishing from research subjects what it is that they want and need from social research. Most often this will be an analysis of the structures that marginalise them and ideas for social change (Harding, 1987: 8–9). Finally, to create trustful coalitions the researcher must always be self-reflexive, showing awareness of how her own social position and politics affects her analysis (Harding, 1987: 8).

All of this seems eminently sensible as a way to manage the unequal power relationships which inevitably exist between researchers and researched and as a means to produce research which will be useful to its subjects. However, trying to adopt such a methodology is extremely problematic when researching trafficking. Quite simply, it is difficult to establish a coalition with trafficked women, for many of the reasons touched on earlier. Instead, the creative and sensitive way forward is for academic researchers and *Ireland en Route* to cooperate in a research partnership. By working collaboratively to set a research agenda which meets the needs and interests of all concerned, a trustful relationship between researcher and researched should be established. The shared knowledge such research then produces will be used by the network as they seek to further their other aims: providing best practice in service provision to trafficked women and children and possessing sound information which can be used to lobby government for appropriate legislative changes.

Conclusion

It is a far from simple task to collect data on any form of human trafficking, including the extent of trafficking in women and children for sexual exploitation. It is widely acknowledged in the existing international literature that such research is beset by problems associated with the criminality of the act, the vulnerability of the trafficked, confusion surrounding defining trafficking, the lack of systematic collection of information and the politics of publishing data. This chapter has shown that these problems frustrate data collection on trafficking at all levels, from the global to the local. Awareness of all these complications could paralyse further research attempts. Yet, to allow this to happen would be ethical evasion, with the 'darker corners of society' (Lee, 1993: 4) where trafficking occurs being left unilluminated and the human rights abuses connected with it going unchecked. What is needed then are creative and ethical research methodologies, perhaps along the lines outlined here, which can uncover the extent of trafficking, contribute to an understanding of how and why it occurs and hopefully empower those working in anti-trafficking and be of use to trafficked women, children and men themselves.

Notes

1. Kelly and Regan (2000) are making reference to IOM's 1998 Final Report to the EU's STOP Programme.
2. Although as Kyle and Koslowski (2001: Introduction) explain, the two categories often collapse into each other in practice.
3. For example, the number of 500,000 women trafficked across Europe for sexual exploitation appears in the report of the Irish Observatory on Violence against Women (O'Connor, 2004) and in the Conference of European Churches Report of its Driebergen Consultation on trafficking (Driebergen Consultation, 1999) and its follow-up resource book for the European Churches (Vogel-Mfato *et al.*, 2003).
4. See http://www.ruhama.ie/aboutus.htm.

5. For the foundational statements of these contrasting views of the relationship between trafficking and prostitution see Barry (1979; 1995) as compared to Kempadoo and Doezema (1998).
6. Personal communication.
7. Membership of Ireland en Route includes the following NGOs and statutory agencies: Cairde, Copine (Combating Paedophile Information Networks in Europe), Garda National Immigration Bureau, Holy Child Sisters, Immigrant Council of Ireland, International Organisation for Migration, Irish Refugee Council, Mercy Open Door, Mercy Sisters, Migrants' Rights Centre, Ruhama, Service for Young People Out of Home (Southern Health Board), Unaccompanied Minors Unit (Eastern Coast Area Health Board), Women's Aid, Women's Health Project (ECAHB). The network can be contacted through trafficking@ruhama.ie.

References

Anti-Slavery International (2004) *What is Trafficking? Q and A.* Available at: http://www.antislavery.org/homepage/antislavery/trafficking.htm-qanda [Accessed 17 May 2005].

Barry, K. (1979) *Female Sexual Slavery*, New York: New York University Press.

Barry, K. (1995) *The Prostitution of Sexuality: the Global Exploitation of Women*, New York: New York University Press.

Connolly, M. (2001) 'Trafficking in Women for Sexual Exploitation: A Human Rights Issue', *Womenzone*, 7 June: 13–15, Dublin: National Women's Council of Ireland.

Conroy, P. (2004) *Trafficking in Unaccompanied Minors in Ireland*, Dublin: International Organisation for Migration Mission in Ireland.

Driebergen Consultation (1999) *Trafficking in Women in Europe*, Papers from an International Consultation held in Driebergen, Netherlands, 27 November–1 December, Geneva: Conference of European Churches.

Ethical Guidelines of the Sociological Research Association UK (2003). Available at: http://www.the-sra.org.uk [Accessed 17 May 2005].

European Parliament Directorate-General for Research (2000), *Trafficking in Women*, Working Paper, Civil Liberties Series, LIBE 109 EN, 3–2000, Brussels: the European Parliament.

Gallagher, A. (2001) 'Human Rights and the New UN Protocols on Trafficking and Migrant Smuggling: A Preliminary Assessment', *Human Rights Quarterly*, 23: 975–1004.

Gibb, J. (2003) 'Sex and Slavery', *The Observer Magazine*, 23 February: 24–9.

Guerin, J, (2002a) 'Lap Dancers Neighbours of McDowell', *Sunday Independent*, 11 August.

Guerin, J. (2002b) 'Lap Dancing Clubs Hit by Permit Ban', *Sunday Independent*, 1 September.

Harding, S. (1987) 'Is There a Feminist Methodology?' Introduction in S. Harding (ed.), *Feminism and Methodology*, Bloomington, IN: Indiana University Press.

Human Rights Watch (2002) *US State Department Trafficking Report: Missing Key Data, Credits Uneven Efforts.* Available at: http://www.hrw.org/press/2002/06/us-report0606.htm [Accessed 17 May 2005].

Human Rights Watch (2003) *Letter to Colin Powell on the Trafficking in Persons Report 03*. Available at: http://www.hrw.org/press/2003/06/us062703ltr.htm [Accessed 17 May 2005].

International Organisation for Migration (1998) *Final Report to the STOP Programme: Analysis of Data and Statistical Resources Available in the European Union Member States on Trafficking in Humans, Particularly in Women and Children for the Purposes of Sexual Exploitation*, Geneva: IOM.

Jaggar, A. (2000) 'Globalising Feminist Ethics', in U. Naranyan and S. Harding (eds.), *Decentering the Centre: Philosophy for a Multicultural, Postcolonial and Feminist World*, Bloomington, IN: Indiana University Press.

Kaye, M. (2003) *The Migration–Trafficking Nexus: Combating Trafficking through the Protection of Migrants' Human Rights*, London: Anti-Slavery International.

Kelly, L. and Regan, L. (2000) *Stopping Traffic: Exploring the Extent of, and Responses to, Trafficking in Women for Sexual Exploitation in the UK*, London: Home Office, Policing and Reducing Crime Unit: Police Research Series Paper 125.

Kempadoo, K. and Doezema, J. (1998) *Global Sex Workers: Rights, Resistance, Redefinition*, London: Routledge.

Kyle, D. and Koslowski, R. (eds.) (2001) *Global Human Smuggling: Comparative Perspectives*, Baltimore, MD: John Hopkins University Press.

Laczko, F. (2002) 'Human Trafficking: The Need for Better Data', *Migration Information Source*. Available at: http://www.migrationinformation.org/Feature/print.cfm?ID = 66 [Accessed 17 May 2005].

Lee, R. (1993) *Doing Research on Sensitive Issues*, London: Sage.

Lentin, R. (1993) 'Feminist Research Methodologies – A Separate Paradigm? Notes for a Debate', *Irish Journal of Sociology*, 3: 119–38.

Lentin, R. and Luibheid, E. (eds.) (2003) *Women's Movement: Migrant Women Transforming Ireland*. Available at: http://www.tcd.ie/Sociology/mphil/dwnl/migrantwomenpapers.PDF [Accessed 16 June 2005].

Lloyd-Roberts, S. (2002). 'Adventures on the Skin Trail: There is a New Route to Sexual Slavery in Europe, and it Leads from the Former Soviet Union to the Sex Clubs of Soho' *The Independent*, London, 22 September. Available at: http://www.friends-partners.org/partners/stop-traffic/1999/1154.html [Accessed 17 May 2005].

Lynch, K. (2004) 'Emancipatory Research as a Tool of Change', in J. Baker, K. Lynch, S. Cantillon and J. Walsh (eds.), *Equality: from Theory to Action*, Basingstoke: Palgrave Macmillan.

McAdam, N. (2002) 'Call for Lap Dance Clubs to be Closed', *Belfast Telegraph*, 18 November. Available at: http://www.belfasttelegraph.co.uk/news/story.jsp?story = 353390 [Accessed 17 May 2005].

O'Connor, M. (2004) *First Country Report from the Republic of Ireland, May 2004*, Dublin: Irish Observatory on Violence against Women.

UNODC (2004) *Fact Sheet on Human Trafficking*, United Nations Office on Drugs and Crime. Available at: http://www.unodc.org/unodc/trafficking_victim_consents.html#facts [Accessed 17 May 2005].

US State Department (2004) *Victims of Trafficking and Violence Protection Act 2004: Trafficking in Persons Report*. Available at: http://www.state.gov/g/tip/rls/tiprpt/2004/ [Accessed 17 May 2005].

van den Anker, C. (ed.) (2004) *The Political Economy of New Slavery*, Basingstoke: Palgrave Macmillan.

Vogel-Mfato, E-S. *et al.* (2003) *Churches in Europe against Trafficking in Women*, Geneva: Conference of European Churches.

Ward, E. (2004) 'Lap-dancing in the New Europe – the Case of Ireland', unpublished paper presented to the Political Studies Association 'Women in Politics' Conference, Queens University Belfast, 21 April.

6
Slavery Legislation vs. Trafficking Legislation in Prosecuting the Crime of Female Sexual Slavery: An International Law Perspective

Adrienne A. Reilly

> ... **slavery**, [the] **holocaust** ... **apartheid** [and] **ethnic cleansing** – have deeply wounded the victim and debased the perpetrator. These horrors are still with us in various forms. It is now time to confront them and to take comprehensive measures against them
>
> (Robinson, 2001)
>
> Sexual slavery is ultimately a matter of human rights
>
> (Tree, 2000)

Introduction

The common link between the most prominent and highly reported atrocities of the twentieth century such as the Holocaust, apartheid and ethnic cleansing is that they have all encompassed gross violations of what is now known as the first true international human right to be covered by international law: The right not to be held in slavery or servitude (Paust, 2000). That slavery has been sustained and re-manifested during eras of the worst kinds of human annihilation is pertinent in that it is thus acknowledged to be an efficient means of control for the benefit of those in power of a given situation. It is somewhat ironic, however, that

89

the twentieth century, in which the formal abolition of slavery was achieved through codified legal instruments and conventions,[1] has also been the century in which slavery re-emerged in new guises of bondage whilst still maintaining the age-old objective of 'slavery' for the purpose of exploitation.

Current trends involving the process of enslavement of women and girls, however, highlight the difficulty in definitively pinpointing the actual exercise of slavery itself. Contemporary examples reveal this challenge: the sex camps reported in the most recent cases of internal armed conflicts of the Balkans and Rwanda, where women were held under the guise of 'internees' (Kunarac, Vukovic and Kovac Case, 2001)[2] and the sex houses more commonly known as brothels where they are held as 'prostitutes' (American Anti-Slavery Group)[3] in major cities around the world, and the marriages where they have been bought through mail order and are held under the guise of 'wives' all ensure continuation of the existence of sexual slavery as one of the most pervasive and subtle forms of abuse to permeate the global economy during times of peace, as well as during periods of conflict, in the contemporary world.

Sexual slavery *per se* involves the 'exercise of any or all of the powers attaching to the right of ownership or control when such exercise involves obtaining or imposing sexual service and/or access through rape or other forms of sexual violence' (McDougall, 1998). This applies to both genders. Protection for female victims of sexual slavery, however, involves more than just literal interpretation of the above definition. It encompasses a deeper understanding of the sociological position of women in societies, as many 'gender abuses are sanctioned or perpetrated by the government, often under the guise of culture, religion or tradition' (Askin, 1997). It involves understanding the cultural implications on women's lives and their societal roles that have many universal backdrops, and taking account of gender and racial discrimination, which has been highlighted by all women's lobby groups which have argued that human rights violations targeted specifically at women because of their 'gender' group have been largely ignored by a male, patriarchal system of legislators. But most importantly for the purposes of this chapter, it involves an analysis of a continual lack of sufficient response from the international legal system to provide sufficiently for female victims of sexual slavery, under its own standard and obligation of protecting those most vulnerable. In brief, this chapter argues that it has done so by shifting the debate on prosecuting the crime of slavery to one on prosecuting the crime of trafficking. This has diluted the debate so that governments and the international community have fewer obligations to prosecute for and protect from the crime of female sexual slavery.

This chapter is divided into two sections. The first outlines how the international community has come to accept the customary and international legality of the abolition of slavery in all its forms. This establishes the right not to be held in slavery as non-derogable. The second section assesses how sexual slavery is still a vast problem in contemporary society and how this issue is being dealt with in international human rights provisions as an issue on trafficking in human beings, and not as an issue of the new slave trade. This section is divided into two sub-sections. The first looks at three major factors that have helped sustain sexual slavery as part of the sex industry: military conflict, poverty and prostitution. The second analyses the existing slavery and trafficking legislation to establish whether this provides sufficient protection and prosecution measures. It argues that the current trend of combating female sexual slavery through reliance on trafficking legislation, whilst *prima facie* sufficient, fails abjectly in its application. This failure is to its continued link with prostitution, its failure to refer explicitly to sexual exploitation with regard to slavery and the fact that the international community itself has never responded to trafficking legislation from a human rights position in favour of victims. It is usually used to stop traffickers and remove illegal immigrants, but not to protect and offer redress to female sex slaves. In conclusion, I argue that the subject of contemporary slavery itself needs to be addressed, and propose that, ultimately, if the re-emergence of the slave trade in all its 'new' forms is to be taken seriously, then a new convention on slavery needs to be considered.

Abolition to re-acknowledgement

International crimes are acknowledged as such because they are considered to be violations of international law, a law derived from a combination of international agreements and customary law (Paust, 2000).[4] The Statute of the International Court of Justice distinguishes customary international law and fundamental principles of law as sources of international law. That slavery and related crimes fall under the category of 'Fundamental Human Rights' is of no surprise, since from 1807 to the first Slavery Convention of 1926 there was a huge upsurge in those who wanted to end 'their nation's involvement in the slave trade' (Lauren, 1998). Viewing it as an international trade 'repugnant to the principles of humanity and universal morality[5] ... [and] irreconcilable with the principles of humanity and justice' (Lauren, 1998), the public voice in all civilised countries called for its prompt suppression.

These slavery instruments and principles contributed to the establishment of the abolition of slavery as customary international law. Article 38 of the Statute of the International Court of Justice[6] recognises that customary law is that which has become a 'general practice accepted as law', comprised of two elements: 1) generally accepted practice or behaviour i.e. what people/governments do; and 2) general acceptance as being law, i.e. *opinio juris* (Steiner and Alston, 2000). Both elements must coincide and, in relation to slavery and the slave trade, it is universally accepted that they do. Furthermore, in order to support the existence and legality of customary international law, slavery is one of the legal issues that legal criminal law writers refer to in order to substantiate the argument, thereby enabling them to rule that a particular law has the force of universal obligation for the international community (Steiner and Alston, 2000).

Customary international law is binding on all states, except in situations where a state consistently and unequivocally refuses to accept a custom in the process of formation (Roberts and Guelff, 2000). Whilst some legal writers may put up a convincing argument that trafficking in humans is not customary law, this is definitely not the case with regards to slavery and the slave trade. Slavery is undisputedly an international crime, whether in times of war or in times of peace (Gutman and Reiff, 1999). As Guelff asserts,

> this formation of customary law requires consistent and recurring action (or lack of action) by states, coupled with a general recognition by states that such action (or lack of action) is required or permitted by international law. In general, the practice of states includes not only diplomatic, political, and military behaviour but also official statements, court decisions, legislation, and administrative decrees.

In relation to slavery this has definitely been the case. Furthermore, since the Second World War all the major international human rights and humanitarian law instruments have provided for prosecuting the crime of slavery, explicitly or implicitly.[7]

It is difficult, therefore, with all this legislation, customary law, regional instruments, slavery conventions and explicit codification, to comprehend that female sexual slavery has existed, and continues to exist, with impunity, especially as there is an obligation on state agents to ensure that slavery abolition is enforced and acknowledged as 'the most fundamental principal of international law is *pacta sunt servanda:* agreements must be observed' (Askin, 1997). Yet the following accounts provide appalling evidence of the continued existence of the new bondage of old slavery with the forcible enslavement of women for purposes of sexual violence and exploitation, at the behest of an arguably patriarchal society that accepts that women and girls are a prize of war, and a free, tradeable commodity during peace.

Grounding the debate

Slavery was the first human rights issue to arouse international concern, yet the persistence of the slave trade, especially in the form of sexual slavery, remains a grave and tenacious problem.[8] Sexual slavery, which relies on the existence of sexual violence and exploitation, is now located within new points of departure within particularised contemporary economic development. Globalisation, mass communication through the Internet, mass migration, transnational corporation monopoly and legal and illegal trading in arms and weapons, all contribute largely to the continuing existence of sexual slavery (Hughes and Roche, 1999). Furthermore, these contributory factors by and large cannot be considered in isolation, as they compound the assumed role of sexual violence and exploitation as an inevitable product, not even by-product, of the new world order. Its more subtle forms are in evidence in our everyday lives – sexual violence on television, in magazine and billboard advertising, on Internet sites, in comic books for adults[9] and through 'acceptable' levels of pornography. In fact, female sexual slavery is enmeshed in a world where it is ever more sophisticated, more globalised and more technical.

Academic researchers support this claim by categorising the more influential factors which help sustain sexual slavery:

- gender-based social and economic inequality in all areas of the globe (United Nations, 1995), assuring a supply of women, especially from developing and new independent states (NIS) in Eastern Europe (Caldwell, Galster and Steinzor, 1997);
- demand for the sex of prostitution and related sexual entertainment (Barry, 1995, in Raymond, Hughes and Gomez, 2001; Bishop and Robinson, 1998:67; Thanh-Dam Truong, 1990, in Raymond, Hughes and Gomez, 2001);
- macroeconomic policies, promoted by international lending organisations, that mandate 'structural adjustments' in many developing

regions in the world, pushing some countries (e.g. the Philippines) to export women for labour, making them vulnerable to trafficking; or to develop economies based on tourism (e.g. Thailand), including sex tourism (Bishop and Robinson, 1998, in Raymond, Hughes and Gomez, 2001; Daguno, 1998, in Raymond, Hughes and Gomez, 2001);

- expansion of transnational sex industries and increasingly sophisticated predatory recruitment techniques and networks (Gutner and Corben, 1996, in Raymond, Hughes and Gomez, 2001; Kaihla, 1991, in Raymond, Hughes and Gomez, 2001; Vatikiotis, 1995, in Raymond, Hughes and Gomez, 2001);
- globalisation of capital and information technology (Hughes, 1999, in Raymond, Hughes and Gomez, 2001; Santos, 1999, in Raymond, Hughes and Gomez, 2001);
- armed conflict, military occupation and concentration of military and militia bases in various parts of the world (Moon, 1997, in Raymond, Hughes and Gomez, 2001; Raymond, Hughes and Gomez, 2001; Sturdevant and Stoltzfus, 1992, in Raymond, Hughes and Gomez, 2001).

Here, I focus on the link between three scenarios; military conflict, poverty and prostitution. However, I take other factors into consideration as some are pervasive elements that transcend most situations – for example, gender-based social and economic inequality.

Military conflict

The historical genesis of sexual slavery is deeply rooted in military occupation with so-called 'military brothels' the 'oldest form of sexual manipulation on a massive scale' (Leidtholt, 1999). However, unlike the overt conditions of sexual slavery during incidences of armed conflict, irrespective of state denial by both military and political structures, sexual slavery during peacetime is a covert regime under a cloak of many layers. With a thriving international sex industry, sexual slavery is more difficult to identify and prosecute, as sex business flourishes in all major cities around the world. Furthermore, at an alarmingly increasing rate there has also been a rise in the recycling of women that men no longer need after war from the military market to these major cities. This reinforcing of continual abuse of women as 'sexual commodities' involves a perpetual cycle of perpetration, from war to peace.

The military tourist trail: the increase of female sexual slavery

The contemporary existence of sexual slavery in Thailand is arguably 'born from the seeds of Western capital' (Rho-Ng, 2000). Created from the backdrop of the Vietnam War which culminated in the '1967 R & R [Rest and Recuperation] Treaty',[10] the demand for sexual services by US servicemen transformed an already existing Thai prostitution market into what has become a lucrative international sex tourism enterprise. From the 1960s Thailand was open to new development and economic benefit from the 'R & R' industry. By 1967 the industry was worth £5 million as the presence of American soldiers subsidised hotels, night-clubs, video parlours and venereal disease counselling business. The treaty has had lasting repercussions on the economic and political climate in Thailand, and their economic ties with the United States. Elizabeth Rho-Ng's report on this connection, and its advancement of the sex industry in both countries, reveals how much impact these policy agreements have on the global structure of trade and tourism that increasingly informs how the sexual slavery criminal industry remains an appalling problem:

> Between 1960 and 1972, an estimated $4 million was loaned by a financial consortium, which included such major American investors as Bank of America Corporation and Chase Manhattan Corporation, to a handful of Thai companies providing 'personal services' ... Robert McNamara, who had served as the U.S Secretary of Defence during the signing of the R & R Treaty, became the President to the World Bank in the early 1970s. In this capacity, McNamara helped charter an international capital venture, infusing Thailand with investment dollars, many of which were US dollars. That 'the World Bank's agreement was negotiated by the same executive who ... oversaw the R & R [Treaty]' demonstrated how the special kind of tourism envisaged was virtually a foregone conclusion.
>
> In light of the World Bank report recognizing Thailand's 'growth potential of tourism as part of the export strategy' the National Plan of Tourist Development hoped to attract wealthy foreign visitors and tourists. The hope was to recapture the R & R entertainment market in order to maintain the operation of the tourist infrastructure for sustained investment. Arguably such economic strategies for developing tourism led to the current day Thai sex tourism boom.

However, development and survival of the 1967 R & R Treaty[11] hinged on the 'availability of women as providers of "personal services" or "special services" ' (Bales, 2000) to US citizens. That these girls were readily available is not a matter of chance, but characteristic of the social status accorded to women in many states. Sadly, the only thing that separates these women and girls as 'victims' is demographics. What bonds them as 'slaves' is the specific vulnerability that has led them to captivity.

Poverty

The UN human rights bodies, along with the Working Group on Contemporary Forms of Slavery and many NGOs, report extreme poverty as a common link between all forms of slavery. According to Turnbull, poverty, along with high levels of unemployment among women and, concomitantly, the declining social status of women, constitute the *major* 'push factors' (Turnbull, 1999). For Thai women, declining social status has never been an issue, as women in Thailand are essentially viewed as '*things*, markers in a male game of status and prestige' (Bales, 2000). Thus vulnerable Thai women and girls not only have to cope with poverty, but also with being commodities because of their impoverished status.

In the past many struggling Thais were forced to make harsh decisions to survive, especially those in the northern region where in certain situations families were reduced to using their children as commodities. This, according to Bales, was 'a life choice, not preferred but acceptable, and one that was used regularly'. Many of these sales fed a 'small, steady flow of servants, workers, and prostitutes south into Thai society'. Arguably, however, Bales asserts that there is an increase in the sale of girls as some parents have come to realise the money to be made from selling their children. Pressurised by modernisation, parents in northern Thailand feel a greater need to compete on a consumer level, and thus 'the sale of a daughter might easily finance a new television set'. Astonishingly, '[a] recent survey in the northern provinces found that of the families who sold their daughters, two thirds could afford not to do so but instead preferred to buy color televisions and video equipment' (Bales, 2000). It is worth pointing out that it has always been the sale of girls, never boys.

Similarly, in the Newly Independent States of Russia, while 98 per cent of women are literate and a substantial number university-educated, they face 'widespread employment discrimination that is practised, condoned and tolerated by the government' (Caldwell, Galster and Steinzor,

1997) – so much so, in fact, that in 1994 the Minister of Labour, Gennady Melikyan, stated that 'the government would disregard female unemployment until the day arrives when all Russian men are employed' (European Union, 2001). Herein we see that it is accepted as public policy that gender is factored into the poverty equation, exposing the gender discrimination that leads *inter alia* to the entrapment of women in sexual slavery – pushed by the very forces that should serve to redress this situation: government agencies. Unfortunately, many female Russians, just like female Thais and females from transitional or developing countries, end up in horrendous enslavement situations.

The 'pull factors', however, for all these victims, are what have traditionally influenced the migratory patterns of all peoples, never mind impoverished women and girls: 'employment opportunities, higher standards of living, and general economic wealth' (Turnbull, 1999; see also Caldwell, Galster and Steinzor, 1997). For many female victims, however, if they have not been sold outright by families, or taken through kidnapping, the entrapment procedure is basically the same. This system, known as 'debt bondage', irrespective of a sexual exploitation nexus for enslavement, is now formally recognised by all human rights agencies as one of the many forms of contemporary slavery.

Many women living in poverty understandably wish to leave or change the conditions in which they are forced to live. For those who wish to leave their country one of the few avenues open to them is to use the services of 'illegal'[12] smugglers to secure visas, work permits and airline/train tickets in order to get to their country of choice. In the majority of cases these women and young girls, and their families, are under the illusion that they are going to work in bars, restaurants, factories or as domestic servants (Williams, 1999). While some are aware that they may have to work as prostitutes to pay off the debt incurred to procure their passage and permits, many are unaware of the risk of ending up as sex slaves as part of the deal. In fact, nobody expects to end up enslaved, shackled like an animal, locked in a room, in some instances chained to a bed and sexually abused through systematic and repeated instances of rape, torture, mutilation or misogynist mistreatment by a male clientele, who accept this as a 'service'.

One report noted 'a crackdown on brothels' to target the East Coast of America, where there were accounts of 'a stable of sexual slaves' in New York. Herein, 'thirty Thai women ... smuggled in to serve as sex slaves ... were referred to by numbers instead of by names. Bars covered the windows and buzzers operated and controlled the doors so that women were prevented from leaving'. It is difficult to comprehend that women and girls can retain any level of sanity, or even cooperate in such circumstances. However, before they even reach this stage, many have been exposed to physical and psychological abuse of the worst kind (Hughes and Roche, 1999).

In order to make female sex slaves compliant, their captors usually use violence as a form of oppression. Where this does not work, they threaten to kill, maim or report the 'work' of the female victims to their families. Indeed, in many cases victims know that if they try to escape, their captors will seek financial payment, or otherwise, from their family. This is usually too much for them to bear, so compliance is easy to secure. Furthermore, most women have their passports removed, are told that they are in the country illegally and that even if they go to the authorities that they will be arrested, held and prosecuted as illegal immigrants (Human Rights Watch, 2000). It is important to stress that such threats are by no means imaginary. It is an all too familiar story that state agents and police who are supposed to control incidences of human trafficking are very often complicit actors in the procurement, use or trafficking of the victims. According to Williams, 'agents and police in Thailand ... receive benefits from four major inbound and outbound flows estimated at somewhere between 200 and 280 million U.S. dollars'. Herein lies their incentive.

Furthermore, even when women have free movement it does not necessarily mean that they can escape. Proving they are being held as slaves is often hard to establish when they appear to have free movement. Many women and girls, even if they could escape, do not speak the language of their country of destination. Sometimes they end up not even in the country they thought they were going to. The Coalition Against Trafficking reported that they interviewed 15 foreign women 'trafficked' in the US, of whom 40 per cent spoke no English, and 33 per cent had very little language understanding or speaking ability. In one incident a Sri Lankan woman reported that she was kept in 'extreme conditions of confinement, told of the isolation that lack of English language proficiency caused and how it hindered her escape' (Hughes and Roche, 1999). It was not until she took her son to hospital and met a medical assistant from Sri Lanka that she told her story and got refuge in a battered women's shelter.

Despite these dangers, for many the opportunity of going to a wealthier nation such as Japan to earn a good salary by most standards is very appealing. For women from countries with weak economies this is especially so. However, the Human Rights Watch report on 'Thai women Trafficked into Debt Bondage in Japan' gives an extremely detailed account of women and girls who end up as sex slaves due to their vulnerability in having to rely on criminals to get to Japan in the first place. The following is a brief summary:

> Our findings have been corroborated by researchers, advocates, and government official in Japan and Thailand. The women's shelter Saalaa, found that of the Thai women who worked in Japanese snack bars,[13] more than ninety-five percent arrived in debt. Moreover, in ninety-five percent of those cases the women 'owed' more than 3 million yen (US$24,000), which they were forced to reimburse through sex work under highly coercive conditions. Saalaa published a report on these findings, which points out that although this amount is called a 'debt', this is a misnomer, as the women have not actually borrowed the money.

Human Rights Watch found that while the crime of debt bondage was closely linked to the crime of trafficking – as women were placed into debt bondage by the same networkers that arranged their travel to Japan – women also could be 'sold' into debt bondage in snack bars by persons unconnected to their travel into the country (Hughes and Roche, 1999).

Ironically, much of this sex slave industry in Japan also has links to the military. As Human Rights Watch reports, in the late 1960s 'sex tours, primarily to Thailand and other southeast Asian countries, began growing in popularity among Japanese men' (Human Rights Watch, 2000). Coincidentally, this was at the very same time that the Thai and US governments signed the R & R Treaty, which relied on the provision of girls for 'entertainment' purposes. However, as this activity was frowned on, efforts changed to lure foreign women into the sex industry in Japan, must notably from other Asian countries, and for the most part, by whatever means, they have succeeded.

The Coalition against Trafficking in Women also recognises the international dimension of the military nexus, as they report that, between the 1950s and the 1990s, over 100,000 Korean women emigrated to the US as wives of servicemen. A significant number of these were *kitjich'on* (military camp prostitutes), 'a large percentage of whom were abused and thus separated from their GI fiancés or husbands ... with many now on the sex trafficking circuits in the U.S.' (Hughes and Roche, 1999). This circuit is highly organised and covertly involves the enslavement of women and girls for the purpose of sexual exploitation.

Prostitution

Unfortunately, for women and girls who are enslaved for the purposes of sexual exploitation, there is more often than not an intrinsic link to prostitution, in war and in peace, which weakens both acknowledgement and punishment of the crime of sexual slavery. For, as already noted, we live in a world where commercial sex is accepted and condoned at some level, even when it is illegal. Yet these women are not prostitutes; they are slaves used for the purpose of sexual exploitation. This involves exploitation of their person, based on their gender, for financial or other gain for a slave master. The physical abuser of these slaves is almost exclusively male. The following account highlights the desperate need to ensure that our slavery legislation is more than just theoretically sound. Unless this is done the human rights violations and crime of sexual slavery will persist, enmeshed in the underbelly of prostitution, globalisation and the market economy. Where the crime of sexual slavery is committed against an individual there must be redress for that specific crime to protect the victim of such extreme abuse.

The following account of sexual slavery as documented by Hughes and Roche (1999) exposes the mentality of the perpetrators of such violent exploitation of other human beings:

> When women were brought to bachelor parties or conventions, they might have to engage in sex with up to 20 men. In the men's writings, one man describes a party with over 20 men and one or two women. He writes about it as great fun, but the reality for the woman was most likely quite different.
>
> In the LR [living room] was about 15 guys in towels ... In the room to the left a group of about seven guys surrounded a slender attractive young latino looking girl. She was lying on her back getting fucked ... I stood over the crowd and watched her ... I tried to get down to copa [sic] feel, but I really couldn't get close ... She sucks me for about 10 minutes while 4–5 guys watch in the dimly lit room. I plow her for about 12 minutes ... She kept her eyes closed while I fucked her and didn't say much. Later, I go into the back room and some black guy is giving this girl another plowing ... Most everyone has left. So me and another guy lay her down. I bang her ... finally I slam her hard a few times ... I look in the BR and she's laying there with one leg splayed out and the other is bent at the knee. Her head is turned to the side and her hair is everywhere. She looks like she's been fucked.

Assessing the developments of sexual slavery in contemporary society, it is imperative that the international community seeks to provide legal protections for women against such crimes. Before they ever reach enslavement, these women and girls are at the best of times those most vulnerable. As has been highlighted, albeit in brief, societal structures, macroeconomics, patriarchal military strategies combined with a new global dimension on trading have exposed these women and girls even further to gross violations of many of their fundamental human rights – the most important of which, and presumably most protected, the right not to be held in slavery.

However, observers recognise that the magnitude and violence of these practices of sexual exploitation constitute an international human rights crisis of contemporary slavery. The demand on the international community, therefore, is to provide human rights instruments that protect and offer redress to these victims to solidify their case, not further weaken those already most vulnerable.

Anti-slavery law

As already stated, the right not to be held in slavery or servitude is the oldest international human right in the world, established under customary international law, human rights instruments and codified conventions. However, as none of the major human rights instruments defines sexual slavery, it is necessary to look to the existing conventions to see how they serve female victims of sexual slavery.

The following assesses how the most recognised conventions provide for sexual slavery, and whether these are sufficient to deal with the growing problem of slavery for the purposes of sexual exploitation and violence, in particular to support an ever-growing sex industry.

Slavery conventions

The Slavery Convention of 1926 is the most often cited convention in relation to interpreting what constitutes slavery and servitude.[14] The drafters of the convention recognised the need to offer more 'detailed arrangements' than those already in existence, in order to 'prevent forced labour from developing into conditions analogous to slavery'.[15] This treaty proffers a definition of slavery:

Article 1:
(1) Slavery is the status of condition of a person over whom any or all of the powers attaching to the right of ownership are exercised.

(2) The slave trade includes all acts involved in the capture, acquisition or disposal of a person with intent to reduce him to slavery; all acts involved in the acquisition of a slave with a view to selling or exchanging him; all acts of disposal by sale or exchange of a slave acquired with a view to being sold or exchanged, and, in general, every act of trade or transport in slaves.

This convention calls for all contracting parties, as far as possible, to work to prevent and suppress the slave trade and to bring about the complete abolition of slavery in all its forms as soon as possible. Article 3 confirms that there can be no derogation from the 'principles laid down' in Articles 1 and 2. While the definition in Article 1(1) remains as relevant, the definition of conditions of the slave trade itself under Article 1(2) is not explicit enough with regard to the different types of slavery – hence, recognition by the 1956 Supplementary Convention on the Abolition of Slavery, the Slave Trade, and Institutions and Practices Similar to Slavery[16] that 'slavery, the slave trade and institutions and practices similar to slavery' had not yet been eliminated was imperative in informing a wider remit to address this problem. Included in Article 1 are further definitions of what constitutes slavery:

Section 1 ...
(a) Debt bondage, that is to say, the status or condition arising form a pledge by a debtor of his personal services or of those of a person under his control as security for a debt, if the value of those services as reasonably assessed is not applied towards the liquidation of the debt or the length and nature of those services are not respectively limited and defined;
(b) Serfdom, that is to say, the condition or status of a tenant who is by law, custom or agreement bound to live and labour on land belonging to another person and to render some determinate service to such other person, whether for reward or not, and is not free to change his status;
(c) Any institution or practice whereby:
   (i) A woman, without the right to refuse, is promised or given in marriage on payment of a consideration in money or in kind to her parents, guardian, family or any other person or group; or
   (ii) The husband of a woman, his family, or his clan, has the right to transfer her to another person for value received or otherwise; or

(iii) A woman on the death of her husband is liable to be inher-
ited by another person;

(d) Any institution or practice whereby a child or young persons
under the age of 18 years, is delivered by either or both of his natural parents or by his guardian to another person, whether for
reward or not, with a view to the exploitation of the child or
young person or of his labour.

For the purposes of this chapter the definitions of '(a) debt bondage' and
'(d) ... the deliver[y] of a child or young persons ... [for] exploitation'
are of primary importance, for these are the situations in which most
women and girls who are enslaved for the purpose of sexual exploitation
and violence are more often entrapped. However, the definition of debt
bondage may be too narrow. The definition gives the impression that
this requires or pertains to some kind of 'labour' or 'work' as payment of
a debt. This may be legitimate if the price is not considered too high.
Thus, if 'prostitution' is considered 'work' – as it is by some NGOs, and
in some instances the UN – then elements of slavery in relation to
women who are held in so-called 'brothels' become harder to prove.[17]
Furthermore, as we have seen in the report from the Japanese NGO,
many women do not borrow money, so in many cases it is a fictional
debt the women are repaying.

Section 11 deals with the slave trade, and under Article 3 covers the
criminal offence of conveying slaves. It states that '[T]he act of conveying or attempting to convey slaves from one country to another by
whatever means of transport, or of being accessory thereto, shall be a
criminal offence under the laws of the States Parties to this Convention
and persons convicted thereof shall be liable to very severe penalties.'
Thus the convention explicitly criminalises trafficking. However, it is
important to note the reference 'from one country to another' as this
highlights the difficulty of women who are enslaved within their own
countries and women or girls who are brought into the European Union
and enslaved throughout the member states.

Another problem is that the language of the provisions suggests slave
trading en masse. For example, Article 2(a) states that 'The States Parties
shall take all effective measures to prevent ships and aircraft authorized
to fly their flags from conveying slaves and to punish persons guilty of
such acts or of using national flags for that purpose.' However, irrespective of this, it is obvious that the drafters of the agreement meant for any
persons engaging in or acting as an accessory shall be found guilty of the
criminal offence of trading in humans for the purpose of enslaving

should be subject to severe penalties. Section IV defines slavery as defined in the 1926 Convention.

Supplementing both the Slavery Conventions are two Forced Labour Conventions. The first is the Forced Labour Convention (No. 29).[18] Herein 'forced or compulsory labour' is defined as all 'work or service ... exacted from any person under the menace of a penalty' and which has not been offered voluntarily by said party.[19] The rest of convention relates to trade and industry, but if prostitution and/or sex is considered a 'service', then aspects of this convention could apply. The second is the Abolition of Forced Labour Convention of 1959.[20] This recognises the Slavery Convention of 1926, but is mainly concerned with 'forced or compulsory labour', and also takes into consideration the aforementioned convention. However, it is important to note that Article 1 states that:

> Each member of the International Labour Organisation which ratified this Convention undertakes to suppress and not to make use of any form of forced or compulsory labour:
> (b) As a method of mobilising and using labour for the purposes of economic development. ...
> (c) as a means of racial, national or religious discrimination.

Arguably paragraph (b) could be used against countries such as Thailand which have set up sex tourism as a form of economic development. However, this would mean that 'prostitution' would have to be recognised as a form of illegal or legal labour, and, as already noted, this causes a divide between human rights activists and legislators on sexual slavery. Similarly, a gender inclusion in Article 1(e), the idea of which is becoming more and more prominent in the debate on violence against women,[21] would help protect those enslaved for sexual purposes; however once again the 'labour' nexus prevails, thus creating difficulty.

These conventions arguably are not sufficiently explicit in their provisions to provide prosecution of, or protection from, sexual slavery. However, despite the fact that the right not to be held in slavery or servitude is a fundamental guarantee enshrined in all major human rights instruments and explicitly recognised in the above conventions, the international community has sought to provide for the prosecution of sexual slavery under trafficking legislation.

Trafficking and trafficking conventions

As slavery has historically been associated with 'trading', it is hardly surprising that international instruments dealing specifically with trafficking in humans for profit emerged alongside those dealing with the act of slavery. The first international anti-trafficking convention adopted in 1904 was specifically to eliminate the trafficking of white women and children for the purposes of prostitution, and the immediate link here was with sexual exploitation. Nearly 100 years later, as a sad reflection of the Western world, trafficking in women and children 'arguably has the highest profit margin and the lowest risk of almost any type of illegal activity. In the past decade alone, an estimated 30 million women and children may have been trafficked in and from South-East Asia for sexual exploitation and sweatshop labor' (Human Rights Committee, 2001). The following is an account from this UN report:

> Para 4. The efficient, brutal routine endured by trafficked women and children rarely varies in the dozens of countries where trafficking and sexual slavery occurs. Women are held in apartments, bars and makeshift brothels. They are beaten, drugged, starved, and raped into submission. Fifteen-year-old prostitutes in Bangkok service an average of 14 clients a day. They are held captive by debt bondage, violence and fear. Few ever testify against their traffickers and those who do often risk death. In 1998 in Istanbul, Turkey, according to Ukrainian police investigators, two women were thrown to their deaths from a balcony while six of their Russian friends watched. In Serbia in 1998, an escaped Ukrainian woman reported that a woman who refused to work as a prostitute was beheaded in public. (Human Rights Committee, 2001)

The violence of this evidence alone signifies the level of legal security required from any trafficking legislation relied upon to protect and prosecute against slavery, especially sexual slavery.

Until recently, the most notable providing for these violations was the Convention for the Suppression in Traffic in Persons and of the Exploitation of Prostitution 1949.[22] The preamble to this convention opens as follows:

> Whereas prostitution and the accompanying evil of the traffic in persons for the purpose of prostitution are incompatible with the dignity and worth of the human person and endanger the welfare of the individual, the family and the community.[23]

The main focus of this convention is punishing the person who, for the gratification of others, 'procures, entices or leads away, for purposes of prostitution another person, even with the consent of the person or exploits the prostitution of another person, even with the consent of that person',[24] and to punish those who knowingly finance or take part in financing a brothel, or rent a building for the purpose of prostitution.[25] This convention does not prohibit prostitution itself, but yields to state parties whether it shall be legal or prohibited.

It is worth noting that this convention does not have an international border requisite, as many states have internal trafficking which leads to sexual slavery. Furthermore, this convention refers to the rights of the victims, and states that aliens are entitled to the same remedy as nationals. These are considered extraditable offences, or where states are not party to extradition, they shall be punished by their own states on return.[26]

However, as 'human trafficking is widely recognized in the international community as the fastest growing form of transnational criminal activity',[27] there has been much criticism of this document's ability to curb trafficking. First and foremost, from a lawyer's perspective, it does not help that there was no definition of what constitutes trafficking. For human rights lawyers the problem is that 'victims do not have any procedural rights to participate in proceedings against trafficking unless the national law of the state party affords them that right' (Caldwell, Galster and Steinzor, 1997). Also, this convention fails to incorporate lack of consent or coercion in its definition of trafficking. Thus if a party to the proceedings said that any woman or girl was participating in, for example, prostitution voluntarily, then there was little or no grounds to prosecute for either trafficking or sexual slavery; instead, as is often the case, the victim is prosecuted as an illegal immigrant, along with the owner for running an illegal brothel, if this is the case.

However, recognising the huge increase in the number of women and children being exploited at the hands of traffickers, the international community pushed for a convention with a definition to 'encompass the full nature and scope of the abuse' (Human Rights Watch, 2000). Thus this has followed the preceding convention with the Protocol to Prevent, Suppress and Punish Trafficking in Persons, Especially Women and Children, supplementing the United Nations Convention against Transnational Organised Crime.[28]

The Preamble opens as follows:

Declaring that effective action to prevent and combat trafficking in persons, especially women and children, requires a comprehensive international approach in the countries of origin, transit and destination that includes measures to prevent such trafficking, to punish the traffickers and to protect the victims of such trafficking, including by protecting their internationally recognized human rights.[29]

Taking into account the fact that, despite the existence of a variety of international instruments, containing rules and practical measures to combat the exploitation of persons, especially women and children, there is no universal instrument that addresses all aspects of trafficking in persons.

Concerned that, in the absence of such an instrument, persons who are vulnerable to trafficking will not be sufficiently protected.

This Protocol 'promises to contest the world's organized crime networks and combat the trade in human beings and transnational prostitution' (Raymond, 2001).

The purpose of this Protocol is laid down in Articles 2 and 3:

2 (a) To prevent and combat trafficking in persons, paying particular attention to women and children.
  (b) To protect and assist the victims of such trafficking, with full respect for their human rights.
3 [Herein the working definition of trafficking is provided under 'Use of terms']:
  (a) Trafficking in persons shall mean the recruitment, transportation, transfer, harbouring or receipt of persons, by means of the threat or use of force or other forms of coercion, of abduction, of fraud, of deception, of the abuse of power or of a position of vulnerability or of the giving or receiving of payments or benefits to achieve the consent of a person having control over another person, for the purpose of exploitation.

Exploitation shall include, at a minimum, the exploitation of the prostitution of others or other forms of sexual exploitation, forced labour or services or practices similar to slavery, servitude or the removal of organs;
  (b) The consent of the victim of trafficking in persons to the intended exploitation set forth in subparagraph (a) have been used;
  (c) The recruitment, transportation, transfer, harbou ing or receipt of a child for the purpose of exploitation shall be considered

'trafficking in persons' even if this does not involve any of the means set forth in subparagraph of this article.

As there was no working definition on trafficking it was important that a new provision would be included. This definition is important for victims for a number of reasons: they will in theory no longer be viewed as criminals but as victims of the crime; global trafficking will be answered with a global response; this international definition will serve as a basis to harmonise national laws; all victims of trafficking are to be protected, not just those forced (Article 3(a) and (b)). This is very important, as it has an impact on those who end up as sex slaves.

The consent of the victim to be trafficked is irrelevant (Article 3(b)). Furthermore, it takes into consideration the abuse of a victim's vulnerability, which is also important for women and young girls (Article 3(a)). Similarly, it helps to ensure that victims of trafficking do not share the burden of proof (Article 3(b)). It recognises that it is not necessary for a victim to cross a border, so trafficking within countries, or specific regions such as the EU, can be prosecuted. This is important in relation to the EU as there has been a huge increase in women and girls being bought and sold throughout Europe for the purpose of sexual exploitation. In order for victims to be protected under the 1949 legislation they would have to prove that they were third country nationals, especially as the Schengen Treaty removed internal borders.[30] Furthermore, even the European Union Parliament asserted in 1995 that there had to be a foreign border crossing for 'trafficking' in persons to have taken place. It is therefore possible to see the difficulty arising for those who have been bought and sold around a state or region. Most importantly, however, is that the exploitative purpose of the crime is explicitly recognised so that crimes such as slavery, not the movement of the victim, become the issue (Article 3(a)).

Problems providing for victims through trafficking legislation

However, once again this legislation fails to provide sufficiently explicit recognition of the conditions for female victims of sexual slavery. Nowhere in the Protocol is there a definition of slavery, or practices similar to slavery, servitude or 'other forms of sexual exploitation'. The only explicit connection to any form of sexual exploitation is that directly connected with exploitation and prostitution. As noted this causes a deep divide between some NGOs, and between governments, as their interpretation of prostitution varies. Indeed, in relation to the Protocol it too was the source of a lot of debate.

In her position paper to the Ad Hoc Committee,[31] the UN Special Rapporteur on Violence against Women argued that the terms 'victims' and 'sexual exploitation' should left out of the Protocol. Furthermore, she questioned whether all activities in the sex industry constitute 'sexual exploitation' *per se*, or whether only sex work under exploitative or slavery-like conditions could qualify. The problem, however, is that prostitution and most 'sex work' is legal in only a handful of countries, although it is available in all. So how can we make such provisions for a 'job', regardless of complicity, that is illegal?

Similarly, the Special Rapporteur along with the UN High Commissioner for Human Rights, Mary Robinson, was in favour of deleting the term 'sexual exploitation' as it was 'imprecise and emotive' (1999). Instead, it was suggested that reference be made to trafficking for 'forced labour and/or bonded labour and/or servitude' – terms that explicitly include coercion and can be applied to any type of labour or service – thus forcing the issue of 'work' and its tenuous link to 'prostitution' to the forefront of the debate. Whether this is/was their intention is irrelevant. Of most relevance, however, is that such an interpretation weakens the issue of sexual slavery and forces it to become one about trafficking or prostitution. While the UN Group on Contemporary Forms of Slavery has expanded the definition of slavery to include trafficking in women and children who are then forced into sexual slavery, trafficking in and of itself is not slavery. It is the vehicle, the modus operandi, the cargo truck, but not the crime that has been perpetrated against sex slaves. The crime of sexual enslavement occurs *after* they have been trafficked.

Ironically, in terms of the fact that militarism has played such a huge part in the increase of sexual slavery, it is unfortunate that international humanitarian law (the law of war) provides better protection for female victims of sexual slavery. Under the statute of the International Criminal Court, trafficking is recognised as a facet of the crime of enslavement as a crime against humanity.[32] Whilst there is a difficulty in that crimes against humanity must be widespread or systematic for prosecution purposes, it is clearly accepted in the international forum that crimes against humanity can occur in peacetime as well as in conflicts. Furthermore, Article 7(g) explicitly refers to sexual slavery as one of these crimes. This codified definition of enslavement and the elements thereof is of utmost importance for prosecuting sexual slavery. Similarly, the inclusion of trafficking as an element of enslavement would help in the prosecution of traders in peacetime. This should serve as a beacon to the international community with regards to which element of the crime should be recognised as the more serious – trafficking or slavery.

There is a need for the international community to address the issue once more, taking into consideration the work already done in relation to codifying contemporary forms of slavery. The starting point is the 1956 Convention which codified debt bondage and serfdom. Furthermore, the crime of female sexual slavery needs to be codified in respect of the technology of its time – in the twenty-first century it needs to take into consideration the Internet and pornography, as well as prostitution, sex work and debt bondage, militarism, poverty, mass migration and gender.

Conclusion

Slavery is illegal. Customary and codified law ensures that this is a fundamental human right. Yet not only does it continue to exist in contemporary society, it has also re-manifested as an intrinsic part of an exploding global trade in humans, analogous to slave trading in the past. The trade in female sexual slavery involves the buying and selling, kidnapping, coercion and fraudulently acquiring of the means of control over the physical integrity of women and young girls. In the majority of cases this is purely for the purpose of sexual exploitation for the benefit of the traders, who earn large sums of money providing sex slaves for a thriving international sex industry.

However, the trade in sex slaves is not new. Irrespective of international laws that render slavery illegal, soldiers have always expected women and girls to be provided for their entertainment during armed conflict. As we have seen, there has been a clear link between what happened in Thailand in relation to sexual slavery to the military and economic strategies supported by the US government and the Thai government during the conflicts in that region in the 1960s and 1970s. This has massively contributed to the acceptance of sex tourism today.

The international community *per se* has responded favourably to acknowledging the upsurge in contemporary forms of slavery in general, and the increase in sexual slavery in particular, and has sought to remedy this problem by addressing the issue through legislation on trafficking. Arguably, trafficking is an element of the crime of enslavement and in and of itself is not a form of slavery. Therefore, relying on trafficking serves to dilute the debate on many fronts, not least because there has always been a prostitution nexus with trafficking. It forces the 'prostitution as slavery' versus the 'legitimacy of sex work' debate to the front of the problem, making it harder for a coherent response to the violent crime of sexual slavery. The emphasis then falls on the trafficking element of the process of the crime of sexual slavery, as opposed to the gross crime that the victims are subjected to. None of the conventions or protocols concerned with slavery or trafficking, however, has included a working definition of sexual slavery, or refers explicitly to sexual violence or exploitation, without a prostitution nexus. Whilst the Optional Protocol on Trafficking asserts that there are no instruments to date that 'encompass the nature and scope of the crime', it is arguable that this very protocol falls far short when it comes to encompassing the nature and scope of the crime of sexual slavery. Furthermore, Ruhama Women's Project in Dublin informs us that the Irish government has a problem with the protocol as it is feared that the wide definition of trafficking could allow for a large number of women to enter the country illegally and seek asylum or protection claiming to be victims of trafficking.[33] Ireland still has not ratified this protocol.

In order to address the crime of sexual slavery the international community must respond with legislation that will name the crime, call it what it is and provide protection from enslavement within the realms of the conditions of vulnerability that leave women and girls susceptible to abuse. As noted, the most progressive codification of enslavement that has recognised trafficking as an element of slavery (as opposed to the other way around) has come not from international human rights law, but international humanitarian law under the Rome Statute of the International Criminal Tribunal under Article 7(c), which deals with crimes against humanity. The challenge, therefore, to the international community is to re-codify international instruments so that they bring the crime of enslavement back into the criminal legal framework with language and laws that are real and meaningful. The only way this can be done is by providing a new slavery convention to codify the new forms of bondage that constitute slavery, and by acknowledging the continued existence of old forms of slavery, such as debt bondage. There is ample evidence to illustrate the overt abuse of women and young girls, especially through the sex industry. If we cannot protect female victims of such overt sexual oppression, then how can the most vulnerable be protected from covert forms of abuse in society in general?

Furthermore, explicitly codifying what constitutes sexual slavery in a slavery convention will serve to challenge existing institutionalised sexual abuse, the most obvious example being the conduct of armed forces throughout the world. It is ironic that in the aftermath of war UN peacekeepers continually use local women as prostitutes (Chinkin, 1999).

Acknowledgement

I would like to thank Professor Fionnuala Ní Aoláin for her constant support in all my endeavours. I would also like to thank Audrey Guichon for consistently encouraging my slavery research. Finally, a heartfelt thanks to my family and friends who got me this far.

Notes

1. The 1926 and 1956 Slavery Conventions have been the most influential in their definition of slavery and servitude.
2. The first case to deal with definition of enslavement as a crime against humanity for the prosecution on sexual slavery were Kunarac, Vukovic and Kovac, *Judgement of Trial Chamber 11*, The Hague, 22 February 2001 JL/P.I.S./666-e at the International Criminal Tribunal for the Former Yugoslavia.
3. American Anti-Slavery Group, 'Trafficking of Women into Sexual Slavery', in *Slavery Today: The Global Tragedy*, 24, School of International and Public Affairs, Columbia University, New York (2000). There exists a significant ideological chasm between two groups working on women's and human rights issues. In one school of thought, the belief is that women are capable of choosing sex work voluntarily as a commercial/financial option and that 'the abuses are neither inherent nor unique to prostitution'. The other camp 'declares that the institution of prostitution itself constitutes a violation of human rights, akin to the institution of slavery. However, members of both camps can acknowledge that there is a group of women and girls who do not choose sexual employment, but rather are forced into the sex industry involuntarily and fall under the terms of modern day slavery and debt-bondage'. It is from this premise that his chapter proceeds.
4. Bassiouni, in Paust (2000: 10 and 11). 'During a study of numerous international criminal law instruments, Professor Bassiouni has recognised that international crimes can be identified on the basis of one or more of ten penal characteristics.' Note, none of these include trafficking, although this analysis only covered up to 1996. And those under 'Fundamental Human Rights' are those most consider the worst forms of human rights breaches, Genocide, Crimes Against Humanity, Apartheid, Slavery and Related Crimes (which could include trafficking) Torture and Unlawful Human Experimentation.
5. Under the Eight Power Declaration.
6. The International Court of Justice is the judicial organ of the United Nations. The Statute of the ICJ was created under the UN Charter 1945.
7. Universal Declaration of Human Rights, 1948, Article 4; International Covenant on Civil and Political Rights (ICCPR) and International Covenant on Economic, Social and Cultural Rights (ICESCR) 1966. These two Covenants place legal obligations on states that have ratified or acceded them. Article 8 of the ICCPR and Articles 6 and 7 of the ICESCR; The European Convention on Human Rights, 1950, Article 4; Convention on the High Seas, 1958, Articles 13, 22, 99 and 110; Draft Articles on the Origin of State Responsibility, 1980, Article 19; American Convention on Human Rights and Protocols, 1969,

Article 6; African Charter on human and Peoples Rights, 1986, Article 5; Charter of the Fundamental Rights of the European Union, 2001, Article 5.

8. United Nations Fact Sheet No. 14, Contemporary Forms of Slavery. Available at http://www.ohchr.org/english/about/publications/docs/fs14.htm.

9. Whilst living in Japan I was astonished to see that there were specific Japanese *manga* (comic books) for men marketed on sexual violence against women. These are sold everywhere and read openly by male commuters.

10. See Rho-Ng (2000). '[A] similar type of accord was reached between the Philippines and the U.S. The U.S. – Republic of Philippines Military Base Agreement, which technically expired in September 1991, represented 40 years of U.S. military presence in the Philippines whereby the main industry around such military bases was the "entertainment" industry.'

11. Ibid., 'Shortly after 1968, the U.S. cancelled Hong Kong and Sydney Australia as alternative R & R destinations, thereby placing greater emphasis on Thailand's main attraction. In 1970 the amount spent ... was 20 million, as much as one-fourth of the total value of rice exports that year.'

12. I emphasise illegal here because, as we will see, while they are illegal, the very system that is supposed to prosecute them is often the same system that provides them with the legal documentation to enable them to conduct their trade.

13. See Hughes and Roche (1999: 84): 'Snack bars, often referred to as "snacks" are a common venue where many Japanese go for relaxation and conversation.' There are many different types and the ones used for *baishun* (prostitution) are known to locals, but would not be recognised as such by foreigners. Some are known as 'dating' snack bars where the clients may take the girls out of the snack bar for sexual services. The women here are known as 'hostesses', and clients 'can choose a hostel for two hours or the whole night'. A hostess is usually taken by the client to a nearby hotel, the client pays for all the services, and returns the hostess to the snack bar or apartment when he is finished. According to the women interviewed by HRW, 'the average fees were 20,000 to 30,000 [yen] (US$170–250) for two hours and 30,000 to 40,000 yen (US$240–340) for the night, and the money was given directly to the mama [the woman who runs the snack bar; also locally known as the *Mama-San*]'.

14. Entered into force 9 March 1927, in accordance with Article 12 of same. See http://www.unhchr.ch for the full treaty. The treaty refers to the influence of earlier conventions such as the General Act of the Brussels Conference of 1889–90 which sought to put an end to the African slave trade, the Convention of Saint-Germain-en-Laye 1919, which revised the General Act of Berlin of 1885, and the General Act of Brussels of 1890, to attain the 'complete suppression of slavery in all its form and of the slave trade by land and sea.' Furthermore, it also refers to the Temporary Slavery Commission appointed by the Council of the League of Nations on 12 June 1924.

15. Preamble to 1926 Slavery Convention.

16. Adopted by a Conference of Plenipotentiaries convened by Economic and Social Council resolution 608 (XXI) of 30 April 1956 and done at Geneva on 7 September 1956 entered into force on 30 April 1957, in accordance with Article 13 of same.

17. Especially as the debate on legalising prostitution versus prostitution as slavery, has yet to reach any conclusion. Yet where prostitution has been

legalised, most notably Belgium, Germany, Norway and Victoria, Australia, NGOs have argued that there has been an *increase* in the number of women being bought and sold into prostitution.

18. Adopted on 28 June 1930 by the General Conference of the International Labour Organisation at its fourteenth session, *entry into force* 1 May 1932, in accordance with Article 28 of same.

19. Ibid., Article 2(1)

20. Convention (No. 105) Concerning the Abolition of Forced labour. Adopted on 25 June 1957 by the General Conference of the International Labour Organisation at its fortieth session, entered into force, 17 January 1959, in accordance with Article 4 of same. See http://www.unhchr.ch for Convention.

21. World Conference Against Racism, Racial Discrimination, Xenophobia and Related Tolerance, Durban, South Africa 31 August-7 September 2001, p. 14. 'An expert group meeting on gender and racial discrimination (Zagreb, Croatia, 21–24 November 2000) recommended that the World Conference pay specific attention to the issue of gender in considering its themes and to take into account the intersection between gender discrimination and racial discrimination.'

22. Approved by the General Assembly resolution 317(IV) of 2 December, entered into force 25 July, 1951, in accordance with Article 24.

23. The international instruments that are in force and recognised in this preamble are as follows:

    (1) International Agreement of 18 May 1904 for the Suppression of the White Slave Traffic, as amended by the Protocol approved by the General Assembly of the United Nations on 3 December 1948.

    (2) International Convention of 4 May 1910 for the Suppression of the White Slave Traffic, as amended by the above-mentioned Protocol.

    (3) International Convention of 30 September 1921 for the Suppression of the Traffic in Women and Children, as amended by the Protocol approved by the General Assembly of the United Nations on 20 December 1947.

    International Convention of 11 October 1933 for the Suppression of the Traffic in Women of Full Age, as amended by the aforesaid Protocol.

24. Article 1(1) and (2).

25. Article 2(1).

26. Articles 5 and 8.

27. 'Global estimates of the scale of trafficking in women and children were prepared by the US Government. It was estimated then that between 700,000 and 2 million women and children are trafficked across international borders annually, although the calculations used to arrive at these figures are unclear.' US Department of State, International Information Programs, 25 April 2001.

28. In December 2000, 148 countries gathered in Palermo, Italy to attend a high-level conference opening the new UN Convention for signature. Of the 148 countries present, 121 signed the UN Convention against Transnational Organised Crime, and over 80 countries signed one of its supplementary this supplementary protocol; This convention has been a culmination of lots of regional and national governments increasing recognition of this new trade

in humans. Ibid., p. 52: 'In a resolution adopted on January 18, 1996, the European Parliament called upon the Commission and member States to 'take action on an international level to draft a UN convention to supersede the obsolete and ineffective [Trafficking Convention]'. See also Article 6 of the Convention on the Elimination of All Forms of Discrimination Against Women which obligates State parties to 'take all measures, including legislation, to suppress all forms of traffic in women and exploitation of prostitution of women,' whether violations of governmental or private acts.
29. My emphasis.
30. Schengen Treaty on the Gradual Abolition of Border Checks, 19 June 1990, signed by France, Germany and the Benelux States. At present these countries and Greece, Spain, Finland, Portugal, Sweden and Austria are parties to the agreement. Ireland and Britain are not.
31. 20 May 1999.
32. Rome Statute of the International Court, 37 I.L.M. 999 (1998); 7(c) 'Enslavement' means the exercise of any or all of the powers attaching to the right of ownership over a person and includes the exercise of such power in the course of trafficking in persons, in particular women and children.
33. In Interview with Ruhama Women's Project, a group who work with street prostitutes in Dublin, Ireland, 15 September 2001.

References

American Anti-Slavery Group (2000) 'Trafficking of Women into Sexual Slavery', in *Slavery Today the Global Tragedy*, School of International and Public Affairs, Columbia University, New York: 24.
Askin, K. D. (1997) *War Crimes against Women: Prosecution in International War Crimes Tribunals*, Dordrecht: Martinus Nijhoff.
Bales, K. (2000) *Disposable People: New Slavery in the Global Economy*, Berkeley: University of California Press
Bassiouni, M. Cherif (2000) in J. Paust (ed.) *International Criminal Law, Cases and Materials*, Durham, NC: Carolina Academic Press
Chinkin, C. (1999) 'Women: The Forgotten Victims of Armed Conflict?', in McCormack and Durham (eds), *The Changing Face of Conflicts and the Efficiacy of International Humanitarian Law*, Dordrecht: Martinus Nijhoff.
Gutman, R. and Reiff, D. (eds.) (1999) *Crimes of War, What the Public Should Know*, New York: W. W. Norton
Hughes, D. and Roche, C. (eds.) (1999) *Making the Harm Visible: Global Sexual Exploitation of Women and Girls, Speaking Out and Providing Services*, Rhode Island: Coalition Against Trafficking in Women.
Lauren, P. (1998) *The Evolution of Human Rights: Visions Seen*, Philadelphia: University of Pennyslvania Press.
Leidholdt, D. (1999) 'Prostitution: A Form of Modern Slavery', in D. Hughes and C. Roche (eds.), *Making the Harm Visible: Global Sexual Exploitation of Women and Children*, Rhode Island: Coalition Against Trafficking in Women, p. 49.
McDougall, *see under* UN Reports and press releases.
Paust, J. (ed.) (2000) *International Criminal Law, Cases and Materials*, Durham, NC: Carolina Academic Press.

Roberts, A. and Guelff, R. (eds.) (2000) *Documents on the Laws of War*, Oxford: Oxford University Press.

Robinson, M. (2001) *Tolerance and Diversity - A Vision for the 21st Century*. Available at: ww.un.org/WCAR/e-kit/vision.htm [Accessed 26 September 2005].

Rho-Ng, E. (2000) 'The Conscription of Asian Sex Slaves: Causes and Effects of U.S. Military Sex Colonialism in Thailand and the call to Expand U.S. Asylum Law', *Asian Law Journal*, 7: 103–30.

Steiner, H. and Alston, P. (eds.) (2000) *International Human Rights in Context: Law, Politics and Morals*, Oxford: Oxford University Press.

Tree, T. (2000) 'International Law: A Solution or a Hindrance towards Resolving the Asian Comfort Women Controversy?' *UCLA. Journal of International Law and Foreign Affairs*, 5: 461–98.

Turnball, P. (1999) 'The Fusion of Immigration and Crime in the European Union: Problems of Cooperation and the Fight against Trafficking in Women', in P. Williams (ed.), *Illegal Immigration and Commercial Sex: The New Slave Trade*, London: Frank Cass, p. 200.

Williams. P. (ed.) *Illegal Immigration and Commercial Sex: The New Slave Trade*, London: Frank Cass.

Cases

Kunarac, Vukovic and Kovac, *Judgement of Trial Chamber 11*, The Hague, 22 February 2001 JL/P.I.S./666-e at the International Criminal Tribunal for the Former Yugoslavia.

NGO reports

Caldwell, G., Galster, S. and Steinzor, N. (1997) 'Crime and Servitude: An Exposé of the Traffic in Women for Prostitution from the Newly Independent States', Washington: Global Survival Network.

Human Rights Watch (2000) 'Owed Justice: Thai Women Trafficked into Debt Bondage in Japan', New York. Available at: http://www.hrw.org/hrw/reports/2000/japan/5-int-stand.htm [Accessed 19 October 2000].

Raymond, J. (2001) 'Guide to the New UN Trafficking Protocol', North Amherst, MA: Coalition Against Trafficking.

Raymond, J., Hughes, D. and Gomez, C. J. (2001) 'Sex Trafficking of Women in the United States: International and Domestic Trends', North Amherst MA: Coalition Against Trafficking.

European Union

European Union, Justice and Home Affairs, Information Sheet to mark International Women's Day, 8 March 2001.

UN reports and press releases

E/CN.4.SUB.2/1998/13, 22 June 1998, Contemporary Forms of Slavery, 'Systematic Rape, Sexual Slavery and Slavery-like Practices during Armed Conflict', Final Report submitted by Ms Gay J. McDougall, Special Rapporteur.

United Nations Fact Sheet No. 14 (1991), Contemporary Forms of Slavery. Available at: http://www.ohchr.org/english/about/publications/docs/fs14.htm [Accessed 26 September 2005]

E/CN.4/2001/NGO/113, 6 February 2001, Commission on Human Rights: Fifty-seventh session. Item 12(a) of the provisional agenda, 'Integration of the Human Rights of Women and the Gender Perspective: Violence against Women'.

A.AC.254/16, 1 June 1999 Ad Hoc Committee on the Elaboration of a Convention against Transnational Organised Crime, Fourth Session, Vienna, 28 June–July 1999. Informal note by the UN High Commissioner for Human Rights.

7
Trafficking in Human Beings: A Comparative Account of Legal Provisions in Belgium, Italy, the Netherlands, Sweden and the United States

Helga Konrad

Introduction

If we use the unveiling of the United Nations (UN) Protocol against Trafficking in Persons (2003) as the starting point of the modern era of confronting human trafficking, trafficking has now received concerted international attention for several years. New anti-trafficking laws were enacted, the funding for anti-trafficking projects and programmes began to flow, and more governments, organisations and individuals dedicated increasing attention to this problem. Yet, despite all these activities, there is little evidence of a substantial reduction in human trafficking, although this is exactly what all our activities are meant to be about.

Some significant answers may be found if we test the assumptions on which we have been conducting our fight. Many destination countries in Europe generally put the emphasis on preventing irregular immigration and on combating asylum abuse. Concentration on border controls, deterrence and immediate repatriation of irregular migrants, including victims of trafficking, is often the beginning of a vicious circle. Studies confirm that up to 50 per cent of those immediately deported are re-introduced into the criminal cycle of human trafficking. Although such measures are obviously short-sighted, it is stubbornly held that they are effective means of self-protection, serving the interests of state security.

So the first lesson we have to learn is that human trafficking must not  be seen primarily or exclusively from the perspective of national security. Moreover, combating human trafficking must not be seen only as a fight against organised crime and illegal migration. It is first and foremost a violation of human rights. It follows that trafficking in human beings (THB) is both a security issue and a human rights concern; there is no either/or. The issues must be tackled together if we wish to be successful in the fight against human trafficking.

The fact that people smuggling is constantly confused with human trafficking and that the two terms are used interchangeably is another problem that stands in the way of effective action against human trafficking.

Some of the victims may well have accepted the services of smugglers to get to a foreign country or they may have crossed borders illegally, but the fact that they are deprived of their freedom and that they are put into slavery-like conditions creates a clear distinction. Trafficking in human beings is distinctly different from human smuggling or illegal migration and as such requires specialised measures for its investigation, prosecution and prevention.

Clarification is also called for with regard to migration. It is true that the movement of people, voluntary or forced, presents multiple aspects, implications and dilemmas for states. Unfortunately, the trend towards establishing a discursive link between irregular migration and international crime is rising.

As a rule, migrants in general and illegal migrants in particular are at the mercy of traffickers and their accomplices. The fact that trafficking has been generally set within the framework of combating organised crime and criminality has caused human rights protection to be subordinated to control and anti-crime measures and has had extremely negative impacts on how human trafficking is approached and on the protection of victims.

When talking of human trafficking what people usually have in mind are prostitutes, economic migrants, illegal aliens or illegal workers. In a nutshell: suspects of all sorts. But what we are actually concerned with are victims of a serious crime, people who have been lured, tricked, deceived or coerced into slavery-like situations, where they are exposed to brutal violence, locked up, intimidated and exploited in the sex industry, in domestic servitude, in sweatshops, and other forms of forced and bonded labour.

Instead of providing appropriate protection and assistance to the victims of trafficking – one of the main points of discussion is an extended stay for trafficked persons in destination countries – they are usually expelled as soon as possible and returned to their home countries. The prevailing practice in most destination countries is to make support for victims – even if they are allowed to stay temporarily – dependent on whether they are willing to cooperate with law enforcement authorities and the extent to which they are considered useful to the prosecution. As a result, victims are often instrumentalised in the interests of the prosecution. State interests take precedence over the right of victims to the protection of their physical and mental integrity. This attitude is also influenced by the assumption that the offer of a temporary stay would attract more migrants and be abused. The lesson we have to learn is that responses to the problem of human trafficking found in the domain of immigration control are almost always inadequate.

As mentioned above, the tendency to view human trafficking primarily or exclusively as a security issue has detrimental implications for the rights and needs of its victims. It tends to detract attention from a victim-centred approach and to concentrate exclusively on a law enforcement strategy. This is not appropriate, since the prosecution depends to a certain extent on the victim's cooperation in establishing a case.

In the interest of a victim-centred approach it would be more useful to employ the legal tools, such as wire tapping, tracking the financial assets of the criminal enterprise, addressing the crime from beginning to end, long-term undercover investigations and/or surveillance, etc., which are used by law enforcement agencies against organised crime but almost never in human trafficking cases.

A particular and problematic issue arises from the interference between various laws, more specifically between the laws on trafficking in human beings and the legislation on immigration. Since in most countries crossing borders illegally is a crime, victims of trafficking are prosecuted for being illegal aliens. This is a serious obstacle to a successful prosecution, because it impedes and prevents cooperation between the victim and the police or the prosecutor. States must ensure that victims of trafficking are not subject to criminal or administrative liability and sanctions for acts arising from the trafficking situation.

There is a role for everyone in a concerted approach to this problem, but the ultimate responsibility for responding appropriately and effectively lies with each individual government. Governments must accept their responsibility and accountability if progress in the fight against human trafficking is to be made.

Trafficking in persons is a very complex problem and cannot be captured in a single 'snapshot'. It is better characterised as a series of actions unfolding like a movie. That is to say, it does not happen in a given moment in time after which it is over, nor does it happen in one place. It is not perpetrated only in the country of destination where the victim is discovered. It is instead a chain, or series, of criminal offences and of human rights violations, starting in the country of origin and extending over time and across countries of transit into countries of destination. Even internal trafficking involves a series of crimes and human rights violations that extend over time. And the various links of this chain require different responses.

While it has almost become a cliché that human trafficking is a transnational crime, the problem is that virtually no one addresses it as such. There are hardly any investigations of human trafficking that link the criminal activity in the countries of origin with the criminals in the countries of destination. And there is hardly any institutionalised and concerted follow-up of victims once they have been returned to their countries of origin.

From all this it is evident that in search of an easy answer, repeated attempts have been made to reduce a highly complex and multidimensional problem to a simplistic, often one-dimensional issue. Such tunnel vision grossly underestimates the complexity of human trafficking and fails to lead to a desirable outcome. All those who work in this area in practice come to realise its breathtaking complexity.

Last but no least, we must find the means to make people internalise the reality of modern manifestations of slavery; we must make them 'see' the problem and understand it. A change in the working assumptions and an improvement in the effectiveness of all programmes and measures will largely depend on making policymakers, donors and others understand the 'why'. Unless they understand that, they will not be convinced of the 'how' or the 'what'. In the final analysis, this is what will ensure that we make the right choices and find the right path to effectively combat this crime.

Within the anti-trafficking community, discussion is widespread on various models for combating trafficking in human beings used in 'Western' countries. The countries selected for this overview – Belgium, Italy, the Netherlands, Sweden and the United States – all have their own approach to combating this modern form of slavery. These national approaches have not only led to intense discussion, but in some cases even to a polarisation of positions. From the very broad definition of trafficking in human beings in Belgium to a more narrow, sex industry-focused approach in the Netherlands and Sweden, and from very liberal procedures with regard to residence permits for victims in Italy to a much more restricted approach in the United States, these procedures all have their supporters and opponents in the international community.

What all these countries do have in common though is that they – as opposed to many countries in Asia, South America, Africa and south-eastern Europe – take their measures from a position of countries of destination, rarely of transit and virtually never of origin. This is reflected in their approaches, and the focus of their legal approach therefore is on measures supporting the prosecution of the perpetrators, the protection of victims and/or witnesses and on supporting the prevention of trafficking in the source countries.

The aim of this overview is to contribute to the debate from a neutral perspective, covering both the positive and the problematic aspects of the various approaches. In this way, discussion can be rationalised by taking it from the more emotional debate to a discourse based on the effects of specific policies in practice.

Legal strategies in the fight against trafficking in persons

Trafficking in persons implies the use of violent, coercive, deceptive or abusive means for the purpose of exploitation, including servitude, slavery and forced labour. It is a serious crime against the person and requires states to adopt specific legislation, policies and measures based on the respect of victims' dignity, status and rights. According to the EU Expert Group:

> Strategies to address trafficking seem to move between two poles. On the one hand repressive strategies, which aim at suppressing those phenomena that are considered to be particularly connected to trafficking in human beings, such as organised crime and (illegal) migration and – depending on ones view – prostitution as such. On the other hand strategies which aim at empowering the persons and communities who are or could be affected by self-organisation, encouraging participation in finding solutions, improving living and working conditions and widening the set of (economic) choices, strengthening rights and increasing possibilities to exercise control over their own lives. (Expert Group Report, 62)

Stakeholders employ a number of approaches to tackle trafficking in human beings (e.g. prostitution, migration, organised crime, human rights, etc.), but they are not always clear-cut in practice since they usually overlap. After all, many responses to this problem seek to combine diverse elements in view of the fact that THB is a multidimensional issue. However, most states would have one overarching approach, which in the case of Belgium, the US, Italy and the Netherlands seems to be migration, while Sweden focuses mainly on the prostitution approach by centring on demand.

In Sweden, the law on Prohibiting Trafficking in Human Beings for Sexual Purpose has been in force since July 2002, yet in 2004 an amendment was made which extended criminalisation to all forms of trafficking in human beings into the national legislation in accordance with the UN Protocol against Trafficking in Persons. In addition, the penal code covering the criminalisation of clients under the Act Prohibiting the Purchase of Sexual Services (January 1999) is used to prosecute cases of trafficking, yet criticism has been made of the fact that there are few arrests and convictions derived from this law due to lack of evidence. Since this Act has come into force, there has been a dramatic drop in the number of women involved in street prostitution. However, statistics on prostitution are highly uncertain, and thus represent only an indication. Moreover, there are no statistics on indoor prostitution – as indicated by the report from the Swedish National Rapporteur, there are no reliable methods to carry out this exercise and it is a very resource-intensive job with uncertain results for the police (National Criminal Investigation Department, 2003/2004). On the governmental side there seems to be a perception in Sweden that trafficking in human beings has decreased compared to neighbouring countries since the Act Prohibiting the Purchase of Sexual Services came into effect, thus leading to a reduction in demand. If, on the one hand, the new law is said to represent a change in paradigm as the number of women involved in the sex trade has decreased or they have at least become less visible, on the other, not everyone shares these conclusions, since identification of victims of trafficking in Sweden seems to be a weak point. One might just as well believe that exploitation has gone deeper underground, thus making the work of the authorities harder. Criminals may have adopted new methods of organisation and exploitation. Overall, the expectation in Sweden is that this approach will establish a social standard whereby prostitution equals exploitation and violence against women. However, for the time being it is difficult to say with any certainty that focusing almost exclusively on demand will effectively curb human trafficking.

Among Western countries the Belgian law on trafficking in human beings has been the first to include in its formulation the broadest definition of trafficking in persons in reference to the UN Protocol. The law on the Suppression of Trafficking of Human Beings and Child Pornography (Law of 13 April 1995, hereinafter the April 1995 Law against Trafficking) amended the Criminal Code and the Immigration Law regarding access to the country, stay, residence and removal of foreigners (Law of 15 December 1980, hereinafter the Immigration Law), as such Article 77*bis* of the Immigration Law describes trafficking in human beings as:

> the situation in which a person, in any way whatsoever, directly or through an intermediary contributes to the entrance, transit or residence of a foreigner on Belgian territory in case he directly or indirectly uses tricks, violence, threats or any other form of coercion with regard to that foreigner or in case he abuses the victim's vulnerable position in which he/she finds him/herself due to an unlawful or insecure administrative situation, due to the fact that the victim is a minor, pregnant, sick or physically or mentally disabled.

While covering most elements of the Palermo Protocol definition on trafficking in human beings,[1] the Article does not consider exploitation a necessary element of its definition of the crime. Therefore, in practice Article 77*bis* is also used to prosecute smuggling in persons, cases involving employment of illegal workers, and letting rooms to foreigners at an exorbitant rent, together with cases involving exploitation that constitutes 'trafficking' in accordance with the definition of the Palermo Protocol. The reason is that penalties under the generic smuggling provision (Article 77) are relatively light. Both trafficking and smuggling are therefore prosecuted under Article 77*bis*, and the two crimes are *de facto* merged under Belgian law. The 'abuse of a vulnerable and precarious position' is interpreted very widely and, as a consequence, the foreigner's illegal residence status is sufficient proof of abuse of a vulnerable position.

In addition to Article 77 a Ministerial Directive, known as the COL12/9920, was issued in 1999 to combat trafficking in human beings more effectively, and its definition is more in line with the UN Protocol definition, covering forms of forced labour in addition to prostitution. The directive highlights the importance of a multidisciplinary approach to counter trafficking including victims' obligation to cooperate and co-ordinate with the local and federal police.

In the Netherlands and Sweden anti-trafficking legislation was initially formulated on the basis of trafficking for sexual exploitation, yet amendments have been made in both countries, leading to a broader definition in line with the UN Protocol. In the US, trafficking in human beings is defined in broader terms, and includes persons under debt bondage and involuntary servitude for labour purposes. In fact, if one compares all the countries cited in this Article, the US legislation offers the broadest and most comprehensive definition when dealing with trafficking for labour purposes.

According to US legislation under section 112 of the TVPA, new criminal offences were introduced, amending the US Code Chapter on Peonage and Slavery, in which trafficking is defined as: 'whoever knowingly recruits, harbours, transports, provides, or obtains, by any means, any person for labour or services, for peonage (holding another against their will to pay off a debt), slavery, involuntary servitude (holding another in service through force or threats of force) or forced labour' (defined below). This definition is in line with the UN Protocol, but requires fewer elements to establish proof and thus covers more cases. Peonage, slavery, involuntary servitude or forced labour can be more easily proved than deception, coercion or abuse of a position of vulnerability. Moreover, the law against forced labour (section 1589) covers:

A person who knowingly provides or obtains the labour or services of a person:
(1) By threats of serious harm to, or physical restraint against, that person or another person;
(2) By means of any scheme, plan, or pattern intended to cause the person to believe that, if the person did not perform such labour or services, that person or another person would suffer serious harm or physical restraint; or
(3) By means of the abuse or threatened abuse of law or the legal process.

This is an important provision because it plugs a gap in criminal law. Previously, psychological coercion was insufficient to prove the crime of involuntary servitude. However, under the current provision, which includes the use of psychological coercion, one can now cover cases in which trafficked persons have been given the following messages by their exploiters: 1) they would earn their own money, once they had cleared their debt; 2) they would be arrested and put in prison if they left; or 3) their families would reject them if they were to return.

In addition, section 1592 of the US legislation covering unlawful conduct with respect to documents in furtherance of trafficking, peonage, slavery, involuntary servitude or forced labour is very comprehensive compared to legislation in the Netherlands, Belgium, Italy and Sweden. Under this section:

> whoever knowingly destroys, conceals, removes, confiscates, or possesses any actual or purported passport or other immigration document, or any other actual or purported government identification document, of another person in furtherance of any of the crimes related to peonage and slavery or in order to prevent or restrict the liberty to move or travel of a victim of a severe form of trafficking, in order to maintain their labour or services is subject to a fine or imprisonment of up to five years, or both.

Trafficked persons are explicitly excluded from prosecution for this offence.

Assistance and protection

Once identified, trafficked persons should be granted with a period of reflection and a package of support and assistance services, which aim at social inclusion. All services should be provided voluntarily, confidentially and in a non-discriminatory and non-stigmatising manner. The provision of legal residence status is among the basic preconditions and intrinsic provisions to ensure the protection and assistance of trafficked persons as victims of a serious crime. In addition, access to assistance, protection and social inclusion programmes should be provided to trafficked persons in accordance with their individual needs, regardless of their willingness or ability to cooperate in investigation and prosecution. This is important to ensure that the granting of residency status will not be used to discredit the victim's testimony in the course of a trial against traffickers, if s/he decides to testify. Furthermore, the provision of a clear legal status and the prospect of social inclusion will help the victims to regain control of their life and encourage them to participate and contribute to successful prosecution. Besides, supporting victims to overcome their vulnerability and marginalisation enables them to become active members of society, which reduces social costs.

In Italy, Belgium, the Netherlands and the US victim care and assistance is under the competency of non-governmental organisations (NGOs), which offer a wide variety of services, ranging from legal assistance and counselling via mental health and other health care, vocational guidance, job training and referral to protection, shelter and follow-up. In Belgium, for instance, specific accreditation status is given to the three specialised centres run by accredited NGOs which are mentioned in the legislation. In Italy, many NGOs are dealing with a variety of issues from immediate assistance to vocational training for victims of trafficking, supported by the government, the European Social Fund and by other donors. The Italian approach has led to a number of innovative initiatives, such as job training and integration of victims of trafficking into the labour market, thus showing very positive results in terms of social inclusion. In Belgium victims holding a temporary permit are officially entitled to work, yet in practice it is very difficult to secure employment given their limited skills as well as the fact that employers view those holding a temporary permit as unstable. In the Netherlands, despite holding a temporary residence permit, which can be extended until the end of the judicial procedure, trafficked persons are not allowed to work, thus leading to a situation of dependency on the social system, as well as hindering their ability to achieve social-economic integration into the community while residing in the country. It is important to highlight that one of the key aspects in the victims' rehabilitation process is the restoration of a normal life, which includes being an active member of society, while having the means to become fully empowered in order to make their own decisions.

Sweden, conversely, due to its decentralised system of welfare, has no institutionalised cooperation with specialised NGOs as service providers for supporting victims during their stay in the country. Experience from Belgium, the Netherlands and Italy shows that specialised anti-trafficking services and well-trained personnel are key to a more sustainable approach and have a positive impact on the lives of trafficked persons.

Recovery period/period of reflection

As victims of a serious crime, trafficked persons need time to recover from their trauma and to be fully informed about their legal rights in order to be able to make informed choices and actively participate in proceedings, recall what has happened and be able to present their account in a systematic way. Thus their re-traumatisation can be avoided and they will be able to give a full and consistent testimony, which is often crucial for a successful prosecution. Therefore, immediately after identification as a victim of trafficking, the person should be provided with a reflection and/or recovery period, to build their self-confidence and trust in the state authorities' support offered before voluntarily identifying themselves as victims of trafficking. This will enable them to make an informed decision about their future, such as whether to assist in or pursue criminal proceedings, to claim compensation, to enter a social protection programme or to opt to return to their home country.

The Netherlands has been the first country to adopt and implement this policy. It is an automatic right for presumed victims of trafficking for sexual exploitation. The reflection period is granted for three months and enables those who have allegedly been trafficked to recover and to decide whether they wish to report their trafficker to the police. The regulation is laid down in the Circular for Immigrants, Regulation B9 (2000) (formerly B17 [1988]), which aims to facilitate both the investigation and prosecution of trafficking cases and to offer support and protection to trafficked persons.

In the Netherlands, Belgium and the US such a reflection delay is clearly specified in legislation. In Italy where such provision is not envisaged in law, victims have no defined status but are tolerated and may remain in the country under the care of NGOs. In Belgium, a period of reflection is provided under the procedure in which identified/ presumed victims of trafficking are issued with an 'order to leave the territory' within 45 days, provided they leave the 'exploitative environment/network' and are assisted by one of the three specialised centres. During this period the victim can decide whether she or he will lodge a complaint against the traffickers, and if the judicial system considers them useful for the prosecution, an application for a three-month stay can be filed. This period can be extended until the end of the judicial investigation. It is important to highlight that the Belgian, American, Dutch and Italian systems all call on the authorities to advise victims of trafficking of their options and resources available to them, including assistance from NGOs.

Temporary or permanent residence permit

Temporary residence permits for trafficked persons should be renewable and allow the holder to work or study. In practice, residence permits are offered to victims of trafficking on successful completion of a social assistance programme and/or integration into the labour market, on cooperation with the judiciary, on refugee status and on humanitarian grounds.

In Italy, under the Law on Immigration Article 18 (LD n. 286/1998) the police may issue a special residence permit to a foreign person who is a victim of coercion or serious exploitation, and whose safety is endangered as result of his/her attempt to escape pressure from the exploiter(s) or of statements made in pre-trial investigations. The permit can be issued based on a double procedure: the judicial and the social one, i.e. as victim-witnesses in legal proceedings, and as victims, regardless of their witness status. In both cases, the granting of a residence permit is dependent on participation in a social integration programme. Applications can be made by police, public and social services, as well as accredited NGOs. However, in the practical implementation of the law there appears to be a tendency to implement mostly the judicial procedure and link the provision of support and protection to the cooperation of the victim with investigative and prosecutorial authorities.

Among the innovative and positive aspects of the Article 18 system is the fact that trafficked persons are granted a residence permit for six months and have access to education, vocational training and employment. This permit can be renewed and converted into a regular labour permit. NGOs and local authorities closely cooperate and accompany the trafficked persons through the process of social inclusion. They provide a wide range of services, from safe and suitable accommodation, to health care, social and psychological counselling, legal assistance, and assistance in the residence permit procedures, educational and vocational training activities, job counselling and especially support to enter the labour market.

The Italian Article 18 system is based on close multidisciplinary cooperation between NGOs, police and the judiciary, as well as on cooperation with local authorities and the national Inter-ministerial Committee for the Implementation of Article 18. Identification, cooperation, provision of legal status and appropriate referral to victim support services are the core elements of an intervention system to protect victims of trafficking and successfully prosecute the perpetrators. With regard to the protection of victims, it is evident from the Italian experience that a less restrictive approach to victim protection leads to better results in convincing victims to testify. Some 3,000 temporary residence and work permits were issued to trafficking victims in 2002, granting access to legal and medical assistance, employment, education and witness protection via an established network of government-recognised NGOs active in the field of combating trafficking in persons.

In Belgium, the three specialised centres responsible for assisting trafficked persons help trafficked persons/victims of trafficking to apply for documents related to the residence procedure. This procedure applies to victims of trafficking in the broadest sense: trafficking for the purpose of sexual and economical exploitation as well as clandestine immigration.

Under a Royal Decree on financing the reception of victims of trafficking, the residence document entitles the holder to social benefits which are either disbursed by the specialised reception centre or by the Public Social Welfare Commission. Trafficked persons can request permanent residence at the end of the criminal proceeding. The Immigration Office – based on information from the Prosecutor's Office – will decide on the significance of their information for the criminal procedure against the trafficker and will also consider the degree to which the trafficked person has adjusted to Belgian society. One of the advantages of the Belgian system in comparison to the Italian is the fact that decisions are made by one institution (i.e. the Aliens Office), thus ensuring a more homogeneous implementation/or application of the decision on a case-by-case basis, as opposed to the decentralised Italian system in which results can vary due to different interpretations in the application of the law.

In Italy, renewal of residence documents is determined by the degree of the person's integration into Italian society and on employment. Trafficked persons can also submit applications for asylum on the grounds of fear of persecution and of the absence of provisions of state protection from such persecution. The Italian law does not, however, provide for the protection of family members of trafficking victims nor for family reunification, which is one of the main advantages of the American system. Moreover, the Italian experience has shown that many women who were accepted into social protection programmes without being pressured to testify against their traffickers/exploiters decided to do so after they had gained trust in official institutions. This has been acknowledged by police and public prosecutors, and has led to a considerable rise in arrests and sentencing of traffickers.

Despite the fact that Article 18 covers victims of all the dimensions of trafficking, in practice the programme has mainly been applied to victims of sexual exploitation, unlike the Belgian and American system in which victims of other forms of exploitation have benefited from the system of protection and assistance. In the Netherlands trafficked persons are entitled to a temporary residence permit for the duration of the criminal investigation and the trial, yet there is a difference between law and practice. According to the wording of the national Regulation B9 (2000), the moment the trafficked person presses charges, the report has to be considered as an application for a temporary residence permit. The immigration authorities have to decide within 24 hours whether or not to grant the permit (as is also the case in neighbouring Belgium). The granting of a temporary residence permit does not depend on the prosecutor's decision to start a criminal investigation, although the permit can be withdrawn if the prosecutor decides not to introduce criminal proceedings. In practice, however, immigration authorities or the police often make the granting of the temporary residence permit depend on the decision of the prosecutor to initiate proceedings against the trafficker. This is problematic for various reasons because it contradicts the very essence and intention of Regulation B9 (2000), which is to reduce obstacles to reporting traffickers and to make the victim feel safer to testify. It is essential that the individual can trust that if s/he presses charges against the trafficker, s/he will not face immediate deportation. The permit also needs to be issued as soon as possible, because it affects access to services such as housing and medical care. One of the disadvantages of the Dutch system in comparison to those in Italy, Belgium and the US is that trafficked persons are asked to leave the territory after completion of the judicial process, unless they have applied for permanent residence on humanitarian grounds. Claims on humanitarian grounds are usually dependent on the risk of reprisals, or the risk of prosecution in the country of origin. According to NGOs permits to remain permanently are very rarely granted to trafficked persons and only in exceptional circumstances.

In contrast, the American T visa, which is for a temporary stay, is renewable for up to three years, gives the holder the right to work and can be transformed into a lawful permanent residence permit for humanitarian reasons, which can provide victims of trafficking with a long-term perspective. However, in order to obtain any kind of legal status, the trafficking victim has to prove that s/he will suffer 'extreme hardship involving unusual and severe harm' if s/he is removed from the US. This 'extreme hardship' criterion was included to quell the fears of a multitude of fraudulent claims, yet how the courts will view this is unclear. A narrow interpretation of 'extreme hardship' may be detrimental to trafficking victims and may increase their danger. If a victim comes forward and is willing to serve as a witness, believing that s/he will be granted legal immigration status, but does not meet this higher standard, s/he will be removed and will face a greater risk of retribution in his/her home country. Application of the extreme hardship clause is under close scrutiny, as members of the US Congress have pointed out that the clause implies a 'higher standard' than previous interpretations of 'extreme hardship clauses' used, for example, to overturn removal.

Trafficked persons holding T visas can apply for permanent residence if they have been continuously present in the country for three years, yet critics of the T visa assert that this form of permit falls short of the aim of the US anti-trafficking policy to protect trafficking victims. The more stringent extreme hardship criterion appears unattainable for *bona fide* trafficking victims. The judicial interpretations of what has been defined as extreme hardship give some guidance on what extreme hardship means. Yet the guidance does not appear to give trafficking victims much hope of attaining the criterion required. The traditional criteria used to determine extreme hardship upon removal – 'length of time spent in the United States, special assistance to the United States, family ties and economic situation' – might not meet the high standards of extreme hardship needed to apply for the T visa. Although these factors are not exclusive, and the ordeal and suffering at the hands of captors will be taken into account, it is difficult to see how much weight will be given to past persecution and how that persecution would result in extreme hardship. Fear of retribution on return will play a significant role, but not all trafficking victims will be aware that they will be exposed to such retribution.

As in Italy, Belgium and the Netherlands, the American system of temporary residence permits can be revoked at any time if, for example, the authorities withdraw endorsement of the application or notify the immigration authorities that the person has 'unreasonably refused to cooperate'. This is a serious concern in terms of violating trafficked persons' human rights by making them vulnerable to further harm and danger as a result of being forced to cooperate with law enforcement. What may be considered a 'reasonable request' by investigators may still be unreasonable for traumatised or fearful victims, especially those who have families at risk.

The quota for T visas is 5,000 a year. Both the low number of cases presently under investigation as well as the high standards set to obtain the T visa will prevent this quota from being fully met. Compared with the number of persons trafficked to the US – there is the relatively low State Department estimate of 14,500–17,000 victims per year; other sources put the number closer to 50,000 – the T visa does not seem to be an effective means to protect victims of trafficking.

Conclusion

If countries, individually and collectively, want to be effective in reducing human trafficking, tackling it must not be seen primarily or exclusively from the perspective of national security, the main interest of which is to prevent illegal immigration. Although this has been laid down in international standards or is the expressed political will of many countries, this insight is hardly reflected in practical measures and approaches.

We have to recognise that human trafficking cannot be managed by measures of exclusion and control only. The emphasis on border controls, deterrence and immediate deportation or repatriation of victims of trafficking is often the beginning of a vicious circle.

We must be aware that state policies, which primarily tend towards measures of self-protection as opposed to more comprehensive approaches to the issue, are counter-productive and therefore part of the problem.

Close analysis shows that in practice there is the danger that state interests – which are primarily to control migration and to stress criminal prosecution – run counter to the needs and rights of the victims of trafficking. Practical experience demonstrates that immigration responses to the complex problem of human trafficking are almost always inadequate. It is from the fact that these people are considered to be illegal immigrants and often illegal workers that criminal organisations draw their profits. They take advantage of the demand for cheap, unprotected labour and the promotion of sex tourism in many countries.

Since trafficking victims are currently the primary source of witnesses for the prosecution, a victim-centred approach to law enforcement is not only consistent but logical, if law enforcement objectives are to be achieved. It is, therefore, indispensable to raise awareness of the fact that trafficking in human beings is both a law enforcement issue and a human rights concern, and that it is not a question of either/or. Both issues must be tackled together if we wish to be successful in our struggle against human trafficking.

We must overcome the hangover of the outdated view that the rights and needs of trafficking victims are inimical to effective law enforcement. We must realise that it is impractical and ultimately unacceptable to disaggregate the notion of law enforcement from assisting and protecting victims of this crime.

Thorough training holds a large part of the answer to the continuing need for spreading better understanding. What is called for is intensive training of law enforcement officers, both front-line police and special investigators, and of prosecutors and judges. Team teaching with NGO representatives has proved highly effective and adds a new quality to education and training.

Another factor designed to diminish the conceptual confusion over definitions is the process of criminal law reform in which individual countries must engage vigorously. When countries wrestle with the practical distinctions required to distinguish legally between smuggling, illegal immigration, prostitution and various other offences or crimes and human trafficking, they find it necessary to refine and clarify these distinctions. This impacts not only on criminal law provisions but also on measures for providing assistance and victim/witness protection. The differences between human trafficking, smuggling and illegal immigration again reveal themselves when countries determine which benefits they will provide to human trafficking victims that they will not provide to prostitutes, smuggled persons or illegal immigrants and why.

The assistance and protection of victims of trafficking deserve special attention in the fight against human trafficking. It is a central point which is still largely neglected out of fear that it will be misused. To assist and protect victims – as is the duty of states and governments under human rights norms – is not only called for from the human rights perspective but would also be a major contribution to curbing this crime. Once the victims and their closest relatives are safe and secure, they will be more inclined to support the prosecution of traffickers and to help dismantle their networks.

Although in recent years things have begun to change for the better, and despite increased attention at the political level, victims of trafficking are still frequently seen as perpetrators, and are criminalised. Instead of being taken to appropriate shelters, they are still often put into custody in the receiving countries and/or fined for prostitution and/or immediately returned to their home countries. What is currently offered to protect and assist victims of trafficking is very often human rights-insensitive and not what victims really need.

For victims to be able to free themselves from relationships of violence and life contexts in which they are permanently threatened by violence, they need comprehensive social and economic support, but also legal assistance. The legalisation of the status of a trafficked person is a crucial element in any effective victim and witness protection strategy. A secure and safe legal status of the victims is the prerequisite for support programmes to reach them.

A central issue in this context is the right of (temporary or permanent) residence for victims in the destination countries. A temporary residence permit would also present an instrument for enhancing the prosecution of traffickers and an instrument against organised crime, as it offers trafficked persons time to decide on making a complaint to the police, on cooperating with the investigating authorities and eventually on testifying in proceedings. Ideally, legal residence status should be granted irrespective of the victims' ability or willingness to testify in criminal proceedings. Legal residence status should also imply access for victims to the labour market as well as the right to state welfare benefits and to compensation as victims of crime. Furthermore, the status of victims of trafficking in criminal proceedings deserves particular attention. They must have the right to refuse to testify, and if they agree to testify, they should be able to do so in a non-confrontational environment. In any case, the process of testifying against the trafficker must not re-victimise a victim, but should be an empowering, positive experience.

Effective victim-witness protection does not end at the conclusion of a trial, of course. Research has indicated that in countries of origin, victims and their families are more or less totally unprotected against threats or violence. Therefore, another right should be the right of family reunification. This is often the only way to ensure the security of the closest relatives of trafficking victims.

States must also play a crucial role in changing the perception of victims of human trafficking. Governments must recognise them as victims in the way they treat them. The status and protection of trafficked persons has to be established as being consistent with the status of victims of a serious crime and not with that of criminals. States must ensure that victims of trafficking are not subject to criminal or administrative liability and sanctions for acts arising from the trafficking situation. Governments must, therefore, refrain from immediately expelling (potential) victims of trafficking due to their unlawful entry into the country and to their irregular residence and/or labour status.

A truly comprehensive and multi-pronged approach is called for, if we wish to be successful in combating this scourge – bringing together those who work in poverty reduction, education and human rights protection as well as those who address issues of corruption, organised crime, immigration and legal reform.

Just as we must understand that no country, ministry, organisation or agency can single-handedly put a stop to this appalling violation of human rights, we must understand that no single approach will put an end to it. Trafficking in persons, therefore, cannot be understood solely as a problem of illegal migration, or solely as a labour market issue, or solely as a demand-driven problem, or solely as a problem of organised crime. The multi-dimensionality of the problem must be taken into account. If we wish to reduce human trafficking, there is an equal need for short- and long-term measures. On the one hand, the counter-measures have to be fast-acting. On the other, it is necessary to raise and address the issue of the structural roots of human trafficking – namely, the global inequalities in the allocation of jobs, resources and wealth.

We have no alternative but to engage with the root causes, no matter how complex, difficult and forbidding they may be. Anti-trafficking initiatives must offer real prospects of escaping from the cycle of poverty, abuse and exploitation.

Note

1. The full title of the Protocol is 'United Nations Protocol to Prevent, Suppress, and Punish Trafficking in Persons and the United Nations Protocol against the Smuggling of Migrants by Land, Sea and Air'. The Protocol defines trafficking as 'the recruitment, transportation, transfer, harbouring or receipt of persons, by means of the threat or use of force or other forms of coercion, of abduction, of fraud, of deception, of the abuse of power or of a position of vulnerability or of the giving or receiving of payments or benefits to achieve the consent of a person having control over another person, for the purpose of exploitation'.
   'Exploitation shall include, at a minimum, the exploitation of the prostitution of others or other forms of sexual exploitation, forced labour or services, slavery or practices similar to slavery, servitude or the removal of organs.'

References

Anti-Slavery International (2002) *Human Traffic, Human Rights: Redefining Victim Protection.*
Centre for Equal Opportunities and Opposition to Racism (2002) *Plaidoyer pour une approche intégrée. Analyse de la législation et de la jurisprudence: Lutte contre la trait des êtres humains. Rapport.*
Centre for Research in Ethnic Relations (2003) *Overview Reports on Finland, Ireland and Sweden*, University of Warwick.
Change, Novib, Humanitas (2003) *Report on Victim Reintegration in the European Union.*
Council of Europe (September 2003) *Cooperation against Trafficking in Human Beings. Organized Crime – Best Practice Survey no. 8*, PC-S-CO (2003) 4 E (provisional), Strasbourg.
Dormaels, A., Moens, B. and Praet, N. (2004) 'The Belgian Counter-Trafficking Strategy', in C. van den Anker (ed.), *The Political Economy of New Slavery*, Basingstoke: Palgrave Macmillan, pp. 75–90.
European Commission, Directorate General Justice, Freedom and Security Report of the Experts Group on Trafficking in Human Beings, Brussels (2005).
National Criminal Investigation Department, (2003/2004), 'Trafficking in Human Beings for Sexual Purposes', Situational Report no. 6 for 2003 (2004), and no. 5 for 2002 (2003), National Criminal Investigation Department, National Criminal Intelligence Service, Illegal Immigration Unit.
Nationaal Rapporteur Mensenhandel (July 2004) *Mensenhandel. Derde rapportage van de Nationaal Rapporteur.* [Trafficking in Human Beings. Third report of the Dutch National Rapporteur on Trafficking in Human Beings], The Hague.
Official Journal of the Italian Republic, (11 August 2003) *General series no. 195. Law no. 228 Measures against Trafficking in Persons.*

On the Road, Payoke and De Rode Draad (2002) *Research Based on Case Studies of Victims of Trafficking in Human Beings in 3 EU Member States, i.e. Belgium, Italy and the Netherlands*.

OSCE XIth Economic Forum (May 2003) *Trafficking in Human Beings, Drugs, Small Arms & Light Weapons: National and International Economic Impact. Country Contribution – The Netherlands*.

US Department of Justice (May 2004) *Report to Congress from Attorney General John Ashcroft on U.S. Government Efforts to Combat Trafficking in Persons in Fiscal Year 2003*. Washington DC.

Wetmore, J. M. (2003) 'The New T Visa: Is the High Extreme Hardship Standard too High for *bona fide* Trafficking Victims?' *New England Journal of International & Comparative Law*, 9(1): 158–78.

Wipler, E. (2004) 'Comparison of the Legal Situation for Combating Trafficking in Human Beings in Belgium, Italy, the Netherlands, Sweden and the United States'. Unpublished, August.

8

The Dangers of False Distinctions between Pornography, Prostitution and Trafficking

Julie Bindel

As a feminist who has been involved in the campaign to end violence against women for more than 20 years, I have noticed patterns of understanding change among those in the field. I have been involved in these struggles as an activist, academic researcher and, more recently, an investigative journalist. I have worked on issues such as domestic violence and homicide, child sexual abuse, rape and the international sex industry in many of its manifestations. What has become clear, after many years of feminists and professionals compartmentalising these issues, is that they are *all* interconnected. A woman in prostitution is more likely than not to have experienced child sexual abuse. If she is pimped, she is suffering domestic violence. She will, of course, be raped. If her pimp moves her from one part of the country to another to be prostituted she is the victim of trafficking according to the Palermo Protocol, and it is highly likely that she will, at some stage, be used in pornography, either for men's personal use or to be sold on the open market. Similarly, the men who do the raping, pimping, child abusing and pornography production are often the same. Those that perpetrate these crimes often dabble in a cross-section – progressing from, for example, exposing their genitals to women in public to serial rape and murder.

What led me to working almost exclusively on prostitution in my research and activism, and, to an extent my journalism, was the life and death of a woman called Emma Humphreys. Emma was prostituted at the age of 12, and met Trevor Armitage, a punter, when she was 16 who became her pimp and batterer. Ten months later, after being gang-raped and videoed by three men, and threatened with a 'gang bang' by Armitage, she killed him. This frightened, traumatised 17-year-old was convicted of murder, and sent to prison for life. Seven years into her sentence she contacted Justice for Women, a feminist law reform campaign, and asked for their help. Three years later, after a huge public campaign, Emma walked free from the Court of Appeal having overturned her conviction on the grounds of cumulative provocation. This was a significant change in the law for battered women who kill their abusers. She lived for three more years. At the age of 30, she took an accidental overdose of the prescribed medication that numbed the pain she had become addicted to in prison. During those three years, she talked about the prostitution, and said it was the worst thing that had ever happened to her. Emma had experienced just about every form of sexual violence during her short life, but in the end it was the prostitution that killed her.

Shortly after coming out of prison, one of the sexual predators who had been writing to her since her photograph appeared in a newspaper with the caption 'hooker' invited her to his home and took pornographic photos of her. He did so because he knew he could. Emma was soiled goods in his mind; she had been a prostitute and therefore always would be. This predator knew that pornography would probably not be new to a woman who had been involved in prostitution. He was right.

Shortly before she died, Emma was invited to open a conference in London entitled 'Prostitution: Violence against Women and Children'. There was no question mark at the end. The title caused uproar, and the pro-prostitution lobby sent pimps and prostituted women along to disrupt it. I was hissed at and threatened. Emma had insisted on speaking at the conference, even though she was severely anorexic, doped up to the eyeballs and mentally frail. She asked the audience, 'Why are some people saying prostitution is OK? Do they want to be a spittoon for men's semen like I was?'

Andrea Dworkin gave an interesting example of how she thought women were responsible to campaign against sexual violence. She said that often the best work is done by those with the least resources. For example, if you get to 12 and have not been raped or prostituted, you have more resources than the woman who was. Andrea used the analogy of having a leash around our necks. All women have them, because we are all oppressed, but some leashes are shorter than others. Emma's leash nearly chocked her, and yet she campaigned to change the law of domestic homicide, spoke out against prostitution and took the time to tell me and others about her life, in the hope that it would make a difference. The reality is that most work to combat sexual violence is done by women on the shortest leashes. Those with more slack have a responsibility to do more than they currently are.

In this chapter, I will focus specifically on the false distinctions between pornography, prostitution and trafficking, because this is where we are lagging in recognising the connections. The reason for this is mainly ideological, with those who support the sex industry further strengthening the arguments that there are good and bad victims, that some forms of commercial sexual exploitation are harmless, even liberating, and that the only phenomenon worth challenging is trafficking across international borders.

The UK government is currently carrying out a consultation on policy and legislation for the first time in 50 years. While this initiative is welcomed, it is disappointing that they have chosen to focus disproportionately on children and trafficked women. I argue this for several reasons.

First, even if they are being disingenuous, most people would not publicly disagree that prostituting children, or forcing women from poor countries to work under lock and key, with a gun to their head, is atrocious. Clear legislation and policy direct the police and courts in how to deal with these crimes. Application of the law, and prevention and protection in both areas are lacking. But on paper, we understand that prostituting children and trafficking women across borders are serious criminal offences, even if we do little about them.

The situation regarding adult women in local sex industries is not at all clear though. Most people, even among feminists, do not accept that prostitution itself is violence and abuse. The debate is so heated, and positions so polarised, it is almost impossible to make progress. As a result, many individuals, and some organisations, decided to go down the route they believed was strategic – that is, to introduce the public to how terrible commercial sexual exploitation is by giving them the worst stories. Children being passed around and sold like objects; women being dragged from poor villages in Albania, bundled into lorries, sold like cattle and locked in a brothel. Legislation is already in place to deal with these offences. In 2004, trafficking of human beings became a specific offence in England and Wales, carrying a maximum sentence of 14 years. If a man has sex with someone under the age of 16, in the UK he is guilty of child sexual abuse.

What we now have is reluctance from governments and citizens to engage with the notion that adult, local women in prostitution are also grossly abused. Their sympathy cannot extend beyond children and 'shackled' women.

In the UK, unless you talk about a trafficked woman as being forced, she will be called a migrant sex worker, yet the Palermo Protocol makes it clear that whether or not the victim of trafficking has consented, her human rights have still been violated. Adult women in local sex industries are always seen to have consented, because we believe that accepting money for services amounts to consent. But also because we have this distinction between forced and chosen prostitution, force has to look like real force, not lack of consent. One of the reasons there is such a low conviction rate for rape is because often to survive the victim does not struggle, or suffer additional injuries. Our courts cannot distinguish between lack of consent and force.

With the emphasis on forced prostitution – namely children who *cannot* consent, and women who are described by governments, journalists and many NGOs as 'slaves' – it is easy to create the dichotomy of 'good' and 'bad' victims. Local adult women are seen as bad, whereas children and sex slaves merit some sympathy.

Although there is organised child prostitution in the UK and an increase in the numbers of trafficked women being brought in, neither group is as large as the local, adult women who are prostituted in droves. For example, in Glasgow, which has a population of 600,000, there are an estimated 1,400 women on the streets. None has been identified as trafficked, and only a handful are under-age. In London alone, there are at least 600 brothels, over 100 lap-dance clubs, and between six and ten sites where street prostitution occurs. The sex industry, which now accommodates hundreds of trafficked women, and, to a lesser extent, children, has been allowed to flourish because no one has ever cared about the local, adult women who traditionally populated these venues. Attention is now being paid to the scale of the industry, because the government is aware that illegal immigrants are involved.

The lack of clarity on the part of the general public and policymakers on what to do about local women in prostitution, and the men who use them, means we have allowed new forms of sexual exploitation – trafficking – to flourish. Once trafficked, prostituted women are being sidelined for support, sympathy and understanding, on the false premise that trafficked women and children are more deserving victims even though, in reality, trafficked women and prostituted children get very little support.

One stark example of the way that trafficking is seen as different from and much worse than prostitution *per se* is this. A senior member of the UK government recently suggested that men who buy sex from trafficked women be charged with rape. It sounds good in theory, and at least she is focusing on demand. But what does this mean? First of all, the human rights lawyers would tear it apart. Second, how would you prove the woman is trafficked and that the men knew this to be the case? Third, why not prosecute *all* men who buy, or attempt to buy, sex from women in prostitution? Many men, when they go to a brothel, don't care what nationality the woman is from whom he buys sex. Some do, but others just want to buy any woman who takes their fancy. Why is it acceptable to buy sex from Emma Humphreys, a pimped, abused and exploited woman who experienced all sex with punters as rape, but not with her Serbian or Thai sister in the brothel next door? What are we saying to men? Trafficked women are abused, but not women in local prostitution? And why charge them with rape? Less than 6 per cent of reported rapes in the UK end in a conviction. Do we really want to put these women through a rape trial just to see the defendant walk free, before we have educated the public and the judiciary about what consent really is and is not? I have recommended to the minister that the government adopts the Swedish model and simply criminalises the buying and attempted buying of sexual services *per se*. While trafficked women suffer horrendous abuse and need protection and advocacy, so do all women in the sex industry. Separating them will only add to the attitude that trafficking is a sexy subject and worthy of attention, but regular prostitution is not.

Those in the media have to face responsibility for much of the distinction between trafficking and other forms of prostitution, and of exaggeration in order to run a 'sexier' story. If we see a headline in a national newspaper entitled 'Sex Slaves Sold to Evil Albanians', we will consider the woman is a victim. If, however, the trafficker gets to court and we hear evidence that she agreed to come to the UK, or Chicago, or wherever, from Albania to work in the sex industry, we will start to doubt her. What has been created by those who distinguish between prostitution and trafficking is an almost total necessity for the woman to prove she was forced, the very thing we argue against when it comes to local women. We require evidence of a gun to her head, being bundled into the back of a transit van and taken clandestinely across borders; of her being locked in a brothel and tied to a bed. Research shows that, although there are significant numbers of trafficked women who are kidnapped and forced, they are in the minority. The majority are deceived, or know they will be prostituted to make money, but are so desperate they go ahead anyway. What they can't know, of course, is how truly horrific it is until it is too late to return.

Ideological debates about prostitution – that it is choice and work on the one hand, or violence and exploitation on the other – are now serving to polarise even further discussions about trafficking and local prostitution. The pro-prostitution lobby calls prostitution 'sex work', child sexual exploitation 'juvenile sex work' and trafficking 'migrant sex work'. The only time the lobby concedes that prostitution is abuse is in those cases of what they now call 'forced trafficking'. In the attempt, by the pro-prostitution lobby and much of the international community serving in post-conflict zones, to identify only forced trafficking as abuse, it can look like local, non-trafficked women are having a picnic.

Unfortunately, the British government refused to include pornography in either the legislation, introduced in 2004, on sex offences, or in the consultation on prostitution. I think they worried that there would be too much strong opposition from the libertarians. They were right, of course, but wrong not to take them on. They also believed, in their wisdom, that pornography is an issue of morality and indecency, and according to religious conservatives they are right. But how can they possibly refute the argument that pornography and prostitution are not only linked, but are one and the same thing? How can pornography be produced without prostituted women and men?

Ray Wyre, a profiler who has worked extensively with men who have committed the entire range of atrocities against women and children including rape, child sexual abuse, murder and torture, has written of the harm in pornography and the links between sex crime and its consumption. When he was 16 years old he worked on a ship. It was his job, at night, to present a slide show of pornography to his male colleagues. He remembers being offered prostituted children, as young as eight, by local men. Ray made the connections early on in life, but often wonders what stopped him from saying 'yes' to the eight year old or enjoying the pornography. It is a question we should be asking more and more. Why *don't* some men do it?

But the British government, along with many others, do not want to enter the murky waters of pornography. Or if they do, it is framed in the language of obscenity and morality. This is in direct contradiction of a feminist analysis of pornography. Regardless of how much funding for anti-porn and prostitution work the US and UK governments make available, if campaigners against trafficking and prostitution are required to get into bed with right-wing moralist Christians to do the work, the main agenda, that of women's human rights and gender equality, will be lost.

Because of feminist campaigns against pornography, we can no longer pretend that it just consists of 'dirty pictures' or mere representation. The police know this – the paedophile unit at New Scotland Yard stopped referring to child porn as such some time ago. They refer to it, correctly, as 'records of child sexual abuse' and of a 'crime scene'. We should be advocating extending this to pornography of adult women, and men also.

Research conducted into lap-dancing in the UK clearly highlights the links between prostitution, pornography and trafficking. Visiting the clubs with a male colleague posing as a curious couple the researcher was able to spend a lot of time talking to the dancers and customers. Two of the women said they did 'glamour modelling' and said there were other dancers who did this. One explained that the club owners encouraged the women to model for 'adult' publications as it is good for business. 'If my picture is in the *Sunday Sport* and it says I work at a certain club, the men who like the look of me might decide to come and see me in the flesh. Therefore, the club owns you, because your pictures will be around long after you worked there.'

One woman talked about being 'pressurised' into glamour modelling by management. She also spoke of 'some of the girls' being upset at discovering that their photographs had been used to advertise the club without their knowledge or consent. There was also evidence of some customers having used their mobile phone cameras to take pictures of the women whilst naked. Men were seen taking photos of the women while they were performing. One customer was joking he was going to put a naked picture of one of the women on the Internet. There was nothing to stop him.

There was also evidence that women are being trafficked directly into lap-dance clubs to 'break them in' before putting them in brothels. Taxi drivers would tell the researcher they regularly drove 'Russian' women who could barely speak a word of English to the clubs. Several women who were foreign, some of whom will have been trafficked, said the club owners move the women round, often from country to country, because regular customers want 'new women'.

In terms of resistance to recognising these connections we need look no further than countries that have legalised prostitution. The Netherlands, Germany and some states in Australia should hang their heads in shame for introducing the legal abuse and rape of so many women. Everyone knows how easy it is to get hard-core pornography in all its forms in those countries, and research has shown conclusively that legalisation is a green light to any trafficker. Police and policymakers in those countries promised that legalisation would help eradicate trafficking. The opposite has happened, and why wouldn't it? They are the same thing. Talking about legalising prostitution so that trafficking can be better dealt with is like saying we should legalise wife beating so more attention can be paid to domestic homicide, or that acquaintance rape should be decriminalised so we can catch the hooded psychopaths. The myth that to be beaten or raped by your partner is less harmful and traumatic than if a stranger does it, or if you are a foreign national, is risible. Yes, it is horrific to be prostituted in an unfamiliar country, where you don't speak the language, are frightened of the police, are isolated and are being grossly abused by your trafficker and customers. But aside from the language barrier, that is the lot of all women in prostitution, trafficked or not.

Research conducted into prostitution in Australia, Ireland, the Netherlands and Sweden found that trafficking increases in countries that have legalised prostitution.

The connections between organised crime and the sex industry have not diminished. Reports from Australia and the Netherlands highlight that legalisation has, in some respects, strengthened links. In October 2003 Amsterdam City Council took the decision to close the street tolerance zone; Mayor Job Cohen noted that the situation was 'a devil's dilemma' because 'it appeared impossible to create a safe and controllable zone for women that was not open to abuse by organised crime' (Editorial, *Het Parool*, 2003).

Legalisation encourages the growth of the sex industry. There has been a significant increase in the number of brothels in Victoria, Australia, since legalisation. Indeed, the number of legitimate brothels grew from 40 in 1989 to 94 in 1999 (Raymond, 2002).

The difficulty of policing the industry, and the lack of support/resources given to local authorities to carry out licence checks and ensure that health and safety requirements are met, have been cited as a main reason for the apparent failure of introducing legalisation as a method to eradicate trafficking. As Janice Raymond (2003) points out:

In New South Wales, brothels were decriminalized in 1995. In 1999, the numbers of brothels in Sydney had increased to 400–500. The vast majority have no licence to operate. To end endemic police corruption, control of illegal prostitution was taken out of the hands of the police and placed in the hands of local councils and planning regulators. The council has neither the money nor the personnel to put investigators into brothels to flush out and prosecute illegal operators.

Because of the more stringent police-control the new regulations also resulted in the relocation of activities within the prostitution sector: criminal forms of prostitution moved to places where there are fewer or less stringent checks.

In other words, the criticism often levelled at those advocating removing prostitution from particular localities – that it will be displaced – seem to apply to legalisation too.

A report by the Platform Organisations Shelter for Prostitutes presented to Parliament in December 2003 concludes that three-quarters of women in prostitution in the Netherlands wish to attend exit programmes to enable them to leave. The report is a response to an evaluation on the lifting of the brothel ban in October 2000, which claims that in the main, there have been few problems since the new laws were enacted, but illegality and coercion still dominate the industry (Reformatorisch Dagblad, 2003).

Legalisation is a 'pull factor' for traffickers. Project Respect estimates that 'at least seven licensed brothels in Victoria have used trafficked women in the last year'. An Australian Institute of Criminology study estimated that Australian brothels earned $1 million a week from illegal prostitution. Mary Sullivan and Sheila Jeffreys point out that, 'Legalisation was intended to eliminate organised crime from the sex industry. In fact the reverse has happened. Legalisation has brought with it an explosion in the trafficking of women into prostitution by organised crime. Convicted criminals, fronted by supposedly more reputable people, remain in the business' (2000: 12). In Victoria estimates from the police and the legal brothel industry put the number of illegal brothels at four times higher than the legal ones (Murphy, 2002).

Child prostitution in the Netherlands has significantly increased during the last ten years. The ChildRight organisation in Amsterdam estimates that there are now more than 15,000 children (primarily girls) being prostituted, an increase of 11,000 since 1996; 5,000 of these children are thought to be from other countries, mainly Nigeria (Tiggloven, 2001).

One of the most significant limitations of legalisation in the two countries examined is that it excludes street prostitution. In this sense, these regimes further marginalise the most vulnerable and exploited women, who certainly do not benefit from this approach. It serves as further legitimisation of targeted 'crackdowns', which criminalise them, and for many, result in deportation. Furthermore, legalisation has not reduced street prostitution. There has been a significant *increase* in street prostitution in Victoria, especially in St Kilda, along with increased levels of rape and violence.

Legalisation opens more opportunity for entrepreneurial pimps. A drive-in brothel that features eight garages into which buyers drive to buy sex has become a huge success in Cologne. Profits have risen so fast that this style of brothel may be expanded to other cities. Germany has a significant and growing problem with women being trafficked into its towns, cities and even villages. What does the government do? Plenty compared to other European countries, including my own, to investigate the criminals involved and assist the women if detected. This is rather like building a bridge at night and blowing it up the next day. The reason why they have such a big problem is because the local sex industry is thriving.

Within the international community, there are those lobbying to redefine the terms 'choice' and 'abuse' within the sex industry. The same people are also movers and shakers in the drive to legalise prostitution, arguing that freeing up police time in dealing with 'harmless' local prostitution will mean better resources in fighting trafficking. That is not how it works. Traffickers import women to countries where there is a friendly, thriving sex industry, not to those where police are actively monitoring brothels and other sex establishments. But the Dutch, Germans and Americans give a lot of money to inter-governmental and non-governmental organisations in the Balkans and elsewhere, and they are the ones putting pressure on local government, police and citizens to support this approach. One feminist activist in Croatia said, just after the war, that she could not bear the idea of legalised prostitution because:

My beautiful country would become a destination for sex tourists. The beaches would get busy again, but we wouldn't be able to take our children to them, because they would be full of sexual predators.

What about women who are returned after being trafficked? What if the country they return to, dishonoured and stigmatised because they have been prostituted, has a thriving sex industry of its own? There are countless stories of women in the Balkans being returned and ending up working in local prostitution. Where there is monitoring of local sex industries, traffickers will consider it unsafe to bring women in. Unfortunately, the only example we have of the latter is Sweden, but it is known to be true. If returned trafficked women were properly supported, they would be less likely to end up in the brothel down the road, or re-trafficked out of the country.

The majority of funding for return and reintegration programmes goes to the International Organisation for Migration (IOM). They are very good at the return, but seemingly poor at the reintegration, because they refuse to enter the murky waters of prostitution. They will not engage with the stigma and shame felt by the women who have been prostituted.

The IOM maintains it has no policy on prostitution. Strange how it is only those who believe that prostitution is abuse who are seen to have a position. It is not the only organisation that refuses to acknowledge the abuse in non-trafficked prostitution. The field offices of IOM in Macedonia and Kosovo said much the same. Yet in the Balkans, local activists and professionals are keen to talk about prostitution, in order to help them understand the issues of stigma and shame the women feel on return, and to unpick the complexities of this form of trafficking as opposed to others.

Feminist analysis of pornography provokes similar reactions, with much of the Left considering it a bourgeois indulgence to get worked up about it, even when it involves children. Yet we are only too aware of the role pornography plays in other sex crimes. Take the case of Fred and Rose West in England. In 1995 police dug up their garden and cellar to find the remains of ten girls and young women. All had been sexually assaulted and killed by Fred or Rose or both. We will never know the true extent of Rose's complicity in the crimes because Fred West committed suicide while awaiting trial. What we do know is that the West house had become a haven for girls on the run from local care homes. Fred prostituted Rose and some of the young women who came to stay with them. He made pornography out of them, as well as using violent, sadistic hard-core pornography himself, making Rose and others re-enact scenes from it. He would send pornographic photos of Rose to contact magazines in order to advertise her services. When police first visited the house after a complaint about a missing girl, they described the house as being 'awash with porn'.

Take the case of the Belgian Marc Dutroux. Two girls, abducted by Dutroux and an accomplice, were found starved to death in his home, another two were rescued and two, known to be abducted by the men, were sold into a pornography and prostitution ring in the Czech Republic. One of his victims testified in court that, 'I was allowed to watch a bit of TV when I had given pleasure to the monsieur. Marc Dutroux made me watch pornographic films but they didn't interest me. I had all of that live.' There we have it, pornography, prostitution and trafficking. Sexual sadism in all its forms.

It is also evident that the fashion industry is promoting pimping, prostitution and pornography as the new chic. In the UK, in 2003, two 11-year-old girls were sent home from school for wearing thongs. Earlier that year, BHS brought out a range of underwear for girls under 10, which included thongs emblazoned with the slogan 'Little Miss Naughty'. This is just the tip of the iceberg – 'Porn Star' and 'Pimp It' are clothes labels targeted at teenage girls and boys. Around the same time, the American company Abercrombie and Fitch introduced thong underwear for 7–14-year-olds with the words 'Wink Wink' and 'Eye Candy printed on them. After protests, the company removed them.

This spin on fashion, following closely on the heels of mid-1990s 'heroin chic', is nothing but pseudo-porn. Sex and sexual violence are being used to sell everything from *Pot Noodles* to children's clothes. Pimp and hooker chic is in, demonstrated by the likes of the rap star P. Diddy, with his fur coats and lyrics peppered with references to 'ho's; and Britney Spears and Christina Aguilera, who seem to celebrate dressing like street prostitutes. Things are getting worse, but it is hardly a new phenomenon. In the late 1990s, George Michael filmed actual street prostitutes from Amsterdam for his video to accompany the cover version of 'Roxanne', the Police song about a streetwalker. They were portrayed applying make-up and walking around in nothing more than underwear, looking healthy, happy and glamorous – not quite the reality you would face walking through King's Cross late at night, where desperate women will do pretty much anything for a bag of crack.

We need to ask ourselves what effect the pressure on girls to dress like hookers, and the glorification of some of the worst scum of the earth – pimps – can have. Many fashion editors and models believe that they are responding to 'supply and demand'. What a sick excuse! Have we not heard this from peddlers of drugs and hard-core pornography? Since the seminar, things seem to have got worse, not better, which leaves us wondering if the government was simply paying lip service to criticisms of a largely unregulated industry.

Pressure on younger and younger girls to have sex has increased as a result of being influenced by the 'I'm a total slut' look currently peddled by many designers. The singer Charlotte Church was photographed recently wearing a T-shirt with the slogan 'Barbie is a Crack Whore'. Pornography blends into the fashion industry, which in turn hugely influences the behaviour of those who wish to fit in. Let's not pretend that this growing culture has not had an effect on sexual behaviour. Since 1992, the Office of National Statistics has recorded a significant rise in teenage pregnancy and abortion, including among those aged 14 and under. In 2004 it was revealed that the UK has one of the highest teenage pregnancy rates in the developed world. We have also seen a dramatic rise in STDs, including HIV, among young women in recent years.

The fashion industry may not care, but that should not stop activists from doing something. Many of these designers are extremely rich and powerful – often paraded by governments as ambassadors for their country. As well as holding them accountable for their product, let's insist they put money into solving the problems that so many of them have helped create, such as setting up clinics for young girls with eating disorders. It is up to feminists to make the industry, and governments that let them get away with it, think twice before we see nappies with 'Little Miss Naughty' emblazoned across them, and diets aimed at three year olds.

Children are also becoming used to pornography, including creating their own, with the help of mobile phone companies downloading porn onto handsets, and video games such as 'Grand Theft Auto: Vice City', which sold out of its 300,000 stock in its first two days in the UK. It involves tracking down and beating to death a street prostitute for additional points. And now a new craze has caught on among urban schoolchildren. 'Happy Slapping' is where the perpetrator, usually a boy, attacks and sexually assaults a girl or woman and films the attack on his mobile phone.

Children, of course, are more likely to be victims than perpetrators. Over half of the Internet child porn industry is based in the United States, with Russia coming second at a quarter, according to the UK children's charity National Children's Homes (NCH), which says such sites are directly to blame for the rise in child sex offences.

However, people from all over the world are accessing these sites. It used to be much harder to get hold of – you had to be in a child abuse ring. But now anyone with mild curiosity or no awareness at all can find child pornography on the Net.

Approximately 550 child pornography offenders were either cautioned or charged in Britain in 2001, compared with only 35 in 1988. Surveys of convicted child abusers revealed that up to 70 per cent were inspired to commit their crimes after viewing child porn on the Internet.

The demand for children to work in the sex industry, caused by the dramatic rise in the number of child sex abusers is being increasingly handled by organised crime. Crime gangs, especially in Russia and Eastern Europe, are systematically recruiting children to be filmed having sex, whereas six to seven years ago there was little commercial market for it.

In his address to the World Congress against the Commercial Sexual Exploitation of Children in Stockholm in 1996, the Swedish Prime

Minister Goran Persson said, 'The plague of child prostitution, pornography and the traffic in children has increased dramatically in the past few years. Millions of children around the world are being abused. We must put an end to it.' I suggest we stop it for adult women at the same time.

If we are to eradicate the false distinctions between pornography, prostitution and trafficking, we must resist any alliance with the Moral Right, who make clear distinctions between these issues, and also resist claiming one is 'worse' than the others. To focus disproportionately on trafficking for prostitution, we do the non-trafficked, but nevertheless abused, prostituted woman a grave disservice. To focus exclusively on prostituted children, we are effectively turning our back on them once they reach the age of 18. To neglect looking at the production of pornography as being a direct record of prostitution, we are prolonging the abuse the victims are suffering. If we make the mistake of talking about child prostitution and trafficking as 'worse' than other forms of sexual exploitation, it will not serve to educate sceptics about the abuse in the sex industry in general. It will merely give them their nice, innocent victims to weep over, while they turn their backs on those they consider to have colluded in their own oppression – the adult, non-trafficked prostituted woman who already has almost nowhere to go.

9
Triply Exploited: Female Victims of Trafficking Networks Strategies for Pursuing Protection and Legal Status in Countries of Destination

Anna Marie Gallagher

Teresa, a 25-year-old Colombian woman, lived with her child, parents and extended family in a small town near Cali, Colombia. Her family was poor and Teresa had no work. Many young women from the town were moving to Spain to work, and were sending money home to help support their families. Teresa wasn't sure what they were doing, but suspected that they were working as prostitutes. After seeing an ad in the local newspaper from an agency offering work in Spain to young women, Teresa decided to take a chance. She went to the 'travel agency', which offered to arrange travel to Spain and a job as a dancer in Barcelona. Although Teresa was nervous, she decided to take the offer.

After arriving in Spain, she began work as a dancer in a club in Barcelona. Conditions were horrible. She worked twelve hours a day, having sex with many different men daily. She lived in a house with other dancers – all immigrant women from different countries – and received little money. Most of her 'salary' was withheld to pay for her travel and housing expenses. Neither Teresa nor the other women were allowed to leave the home without the 'controller'. Once, one young woman did slip out to meet a friend. When she returned, the controller beat and raped her, leaving her scarred. During the time that she worked in the club, Teresa was not able to send any money home. Depressed and fearful for her life, she decided to flee. Others had escaped before her, including some young women from her home town. After getting away, she managed to contact a group which helped women who had been smuggled or trafficked to Spain. They told her that if she cooperated with the police, she might be able to stay legally in Spain, but they could offer no guarantees. Teresa decided against cooperating and chose instead to return home to be with her family. When she arrived home, she did speak with the local police and told them what had happened. They wrote up a report but told her that they could not investigate the matter because the 'travel agency' had influential and powerful backers.

Six months later, Teresa found out that a young woman who had worked in the same club and had returned to their home town had been murdered. Teresa and others believed that the traffickers had killed her because she had not paid for her passage. A short time later, another young woman was shot in her home; again the people smugglers were suspected. Afraid that she would be next, Teresa borrowed money from family and friends and returned to Spain.

Introduction

'Teresa' is a real person living in Spain. Some of the facts have been changed and, of course, her real name is not used. Teresa, like many other poor women forced to work in degrading conditions, is triply exploited: first, in her home country as a poor, single mother; second, in her destination country as an indentured, undocumented immigrant prostitute; and third, as a woman who may face persecution by her traffickers for her escape and return home. Throughout this chapter, I will refer to this fact pattern to support arguments for asylum and other forms of immigration relief in countries of destination for trafficking victims who want to remain and for those who cannot return home because of fear of persecution by their traffickers.

The purpose of this chapter is to discuss avenues to obtain legal status in destination countries for women who fear returning to their home country or who cannot return because of great economic need. The first section provides general background on trafficking, and includes a discussion of the relevant legal instruments. The second section discusses asylum protection for survivors of trafficking and includes an overview of cases from several countries in which such status has been considered and in some cases granted. The final section provides an overview of selected countries' special trafficking visas, with an analysis of their weaknesses and strengths and suggestions for improvement consistent with human rights concerns.

General background on trafficking and the relevant treaties

Although it is difficult to say with a high degree of certainty, it is estimated that 800,000–900,000 persons – the large majority of whom are women and children – are trafficked across international borders yearly for forced prostitution, labour and other forms of exploitation.[1] Trafficking in women and children is the modern-day form of slavery and violates long-established human rights treaties, standards and norms.[2] The current slave trade in women and children is thriving in both rich and poor countries and has become one of the most profitable of business endeavours, ranking third in profits after the arms and drug trafficking markets.[3] Women and children who are trafficked suffer a variety of human rights violations, including rape, torture, forced abortion, starvation, threats and harassment against themselves and family members by traffickers and others.[4]

The trafficking of women and children has long been of concern to the international community. Beginning in 1904, a series of treaties and agreements was approved requiring states to criminalise trafficking and sexual exploitation – considered to be forms of slavery – and to cooperate in prosecuting smugglers and traffickers and rescuing and protecting the victims.[5] In 1998, the UN General Assembly established the intergovernmental Ad Hoc Committee on the Elaboration of a Convention against Transnational Crime to develop an international regime to address transnational organised crime.[6] After meeting on twelve occasions, the committee concluded its work in 2000[7] and drafted the Convention against Transnational Crime and the Smuggling of Migrants and Trafficking Protocols.[8] The Trafficking in Firearms Protocol was drafted and adopted in June 2001.[9]

The UN Crime Commission, which housed and hosted the Ad Hoc Committee in its headquarters in Vienna, Austria, is not a human rights body.[10] The Convention against Transnational Crime and additional protocols are law enforcement rather than human rights instruments. From a protection perspective, it would have been preferable that the instruments and the body or agency drafting them were located within one of the United Nations' human rights bodies. Because of their crime-focused origins, the documents provide strong law enforcement tools but relatively weak language regarding human rights protections and victim assistance. For example, the law enforcement provisions in both the Convention against Transnational Crime and the Trafficking Protocol contain mandatory language, such as 'state parties shall', whereas provisions addressing assistance and protection contain language such as 'state parties may', encouraging rather than requiring minimum levels of guarantees of protection and assistance for victims of trafficking.[11]

The definition of trafficking – which has three elements – is defined in the Trafficking Protocol as follows:

1) an action, consisting of: recruitment, transportation, transfer, harboring or receipt of persons;
2) by means of: threat or use of force or other forms of coercion, abduction, fraud, deception, abuse of power or position of vulnerability, giving or receiving payments or benefits to achieve consent of a person having control over another;
3) for the purpose of: exploitation (including, at a minimum, the exploitation of the prostitution of others, or other forms of sexual exploitation, forced labor or services, slavery or practices similar to slavery, servitude, or the removal of organs.[12]

The reference to abuse of a position of vulnerability refers to any situation in which the person involved has no real and acceptable alternative but to submit to the abuse involved.[13]

Similar to the Convention against Transnational Crime and the Trafficking Protocol, the early documents focused primarily on law enforcement aspects of trafficking. Despite recognition that the violations suffered by trafficking victims violate a variety of human rights treaties and norms, rights-based arguments to support protection and assistance of trafficked women and children are only beginning to be addressed and considered seriously in devising protection strategies in destination countries.[14] During the drafting process of the Trafficking Protocol, protection and human rights issues were included as a secondary matter. During negotiations, NGOs argued that the Trafficking Protocol should include a right to remain in the destination country.[15] Their position was not supported by governments, which feared that such a right would result in increased illegal migration.[16] Governments have focused primarily on strengthening law enforcement initiatives and migration controls to combat trafficking and smuggling and, to a much lesser extent, on providing protection and assistance to the victims of traffickers. Recently, there has been more discussion on how better to protect the human rights of trafficking victims and develop advocacy efforts on their behalf. Unfortunately, governmental benefits and services provided to victims often depend on their willingness to cooperate in the investigation and prosecution of their traffickers. It is to be hoped that with the development of a human rights-based approach supporting protection of the victims – both in destination countries and upon repatriation to their home countries – and greater advocacy with and on behalf of the survivors, the issue of cooperation will become less and less important in determining ways to remedy the violations that they have suffered.

Asylum and subsidiary protection relief for trafficking victims

Definition of refugee

Persons fleeing persecution in their home country may be entitled to refugee protection under the 1951 United Nations Convention Relating to the Status of Refugees (the 'Refugee Convention')[17] and the 1967 United Nations Protocol Relating to the Status of Refugees (the 'Protocol').[18] The great majority of countries that have ratified the 1951 Convention and 1967 Protocol have also established national laws and norms governing adjudication of requests for refugee or asylum status.[19] In addition to providing protection from return or non-*refoulement*, the Refugee Convention provides for a series of rights which countries should provide to refugees, including education (Article 22), travel (Article 28), employment (Articles 17 and 18), housing (Article 21) and social security rights (Article 24).

Under the Refugee Convention, a refugee is a person who:

> owing to a well-founded fear of being persecuted for reasons of race, religion, nationality, membership in a particular social group or political opinion, is outside the country of his [or her] nationality and is unable, or owing to such fear, is unwilling to avail himself [or herself] of the protection of that country; or who not having a nationality and being outside the country of his [or her] former habitual residence ... is unable or, owing to such fear, is unwilling to return to it.[20]

Therefore, the elements which an applicant for refugee or asylum status must prove are:

- a well-founded fear of persecution;
- because of one of the five grounds: race, religion, nationality, membership in a particular social group or political opinion;
- that she is outside her country of origin; and
- that she is unable to or unwilling to avail herself of the protection of that country.

Based on the circumstances of her case, Teresa may qualify for asylum under the Refugee Convention. She can argue that she has a well-founded fear of persecution of the traffickers in Colombia who arranged for her passage, subsequently held her in slave-like conditions in their club in Barcelona and were responsible for shooting one escapee and killing another in her home town in Colombia. She faces persecution as a member of a particular social group – poor, young Colombian women in the sex industry. She is outside her country of origin, living in Spain and is unable to obtain protection from her own country.

Gender-based claims and trafficking

Historically, the definition of refugee and asylum protection has been interpreted primarily through the experiences of men fleeing persecution. Therefore, many gender-related claims have gone unrecognised. During the past decade, however, the analysis and consideration of gender in the context of refugee protection has advanced in the case law of many countries, in state practice and procedures towards female asylum seekers and in academic scholarship.[21] In light of the special and sensitive issues surrounding adjudication of gender-based claims, Australia, Canada, the Netherlands, Norway, Sweden, the United Kingdom and the United States have drafted guidelines for their adjudicators to use in preparing and deciding such applications.[22] Although gender is not specifically included in the definition under the Refugee Convention or the Protocol, it is widely accepted that it can be considered in adjudicating asylum claims. The UNHCR specifically recognises that gender should be considered in adjudicating asylum claims and the European Union has proposed to its member states that they recognise gender as a basis for asylum.[23]

What do we mean by gender-based claims? The term 'gender-related persecution' is used to address the variety of different asylum claims in which gender is a relevant factor in the determination of refugee status.

Gender-related claims may be brought by men or women.[24] However, due to the particular types of persecution and the particular vulnerability of women during times of conflict and otherwise, they are generally brought by women. Claims of persecution based on gender include acts of sexual violence, family or domestic violence, coerced family planning, female genital mutilation, forced marriage, dowry murder, punishment for failure to obey social norms, honour killing, discrimination against homosexuals and forced prostitution.

The UNHCR has been concerned with the issue of asylum protection for victims of trafficking in recent years.[25] Currently, UNHCR personnel are in the process of drafting guidelines addressing protection and assistance for trafficking victims to provide guidance to adjudicators and policymakers worldwide. These guidelines will be helpful on a number of levels. They will support the idea that victims of trafficking under certain circumstances need international protection as provided under the Refugee Convention. Women or girls who suffer human rights violations as a result of being trafficked do not generally perceive themselves as refugees given the traditional political character and interpretation of the term. Additionally, they often are not viewed as being in need of international protection because trafficking has been considered a law enforcement and migration issue rather than a protection matter. It is to be hoped that these guidelines will help identify and protect this deserving population.

The European Council in conclusions regarding the prevention and combating of trafficking has discussed asylum claims of trafficking victims. The Council recognises that, where an individual is entitled to seek asylum, the fact that the individual is a trafficking victim should not interfere with his or her rights to seek asylum or other available forms of residence.[26] The European Parliament issued a resolution stating that it takes the view that persecution on grounds of sex and, specifically, in trafficking in human beings should justify the grant of refugee status.[27] The European Council conclusions and the European Parliament resolution are especially relevant given many EU member states' reluctance to entertain non-traditional asylum applications such as gender-based claims involving non-state actors. Recognition of gender-based asylum claims is a relatively new development in Europe.[28] Officials responsible for asylum adjudications in many EU member states are reluctant to recognise such claims, arguing that the definition of refugee does not provide protection for such applicants. Additionally, as mentioned below, many adjudicators are reluctant to grant protection in cases involving non-state actors, such as violent spouses, family members or traffickers. Unfortunately, many consider that trafficking cases should be dealt with as a law enforcement rather than a protection issue.

Well-founded fear of persecution

In order to satisfy the first requirement of the definition under the Refugee Convention, Teresa will have to prove that her fear of persecution is well founded. The persecution feared can be either past persecution – something that directly happened to her – or a fear of future persecution.[29] What this means is that, although the frame of mind of the applicant determines her refugee status, this must also be supported by an objective situation. Therefore, the term 'well-founded fear' contains both a subjective and an objective element.[30] The subjective element may be satisfied by proving that the primary motive for her application for asylum is fear and that such fear is reasonable.[31] The objective element can be demonstrated by submitting country conditions information to prove that traffickers operate with impunity and that, therefore, she is unable to reside safely in her country.[32]

Women face particular persecution specific to their sex. The UNHCR, the United Nations and states parties to the Refugee Convention recognise certain forms of gender-specific violence as persecution.[33] The right to protection against rape and other forms of sexual violence is set out in basic instruments of international law, including the International Covenant on Civil and Political Rights and the Convention against Torture, which guarantee protection from torture or cruel, inhuman or degrading treatment or punishment.[34] Forms of gender-based violence constituting persecution include rape, sexual assault, female genital mutilation, honour killing, coercive family planning and domestic violence.[35]

Trafficking for forced prostitution or sexual exploitation can constitute persecution for asylum-related purposes. The UN High Commission for Refugees in its Gender Guidelines specifically includes forced prostitution and sexual exploitation as forms of persecution and states the following:

> Some trafficked women and minors may have valid claims to refugee status under the 1951 Convention. The forcible or deceptive recruitment of women or minors for the purposes of forced prostitution or sexual exploitation is a form of gender-related violence or abuse that can even lead to death. It can be considered a form of torture and cruel, inhuman or degrading treatment. It can also impose serious restrictions on a woman's freedom of movement, caused by abduction,

incarceration, and/or confiscation of passports or other identity documents. In addition, trafficked women and minors may face serious repercussions after their escape and/or upon return, such as reprisals or retaliation from trafficking rings or individuals, real possibilities of being re-trafficked, severe community or family ostracism, or severe discrimination. In individual cases, being trafficked for the purposes of forced prostitution or sexual exploitation could therefore be the basis for a refugee claim where the State has been unable or unwilling to provide protection against such harm or threats of harm.[36]

Teresa can establish a well-founded fear of persecution based on what she saw and experienced working as a prostitute and the subsequent events in Colombia. Specifically, she has a well-founded fear that if she is forced to return to Colombia, the traffickers who arranged her passage, who subsequently held her in slave-like conditions in their facility in Spain, and who shot one escapee and killed another in Colombia, will target her for escaping and failing to pay the amount owed for passage and housing.

Arguments can be developed and evidence produced – through police reports and affidavits – of these events, which prove that the traffickers – whom the local government cannot control – would find and harm her, perhaps even kill her, in Colombia. Her well-founded fear of persecution made her flee her country to seek protection in Spain. In order to satisfy this first prong of the refugee definition, Teresa must prove that what the others suffered – the shooting and murder in Colombia – constitute persecution which Teresa could also suffer if forced to return. Clearly, murder, life-threatening violence, physical abuse and torture – recognised as fundamental violations of human rights – constitute persecution.[37]

Membership in a particular social group

Teresa must also establish that her well-founded fear of persecution – fear of physical violence or death if returned to Colombia – is based on one of the five recognised grounds: race, religion, political opinion, nationality or membership in a particular social group.[38] In this case, we would argue that Teresa is a member of a particular social group targeted for persecution. The UNHCR has defined a particular social group as comprising persons of similar background, habits or social status.[39] In its Guidelines on International Protection, it provides additional guidance on identifying a particular social group for asylum purposes.[40] The Guidelines note that two approaches on what constitutes a particular social group have dominated decision-making in common law jurisdictions. The 'protected characteristics' approach or 'immutability approach' examines whether a group is united by an immutable characteristic or one that is so fundamental to human dignity that a person should not be expected to forsake it. Immutable characteristics may be innate, such as sex or ethnicity, or unalterable, such as the historical fact of a past association, occupation or status.[41] The 'social perception approach' examines whether or not a group shares a common characteristic that makes them a cognizable group or sets them apart from society at large. Women, families and homosexuals have been recognised under this interpretation as particular social groups.[42] Because of concerns regarding potential protection gaps, the UNHCR suggests that the two approaches be reconciled and offers the following definition which incorporates both:

> A particular social group is a group of persons who share a common characteristic other than their risk of being persecuted, or who are perceived as a group by society. The characteristic will often be one which is innate, unchangeable, or which is otherwise fundamental to identity, conscience or the exercise of one's human rights.[43]

Different national courts consider a variety of elements in determining whether an applicant is a member of a particular social group. German courts have looked at the following in determining whether a particular social group exists: 1) the degree of homogeneity among members in the group; 2) the degree of inner structure of the group; and 3) whether the general populace views the collection of people as a group and treats the group as undesirable.[44] According to the Supreme Court of Canada, a particular social group can be defined by an innate or unchangeable characteristic; the group can include members who voluntarily associate for reasons so fundamental to their human dignity that they should not be forced to forsake the association; or, the group members can be associated by former voluntary status, unalterable due to its historical permanence.[45] The High Court of Australia has held that members of a particular social group must have a common, uniting characteristic which sets them apart from society.[46] US courts define a particular social group as comprising persons all of whom share a common immutable characteristic which may be innate, such as sex, race or kinship ties,[47] or as a collection of people closely associated with each other, who are actuated by some common impulse or interest.[48]

Young women from Colombia in the sex industry can constitute a particular social group. They share a similar background and social status – poor, young women who may ultimately suffer sexual exploitation and face persecution if they fail to comply with the traffickers' demands. Teresa, as a member of a particular social group – poor, young Colombian women who escape their traffickers – will face persecution if forced to return to Colombia. The facts in her case prove that at least one other escapee was shot and another murdered by the smugglers, because they escaped and failed to pay their passage. Courts in several countries have considered, and in some cases granted, asylum protection to women victims of trafficking, finding that they suffered persecution because of membership in a particular social group.

Under Canadian gender asylum guidelines and jurisprudence, victims of trafficking may be eligible for asylum protection. Canada's Immigration and Refugee Board (IRB) has considered several claims for asylum filed by victims of trafficking based on membership in a particular social group. In one case, a young Thai woman claimed persecution based on membership in a particular social group: single women suffering from abuse at the hands of their former spouses and single women forced into prostitution. The IRB denied her claim, finding that single women who are forced into prostitution do not constitute a particular social group. In reaching their decision, the IRB found that the applicant was a victim of crime for which there were laws designed to protect such women. Second, her fear of repercussions from traffickers who targeted her because of an outstanding debt had no nexus to the refugee definition. Finally, criminal acts committed by her husband belonged in the realm of criminal law rather than domestic violence, as the couple were then separated.[49]

In the same month, the IRB issued a decision involving a case of another Thai woman seeking protection based on fear of traffickers. In that case, the applicant had been sold to a mafia group that intended to send her to Canada to work as a prostitute. When she discovered that they were to send her to Malaysia instead, she escaped. She was again captured and sold to another mafia group that did send her to Canada, where she paid off her debt by prostituting herself. She claimed asylum because she was afraid that she would be hurt by the first group, from whom she had escaped, if forced to return to Thailand. She claimed membership in a particular social group: single women without protection involved in the sex industry, with an outstanding debt bond. The IRB rejected her claim, finding that her claim of fear was based on what she had done – namely, prostitute herself – rather than what she was, a well-educated woman with varied work experience who could have obtained different types of employment. The IRB found no link between her fear of persecution and a Refugee Convention ground.[50]

However, in another case, the IRB did grant protection to a Thai victim of traffickers. In that case, the claimant, a sex-trade worker in debt bondage, was found to face a serious possibility of harm if she returned to Thailand, either in the form of continued sex trade debt bondage or serious physical consequences for failure to pay off her debt. The IRB found that she feared persecution because of one of the five grounds, membership in a particular social group – women. Alternatively, it found that former sex trade workers comprise a particular social group because they are a group associated by a former voluntary status, unalterable due to its historical permanence.[51]

In Spain, the National Court remanded the case of a Nigerian woman, who was initially denied admission to the refugee status determination procedure by the Office of Asylum and Refugees, for further consideration on the merits of the claim.[52] The woman had been abandoned as a child by her mother, and subsequently sexually abused by her aunt and her aunt's friend. She was later trafficked to Spain, where she was forced into prostitution, imprisoned and threatened by her traffickers. She finally escaped and sought asylum. The lower adjudicating authority, the Office of Asylum and Refugees, ruled the case inadmissible, finding that it did not satisfy the elements of the refugee definition. However, Spain's National Court reversed the decision, finding that the woman could be a member of a particular social group – Nigerian women forcibly trafficked into prostitution – and remanded the matter for adjudication on the merits of the asylum claim.[53]

There have been a number of asylum claims filed by victims of trafficking in Australia arguing persecution as a result of membership in a particular social group. In February 1999, the Refugee Review Tribunal denied asylum to a Ukrainian woman who had been deceived into paying $10,000 for passage and documents for a promised job in Australia as a waitress and traditional dancer.[54] When she arrived at the airport, she was met by men who took her documentation and placed her in an apartment where she was forced to prostitute herself. She was threatened with death if she did not cooperate. Some months later she escaped and reported the traffickers to the police. After that, she moved addresses frequently because she began to be followed. Her family and friends in the Ukraine reported that they had been threatened. The Tribunal, in denying the asylum claim, did find that she had suffered persecution, but found that her fear was not based on a Convention ground, specifically on membership in a particular social group. Rather it was based on the fact that she had reported the matter to the police.

In a second case, decided in September 2000, the Refugee Review Tribunal considered an application for asylum filed by a victim of trafficking from Bosnia and Herzegovina.[55] In this case, the young woman, of Serb ethnicity, in searching for employment, met a group of men who tried to force her to agree to work abroad as a prostitute. Despite her clear refusal, the men continued to harass and verbally abuse her. Upon returning home one day, she was attacked and brutally raped by some of them. When she reported it to the police, they told her she had got what she deserved. She later discovered that one of her attackers was a police officer. In denying her claim for asylum, the Tribunal found her credible, but held that 'women in Bosnia and Herzegovina' or 'young, single women in Bosnia and Herzegovina' do not constitute a particular social group. In reaching this decision, the Tribunal stated that there was no information to support any form of linking or unity of characteristics, attributes, activities, beliefs, interests or goals among women in Bosnia and Herzegovina. It further held there was no evidence to support a finding of discrimination against young women in that society.

There have been several cases of asylum filed in the United Kingdom by women who were trafficked into indentured servitude or forced prostitution. Although in some of the cases, the women were 'willing victims', that is, they paid or intended to pay the smuggler for their illegal passage and work in the UK, they were not prepared for the slave-like conditions in which they lived and were forced to work. Many were kept from escaping these conditions by threats against them or their family – similar to what Teresa suffered.

In 2001, the government granted Exceptional Leave to Remain (ELR)[56] status to two women who were victims of trafficking. The first case involved a Serbian woman abducted in Kosovo where she was forced into prostitution. The second involved a Romanian woman who fled because she feared being trafficked. In both cases, the asylum officers denied asylum relief but did grant ELR status.[57] In several other cases, the UK Immigration Tribunal has found that trafficked women are eligible for asylum based on membership in a particular social group. The Immigration Tribunal granted the asylum appeal of an Albanian woman who had been sold for marriage to a man who intended to traffic her into forced prostitution in Italy. In granting asylum, the Tribunal recognised that the Albanian government could not protect her.[58] In another case, the Immigration Tribunal granted asylum to a Ukrainian woman finding she faced persecution based on her membership in a particular social group: Ukrainian women forced into prostitution against their will.[59] Finally, in a third case, the Immigration Appeal Tribunal recognised a claim for asylum from an ethnic Albanian Catholic woman from Kosovo who based her fear of persecution on membership in a particular social group: women from Kosovo forced into prostitution against their will.[60] The Appeal Tribunal found that the applicant was a member of a particular social group, but denied asylum because it found that the state could in fact provide protection to her upon her return.

There have been several cases for asylum filed by victims of trafficking in the United States based on arguments of fear of persecution because of membership in a particular social group. A US Immigration Judge granted asylum to a 21-year-old Russian woman, who had been abducted by a local crime figure, gang raped by him and his friends and then forced to have sexual relations with him and other men in his home on a nightly basis. The local police refused to intercede and the woman was held as a sexual prisoner. At one point, she tried to escape but was caught and beaten. Her captor gave her to another crime figure in Moscow, who was planning to traffic her to Israel or Turkey for forced prostitution. She was finally able to escape and fled to the United States. The immigration court granted her asylum based on her well-founded fear of persecution as a member of a particular social group, including young women forced into prostitution and threatened with trafficking.[61]

In another case, a US Immigration Judge granted asylum to an Albanian woman who suffered similar abuses. In this case, after the woman's husband had emigrated to the United States, the local chief of police began harassing her. He propositioned her on the street and threatened to send her to Italy for prostitution. She was afraid and rarely left her home. One night, the police chief and three of his friends abducted her from her home and gang raped her. After being held for several hours, she returned home. Soon after, she began to receive threatening calls. She hired a lawyer, but the police chief went to the lawyer's home and threatened and tortured her. The lawyer fled the country and warned her client to do likewise. Shortly thereafter, the woman fled to the United States and applied for asylum. The immigration court, in granting asylum, found that she had a well-founded fear of persecution on account of her membership in the particular social group of women in Albania threatened with being trafficked to Italy to engage in forced prostitution.[62]

In a third case, a US Immigration Judge granted asylum to a young Thai woman who had been given away by her parents to a man named 'Pa'. The young woman was an indentured domestic servant during the ten years that she lived with 'Pa' who during this period of time regularly beat and raped her. He then sent her to Bangkok, where she worked in a beauty salon and was raped and sexually abused by the male customers, including members of the police. Finally, a woman, part of a Thai smuggling operation, approached her and arranged for her travel to the United States. Upon arrival, smugglers were to meet the young woman and force her to work to pay off her passage. The woman accepted the offer. Luckily, at the time the young woman was leaving Thailand, the woman in charge of her travel and subsequent 'work' in the United States was arrested and jailed. After her arrival in the United States, the young Thai woman discovered that the smugglers were looking for her in Bangkok, demanding payment of her passage. In fear for her life, she applied for asylum. In granting asylum, the Immigration Judge found that the applicant was a member of a social group, forced into indentured servitude and trafficked to the United States.[63]

Non-state actor and government failure to protect

The Refugee Convention does not state who the persecutor must be in order for a person to qualify for protection from that persecutor. For many years, the traditional persecutor in the great majority of asylum and refugee cases has been governmental agents, or their representatives, of the country from which the asylum seeker is fleeing. However, as the worldwide geopolitical situation has changed over the years, today many persecutors are non-governmental agents, guerrilla factions, mafia and other groups and individuals from whom governments either are unwilling or unable to protect their citizenry. In gender-based claims, these non-state actors include abusive partners, family members and trafficking organizations.

Most refugee-receiving countries agree that, in addition to governmental agents, persecutors may also include non-state entities or persons that the government is unwilling or unable to control. The non-state actor doctrine is well established in jurisprudence from many state parties to the Refugee Convention, including the United States,[64] Canada,[65] Australia[66] and New Zealand.[67] Many European countries also recognise that asylum seekers who suffer persecution by non-state actors may qualify for refugee protection. However, some countries require that states must be complicit in the persecution, either by encouraging or tolerating it.[68] Others hold the position that if a government is willing but unable to protect, such inability cannot support a claim for asylum.[69] The European Union has proposed that its member states recognise that non-state actors may be persecutors for refugee status determination purposes.[70] The UNHCR, in noting that claims asserting refugee status based on membership of a particular social group often involve claimants who face risk of harm by non-state actors, emphasizes that there is no requirement that the persecutor be a state actor.[71]

Under refugee laws and norms, a state fails in its obligation to its people when it does not provide meaningful protection from harm by non-state actors, even in the absence of active culpability of the state or its agents.[72] Persecution may be found in 'behaviour tolerated by the government in such a way as to leave the victims virtually unprotected by the agencies of the State'.[73] The language of the 1951 Convention refugee definition itself emphasises state responsibility for actions not directly attributable to them by including protection for persons who flee because the state is not only *unwilling* but also *unable* to provide protection.[74] The UNHCR's Handbook notes that private acts of violence 'can be considered persecution if they are knowingly tolerated by the authorities, or the authorities refuse, or prove unable, to offer effective protection'.[75] Principles and basic instruments of human rights law also recognise state responsibility for human rights violations committed by non-state actors.[76] Virtually all human rights conventions and treaties contain language requiring states to control the activities of non-state actors so as to protect against human rights violations.[77]

In Teresa's case, we would argue that the Colombian government was unwilling to provide protection to her from the traffickers. Although the police were willing to take information from Teresa regarding the circumstances of her trafficking and the violations she suffered, they were not willing to pursue any further investigation. Proof of a government's unwillingness or inability to protect can include information relating to failure to prosecute non-state actors who violate human rights, the lack of laws designed to protect persons such as Teresa from the wrath of traffickers, and the ongoing impunity enjoyed by them as evidenced by their successful and ongoing operations.

Asylum should be granted

Spain should grant asylum to Teresa based on the arguments made above. Teresa has a well-founded fear of persecution of the smugglers in Colombia should she be forced to return. Although she travelled to Spain in the knowledge that she would be working as a prostitute, she did not anticipate that she would be working in slave-like conditions from which she would have to escape. Although she hoped to return to Colombia and live in peace, she discovered that others in her situation who had escaped the clubs were targeted. One woman was shot and wounded and the traffickers murdered another. The police have not investigated the cases and no one has been prosecuted. Her persecutors – the traffickers – would target her because of her membership in a particular social group, a young woman who escaped the smugglers. Fearing that she would be harmed, even killed, Teresa fled Colombia and seeks asylum protection from the Spanish government.

The fact that Teresa initially moved to Spain 'willingly' and entered the country illegally should not affect her application for asylum. Under Article 31 of the 1951 Convention, states are prohibited from imposing penalties on refugees for their illegal entry or presence.[78]

Special trafficking visas

Several destination countries have established special trafficking visas, which often provide only temporary legal status, based on the cooperation of the victim in the investigation and prosecution of traffickers.[79] Many of these countries also provide a range of social, medical and housing services in conjunction with NGOs working with trafficked women during the investigation and prosecution of traffickers. Austria provides temporary residence to victims of trafficking, with the possibility of obtaining long-term residence.[80] In Denmark, 15-day permits are granted to permit them to prepare for repatriation. However, many victims are also deported because they have no legal status.[81] In France, temporary visas are granted for cooperation with the police in investigation of trafficking networks. If a trafficker is convicted as a result of such cooperation, a permanent visa is granted.[82] In the Netherlands, deportation of trafficking victims may be suspended for three months during which time the victims can decide whether to report the offence.[83] If the victim does report it, she is given a residence permit for the duration of the investigation and any prosecution of the accused trafficker(s).[84]

In Belgium, once a woman is identified as a possible victim of trafficking, she is given 45 days in which to decide whether she is willing to cooperate with the police in the investigation and prosecution of the traffickers. She is given temporary residence during the period of her cooperation and consequent judicial procedures against the traffickers. Depending on the outcome of the proceedings, she may be eligible to seek permanent resident status.[85]

Practices towards victims of trafficking vary in Germany. Because it is a federal republic, divided into sixteen federal states, laws and procedures differ according to region. Ministries within each federal state are responsible for establishing regulations for the investigation and prosecution of traffickers and for the provision of assistance to victims of trafficking. In all the federal states, there are decrees which recommend limited rights be granted to victims in the interest of pursuing public prosecution of traffickers.[86]

In the UK, the government grants temporary visas for victims of trafficking under certain circumstances.[87]

In the United States, temporary visas are available to victims of *severe* trafficking. In order to prove eligibility for this temporary visa, applicants must establish that they have suffered a severe form of trafficking in persons, that they have complied with reasonable requests for assistance in the investigation or prosecution of acts of such trafficking, and that they would suffer extreme hardship involving unusual and severe harm upon removal. After a period of time, they are then eligible to apply for permanent legal status.[88]

Italy offers the best model for protection of victims of trafficking. It is the only country in the European Union that provides victims of trafficking an unlimited right of residence not dependent on investigative or criminal proceedings against traffickers or the existence of a particularly threatening situation in the victim's home country.[89] Government policy focuses equally on addressing the humanitarian needs of the victims as well as the enforcement concerns seeking to halt trafficking.[90]

On 29 April 2004, the EU Directive on the residence permit issued to third-country nationals who are victims of trafficking in human beings or who have been the subjects of actions to facilitate illegal immigration and who cooperate with the competent authorities entered into force.[91] This directive sets forth criteria for granting a residence permit to victims of trafficking, which requires that they prove a clear intention to cooperate with the authorities. It provides that trafficking victims be given information regarding the residence permit and be provided a period of time to reflect on whether to cooperate.[92] It also advises member states to provide victims with support, access to emergency medical treatment and any special care for vulnerable victims during the reflection period.[93] Where a government determines that a victim meets the criteria, it will issue a residence permit for a period of at least six months.[94] The Directive does not urge member states to refrain from issuing expulsion orders against trafficking victims during the reflection period. Nor does it provide any remedy or relief to trafficking victims who are unwilling to cooperate with authorities. Unfortunately, assistance and residency is predicated upon the victim's willingness to cooperate with authorities.

At the request of the Council of Europe's Committee of Ministers, the Ad Hoc Committee on Action against Trafficking in Human Beings

(CAHTEH) has drafted the European Convention against Trafficking in Human Beings.[95] The recognition of the need to develop further standards to protect victims of trafficking has been welcomed by NGOs throughout Europe. However, they are critical of the lack of transparency in the process of developing the draft. Amnesty International, Anti-Slavery International and several other NGOs had requested hearings before the CAHTEH to share experiences and knowledge on the issue. These requests were denied.[96] Shortly after release of the revised draft, Amnesty International and Anti-Slavery International issued a document which welcomed the CAHTEH's efforts in drafting the draft convention, but voiced concern that it fails to protect victims of trafficking adequately consistent with human rights standards.[97]

Many of the temporary visa schemes of several countries require a high level of participation in the investigation and prosecution of traffickers. For example, in order to be eligible to receive the temporary visa in Spain, victims must cooperate with police investigations and provide testimony before they can receive legal status. Also, the visas are available only to 'innocent victims' who are duped into travelling to Spain.[98] Therefore, even if she agrees to cooperate with the police and provide information regarding labour and human rights violations committed by the club owners, Teresa will most likely not be eligible for this visa because she voluntarily paid a 'smuggler'.

Many of the temporary visa regimes discussed above may fall short of their intended dual goals of assisting law enforcement efforts and providing protection for the victims. First, because of the high level of cooperation required under many schemes, most victims may be afraid to cooperate. Given the precariousness of their legal situation in the destination country, the fact that family members at home often depend on their income, and the very real possibility of serious reprisals should they cooperate, many women forgo such collaboration with the police. This is especially true because granting the visa often depends on variables beyond the victim's control – the determination regarding the 'essential' nature of the information provided by the victim and the conviction of the trafficker. In many cases, the trafficking victim may not have the 'essential' information necessary for the conviction of the trafficker. She may be privy only to general information that the police already have in its possession.

States should revisit the temporary visa schemes in effect in their countries to determine if they are in fact accomplishing the dual goals of improved law enforcement efforts and real protection for the victims of trafficking.[99] In reviewing their visa schemes, states should refer to the

Human Rights Standards for the Treatment of Trafficked Persons,[100] the Model Law to Combat Trafficking in Persons developed by the US Department of State[101] and the system of protection implemented in Italy. Victims of trafficking who are witnesses or potential witnesses should be eligible for witness protection and relocation programmes. Such programmes should include: relocation; new identity documents establishing the identity; new resident, employment and work permits; and protection of confidentiality of identity and location. Additionally, governments should provide victims of trafficking and their accompanying children with appropriate visas to permit them to remain in the destination country while the investigation against the traffickers is pending as long as the victim complies with reasonable requests for assistance in the investigation and prosecution of the trafficker(s). Victims of trafficking and their accompanying children should also be given the opportunity to receive permanent residence in the country under certain circumstances, especially where they would face extreme hardship or harm if returned to their home country. Finally, and most importantly, assistance and legal protection should be provided to victims of trafficking independent of their participation in investigative and subsequent judicial proceedings. Protection in the form of granting legal status and work permits serves as an appropriate remedy for the human rights violations suffered by trafficked women. Countries throughout the world should consider the Italian model in devising their own systems of protection.

Employment-based visas

A discussion addressing whether sex work is a legitimate occupation choice for some women or whether prostitution should be banned is beyond the scope of this chapter. Further, this author is unclear on where she stands on the issue, as there are legitimate arguments on both sides. If we assume, however, that sex work is a legitimate occupational choice and the country in which it is practised does not consider it illegal, then the question is why countries with a shortage of workers in the sex industry do not issue employment-based visas to fill those jobs. Work permits are not issued for purposes of working in prostitution in any of the EU member states, with the exception of Austria.[102]

In Spain, prostitution is not penalised and there is a high demand for prostitutes, especially in the hundreds of clubs in both towns and rural areas throughout the country. A significantly high percentage of prostitutes working in clubs and on the streets are foreign-born.[103] Most are undocumented and have been either trafficked to the country for forced prostitution or smuggled voluntarily with prior knowledge.[104] Given that Spanish nationals are unwilling or unable to perform services in the sex industry, as is evidenced by the high number of foreign nationals working as prostitutes, it seems only logical that Spain and countries in a similar position should consider making employment visas available to women willing to work in the sex industry.[105] The situation is similar in Italy, where it is also estimated that a large majority of prostitutes are foreign-born.[106] Although this alternative would not necessarily solve the issue of trafficking victims into forced prostitution, it would certainly affect the smuggling business. If women could legally apply for employment visas to enter and work legally, using the services of the smuggler would be unnecessary. Women then would not be burdened with huge debt and could, after arrival, exercise their rights to demand fair labour conditions in their jobs.

Conclusions

This chapter does not pretend to address in detail all potential avenues of asylum and immigration related relief for victims of trafficking. Instead, it is intended to promote a discussion on what cracks still exist in systems of protection and assistance and to stimulate brainstorming on more effective ways to provide support, assistance and long term status to trafficking victims. The emphasis on victim assistance and protection in the Italian regime, the US Model Law and the European Council Directive is encouraging. Many assistance and protection programmes, however, often depend on the nature or value of the information or testimony to be provided by the victims, many of whom may not have vital details about the trafficking rings, and the interpretation of 'cooperation' by the investigating authorities. These variables may well result in failure to protect many needy and deserving victims of human rights violations.

In cases where women can prove eligibility, asylum can and should be pursued as an avenue of relief for those who cannot comply with requirements for special trafficking visas. Asylum may be the only relief available to victims of trafficking, many of whom suffer serious violations of human rights subsequent to their arrival in the destination countries.

Finally, in countries where prostitution is legal, governmental authorities should discuss the possibility of providing labour visas for foreign-born women who wish to work as prostitutes. Such visas would greatly reduce the need for smugglers in this area. However, given the dangers that women are exposed to in the sex industry, creation of a labour visa scheme is not enough. Governments should also regularly monitor the labour and related conditions of foreign-born women working in the prostitution trade to guarantee that all of their rights are respected.

Notes

1. US Department of State, Victims of Trafficking and Violence Protection Act of 2000: Trafficking in Persons Report (2003). The United Nations estimates that as of 2000, 4 million women were trafficked around the world. United Nations Economic and Social Council, 2000, p. 24. The International Organisation of Migration estimates that over 500,000 women have been trafficked into Western Europe during the same time period. United Nations Economic and Social Council, 2000, p. 24.
2. From 1815 to 1957, it is estimated that approximately 300 international agreements were passed to suppress slavery. See David Weissbrodt, *Anti-Slavery Int'l, Contemporary Forms of Slavery: Updated Review of the Implementation and Follow-Up to the Conventions on Slavery*, U.N. ESCOR Sub-Comm'n on the Promotion and Protection of Human Rights, 52d Sess., Agenda Item 6, para. 3, U.N. Doc. E/CN.4/Sub.2/2000/3 (2000). The prohibition on slavery and servitude is a non-derogable right under several important human rights treaties, including the International Covenant on Civil and Political Rights, art. 8, 999 U.N.T.S. 171, 175; the European Convention for the Protection of Human Rights and Fundamental Freedoms, *opened for signature* Nov. 4, 1950, art. 4, 213 U.N.T.S. 222 (entered into force September 1953); and the American Convention on Human Rights, art. 6, 1144 U.N.T.S. 123, 146–47.
3. United Nations Children's Fund/United Nations Office of the High Commissioner for Human Rights/Organisation for Security and Cooperation in Europe – Office for the Democratic Institutions and Human Rights (UNICEF/UNOHCHR/OSCE-ODIHR), Trafficking in Human Beings in Southeastern Europe (2002).
4. For a detailed overview of the situation of human rights abuses suffered by women and children victims of trafficking in countries around the world, see The Protection Project Human Rights Report on Trafficking in Persons, Especially Women and Children (SAIS 2d Ed. 2002). This information is available on the website of the Protection Project at http://www.protectionproject.org.
5. See International Agreement for the Suppression of the White Slave Traffic, 18 May 1904, 92 U.N.T.S. 19; International Convention for the Suppression of White Slave Traffic, 4 May 1910, 11 L.N.T.S. 83; International Convention for the Suppression of Traffic in Women and Children, opened for signature 30 September 1921, 9 L.N.T.S. 415; League of Nations Slavery Convention, 9 March 1927, 60 L.N.T.S. 253; International Convention for the Suppression of the Traffic in Women of Full Age, Oct. 11, 1933, 53 U.N.T.S. 49; Protocol to Amend the International Agreement for the Suppression of the White Slave Traffic, 4 May 1949, 92 U.N.T.S. 21; Protocol to Amend the International Convention for the Suppression of the White Slave Traffic, 4 May 1949, 98 U.N.T.S. 103; Protocol to Amend the International Convention for the

Suppression of the Traffic in Women and Children, 12 November 1947, 53 U.N.T.S. 40; Protocol to Amend the International Convention for the Suppression of the Traffic of Women of Full Age, 17 November 1947, 53 U.N.T.S. 50; International Convention for the Suppression of the Traffic in Persons and of the Exploitation of the Prostitution of Others, 21 March 1950, 96 U.N.T.S. 273.

6. *Transnational Organized Crime*, G.A. Res. 53/111, U.N. GAOR, 53rd Sess., 85th plen. mtg., U.N. Doc. A/RES/53/111 (1998).

7. *Report of the Ad Hoc Committee on the Elaboration of a Convention Against Transnational Organized Crime on the Work of its First to Eleventh Sessions*, U.N. GAOR, 55th Sess., Agenda Item 105, at 1, U.N. Doc. A/55/383 (2000) (English version). Reports regarding the work of the Ad Hoc committee are available on the website of the UN Crime Commission at http://www.undcp.org/crime_cicp_commission.html.

8. *United Nations Convention Against Transnational Organized Crime*, U.N. GAOR, 55th Sess., Annex 1, Agenda Item 105, at 25, U.N. Doc. A/55/383 (2000) (English version) [hereinafter *Convention*]; *Protocol Against the Smuggling of Migrants by Land, Sea and Air*, U.N. GAOR, 55th Sess., Annex 3, U.N. Doc. A/55/383 (2000); *Protocol to Prevent, Suppress and Punish Trafficking in Persons, Especially Women and Children*, G.A. Res. 55/25, U.N. GAOR 55th Sess., Annex II, U.N. Doc. A/RES/55/25 (2001) [hereinafter *Trafficking Protocol*].

9. *Protocol Against the Illicit Manufacturing of and Trafficking in Firearms, Their Parts and Components and Ammunition, supplementing the United Nations Convention Against Transnational Organized Crime*, G.A. Res. 55/255, U.N. GAOR, 55th Sess., Agenda Item 105, U.N. Doc. A/RES/55/255 (2001).

10. For information regarding the mandate of the United Nations Crime Commission, visit its website at http://www.undcp.org/crime_cicp_commission.html.

11. *Trafficking Protocol*, art. 6, 7; *Convention*, art. 24, 25.

12. *Trafficking Protocol*, art. 3(b).

13. *Report of the Ad Hoc Committee on the Elaboration of a Convention against Transnational Organized Crime on the Work of Its First to Eleventh Sessions*, Interpretative notes for the official records (*travaux préparatoires*) of the negotiation of the United Nations Convention against Transnational Organized Crime and the Protocols thereto, 55th Sess., Agenda Item 105, at ¶ 63, U.N. Doc. A/55/383/Add. 1 [hereinafter *Interpretive Notes*].

14. See Global Alliance against Traffic in Women, Human Rights Standards for the Treatment of Trafficked Persons (1999). The standards – drawn from international human rights instruments and international legal norms – aim to protect and promote respect for the human rights of victims of trafficking, including those subjected to involuntary servitude, forced labour and/or slavery-like practices.

15. *Revised draft Protocol to Prevent, Suppress and Punish Trafficking in Persons Especially Women and Children, supplementing the United Nations Convention against Transnational Organized Crime*, 11th Sess., Agenda Item 3, at 7, U.N. Doc. A/AC.254/4/Add.3/Rev.7 (2000).

16. See generally Anne Gallagher, *Human Rights and the New UN Protocols on Trafficking and Migrant Smuggling: A Preliminary Analysis*, 23 Hum. Rts. Q. 975 (2001) (summarizing the drafting process surrounding the Protocol).

17. Convention Relating to the Status of Refugees, Apr. 22, 1954, 189 U.N.T.S. 150 [hereinafter 1951 Convention].
18. Protocol Relating to the Status of Refugees, Oct. 4, 1967, 606 U.N.T.S. 267 [hereinafter Protocol].
19. A refugee is someone who satisfies the definition of refugee under the 1951 Convention and who is accepted for admission and residence in another country. Asylum is a process through which persons fleeing persecution seek protection *after* arriving in another country. In order to obtain such protection, the asylum seeker must also satisfy the elements of the refugee definition in the 1951 Convention. The term refugee is often used to refer to those granted asylum, also referred to as asylees.
20. Protocol Relating to the Status of Refugees, Oct. 4, 1967, art. I(2), 606 U.N.T.S. 267 (incorporating by reference Article 1(a)(2) of the 1951 Convention).
21. See E. Dana Neacsu, *Gender-Based Persecution as a Basis for Asylum: An Annotated Bibliography*, 1993–2002, 95 Law Libr. J. 191 (2003).
22. Dept. of Immigration and Multicultural Affairs, Refugee and Humanitarian Visa Applicants: Guidelines on Gender Issues for Decision Makers (1996) (Australia); Immigration and Refugee Board, Guidelines for Women Refugee Claimants Fearing Gender Related Persecution (1993) (updated 13 November 1996) (Canada); Immigration and Naturalization Service, Work Instruction no. 148: Women in the asylum procedure, reprinted in Thomas Spijkerboer, *Gender and Refugee Status* Annex 7 (Ashgate 2000) (Netherlands); Migration Board, Legal Practice Division, *Gender-based persecution: Guidelines for investigation and evaluation of the needs of women for protection* (28 March 2001) (Sweden); Immigration Appellate Authority, *Asylum Gender Guidelines* (November 2000) (United Kingdom); Immigration and Naturalization Service, Office of International Affairs, *Considerations for Asylum Officers Adjudicating Asylum Claims from Women* (1995) (United States), *at* http://www.uchastings.edu/cgrs.
23. UNHCR Guidelines on International Protection: Gender Related Persecution within the context of Article 1A(2) of the 1951 Convention and/or its 1967 Protocol relating to the Status of Refugees, (HCR/GIP/02/01) 7 May 2002. UNHCR Guidelines on International Protection: 'Membership in a particular social group' within the context of Article 1A(2) of the 1951 Convention and/or its 1967 Protocol relating to the Status of Refugees, para. 15 (HCR/GIP/02/02) 7 May 2002. Proposed Council Directive on minimum standards for the qualification and status of third party nationals and stateless persons as refugees or as persons who otherwise need international protection, art. 7(d)(d), art. 12(d), COM(01)510 final.
24. For example, many male homosexuals fleeing persecution in their countries of origin due to their sexual identity have applied for and been granted asylum protection in countries including the United States, Germany, Canada, Australia and the UK. For more on US asylum law and homosexuality, see Jenni Millbank, 'Gender, Visibility and Public Space in Refugee Claims on the Basis of Sexual Orientation', 1 *Seattle J. for Soc. Just.* 725 (2003); Fatima Mohyuddin, 'United States Asylum Law in the Context of Sexual Orientation and Gender Identity: Justice for the Transgendered', 12 *Hastings Women's L.J.* 387 (2001).
25. The UNHCR, evidencing its concern for the issue, addressed the issue of trafficking and asylum in a recent working paper. See Jenna Shearer Demir,

The Trafficking of Women for Sexual Exploitation: A Gender-Based and Well-Founded Fear of Persecution? (United Nations High Commissioner for Refugees, Working Paper No. 80, 2003).

26. Council Conclusions of 8 May 2003 – Brussels Declaration on Preventing and Combating Trafficking in Human Beings, para. 13, 2003 O.J. (C 137) 1. In the recently approved Council Directive on short-term residence permits for victims of trafficking, the Council notes that access to residence under the Directive is without prejudice to protection granted to refugees, to beneficiaries of subsidiary protection and without prejudice to other human rights instruments. See Council Directive on the residence permit issued to third-country nationals who are victims of trafficking in human beings or who have been the subject of an action to facilitate illegal immigration, who cooperate with the competent authorities (2004/81/EC), Preamble (4), 2004 O.J. (L 257).

27. Parliament resolution on the communication from the Commission to the Council and Parliament, entitled 'For further actions in the fight against trafficking in women' (09/08/2000) Bulletin EU 5–2000.

28. For an overview of gender-related persecution claims in Europe, see Heaven Crawley and Trine Lester, *Comparative Analysis of Gender-Related Persecution in National Asylum Legislation in Europe* (UNHCR Evaluation and Policy Unit, Department of International Protection and Regional Bureau for Europe 2004).

29. UN Handbook on Procedures and Criteria for Determining Refugee Status (Geneva, 1979), ¶ 45.

30. UN Handbook on Procedures and Criteria for Determining Refugee Status (Geneva, 1979), ¶ 38.

31. UN Handbook on Procedures and Criteria for Determining Refugee Status (Geneva, 1979), ¶ 41.

32. UN Handbook on Procedures and Criteria for Determining Refugee Status (Geneva, 1979), ¶ 42.

33. UN Handbook on Procedures and Criteria for Determining Refugee Status (Geneva, 1979), ¶ 51. See also n. 22 above (listing guidelines governing gender-based asylum claims in several countries party to the 1951 Convention).

34. International Covenant on Civil and Political Rights, opened for signature 16 December 1966, 999 U.N.T.S. 171, *reprinted in* 6 I.L.M. 368 (1967); Convention Against Torture and Other Cruel, Inhuman or Degrading Treatment or Punishment, *opened for signature* 4 February 1985, 1465 U.N.T.S. 8.

35. These forms of gender-based violence have been recognised as persecution for asylum purposes in several countries. See n. 22 above (listing gender guidelines for several state parties to the 1951 Convention). For US jurisprudence, see Karen Musalo, 'Revisiting Social Group and Nexus in Gender Asylum Claims: A Unifying Rationale for Evolving Jurisprudence', 52 *DePaul L. Rev.* 777 (2003); Stephen Knight and Karen Musalo, 'Steps Forward and Back: Uneven Progress in the Law of Social Group and Gender-Based Claims in the U.S.', 13 *Int'l J. Refugee L.* 51 (2001). For New Zealand case law, see Rodger P.G. Haines, 'Gender-Based Persecution: New Zealand Jurisprudence', *Int'l J. Refugee L.* 129 (Autumn 1997), available at http://www.refugee.org.nz/ Genz.htm. For UK law and gender-based violence as a basis for asylum, see Heavan Crawley, *Refugees and Gender: Law and Process* (2001). For an overview

of EU member states position on gender-based violence and asylum, see Thomas Spijkerboer, *Gender and Refugee Status*, Annex 7 (2000).

36. UNHCR Guidelines on International Protection: Gender Related Persecution within the context of Article 1A(2) of the 1951 Convention and/or its 1967 Protocol relating to the Status of Refugees, para. 18 (HCR/GIP/02/01) 7 May 2002.

37. See James C. Hathaway, *The Law of Refugee Status* 102–103 (1991). Hathaway, in discussing the development of persecution as an element of the refugee definition, notes: 'From the beginning, there was no monolithic or absolute conceptual standard of wrongfulness, the implication being that a variety of measures in disregard of human dignity might constitute persecution.' Under Hathaway's paradigm, physical assault is a first category rights violation. Execution also is a first category rights violation, the risk of which constitutes persecution.

38. UN Handbook on Procedures and Criteria for Determining Refugee Status (Geneva, 1979), para. 66.

39. UN Handbook on Procedures and Criteria for Determining Refugee Status (Geneva, 1979), para. 77.

40. UNHCR Guidelines on International Protection: 'Membership in a particular social group' within the context of Article 1A(2) of the 1951 Convention and/or its 1967 Protocol relating to the Status of Refugees (HCR/GIP/02/02) 7 May 2002.

41. Ibid., para. 6.

42. Ibid., para. 7.

43. Ibid., para. 11.

44. See Judgment of 6 June 1984, No. 1 OVGA 91/82 As, Verwaltungsgericht Hannover (denying asylum to former corrupt official from Ghana); Judgment of 26 April 1983, No. IV/I E 06244/81, Verwaltungsgericht Wiesbaden [Wiesbaden Administrative Court] (granting asylum to an Iranian homosexual).

45. *Canada (Attorney General)* v. *Ward* [1993] S.C.R. 689.

46. *Applicant A* v. *Minister for Immigration and Ethnic Affairs* (1997) 142 A.L.R. 331, [1997] INLR 1.

47. Matter of Acosta, 19 I&N Dec. 211 (BIA 1985).

48. *Sanchez-Trujillo* v. *INS*, 801 F.2d 1571 (9th Cir. 1986).

49. CRDD T98-06446 (3 August. 1999), available from RefLex, Issue 123 (29 September 1999).

50. CRDD T99-01434 (25 August 1999), available from RefLex, Issue 125 (27 October 1999).

51. CRDD T98-06186 (2 November 1999), available from RefLex, Issue 134 (15 March 2000).

52. Matter of —, S 02-03-2001, rec. 1024/1999 (Audiencia Nacional). The Spanish Commission for the Aid of Refugees (Comision Espanola por la Ayuda de Refugiados – CEAR) also reports that its attorneys have represented at least one other claim of a trafficked woman from Mozambique. Memorandum, Meeting with CEAR Attorneys (16 December 2003) (on file with author).

53. For a PDF copy of the decision and English translation, see International Gender Asylum Decisions and Law on the website of The Center for Gender and Refugee Studies, at http://www.uchastings.edu/cgrs.

54. RRT Reference: V97/07831 (11 February 1999).
55. RRT Reference: V00/11003 (29 September 2000).
56. ELR was a discretionary status granted by the Home Secretary to unsuccessful asylum seekers. It was granted for various reasons, but primarily for compassionate or humanitarian reasons. ELR was replaced by Humanitarian Protection and Discretionary Leave in April 2003. See APU Notice 1/2003 available on the website of the Immigration & Nationality Directorate *at* http://www.ind.homeoffice.gov.uk.
57. See Women's Asylum News, Issue 13 (August 2001) available at http://www.asylumaid.org.uk . Several other trafficked persons who testified against their traffickers were granted ELR status or asylum as reported in *Human Traffic, Human Rights: Redefining Victim Protection* 122–3 nn.22–23 (Anti-Slavery International 2002).
58. See *Women's Asylum News*, Issue 34 (July 2003), available at http://www.asylumaid.org.uk
59. *SSHD* v. *Dzhgun* (00TH00728) reported in *Women's Asylum News*, Issue 34 (July 2003), *available at* http://www.asylumaid.org.uk.
60. *Gjoni* v. *SSHD* (Appeal No. UKIAT06307, HX/15098/02), decided 29 January 2003.
61. See Case Summary 275, on the website of The Center for Gender and Refugee Studies, *at* http://www.uchastings.edu/cgrs.
62. See Case Summary 330, on the website of The Center for Gender and Refugee Studies, *at* http://www.uchastings.edu/cgrs.
63. See Case Summary 560, on the website of The Center for Gender and Refugee Studies, *at* http://www.uchastings.edu/cgrs.
64. *In re* O-Z- & I-Z- , 22 I&N Dec. 23 (BIA 1998) (anti-Semitic nationalist groups persecuted applicants); *In re* Villalta, 20 I&N Dec. 142 (BIA 1990) (death squad in El Salvador agent of persecution); *In re* McMullen, 17 I&N Dec. 542 (BIA 1980) (Provisional Irish Republican Army agent of prosecution); *Rosa* v. *INS*, 449 F.2d 199 (1st Cir. 1971) (persecutor does not apply only to state actors).
65. See *Canada* v. *Ward*, 2 S.C.R. 689 (1993) (refugee law requires protection of those whose home state cannot or do not afford protection to them from persecution).
66. See Mary E. Crock, *Immigration and Refugee Law in Australia* 148–49 (1998) (discusses recognition of non-state actor doctrine in context of asylum claims based on domestic violence).
67. See Refugee Appeal No. 2039/93 Re MN, at 17 (Refugee Status Appeals Authority, Feb. 12, 1996) (New Zealand) (accepting that 1951 Convention requires protection from persecution by non-state actors).
68. For an overview of the position of several European countries regarding persecution by third parties, see Ben Vermeulen *et al.*, *Persecution by Third Parties* (University of Nijmegen Centre for Migration Law 1998).
69. ARK 6 June 1996, no. 28. (Switzerland) (Algeria's inability to protect against fundamental Islamists does not support claim for asylum).
70. Proposed Council Directive on minimum standards for the qualification and status of third party nationals and stateless persons as refugees or as persons who otherwise need international protection, art. 9.1 COM (2001) 510 final (12/09/2001).

71. UNHCR Guidelines on International Protection: 'Membership of a particular social group' within the context of Article 1A(2) of the 1951 Convention and/or its 1967 Protocol relating to the Status of Refugees, para. 20 (HCR/GIP/02/02) 7 May 2002; UNHCR Handbook on Procedures and Criteria for Determining Refugee Status under the 1951 Convention and the 1967 Protocol relating to the Status of Refugees, para. 65 (Geneva 1992).
72. See James Hathaway, *The Law of Refugee Status* 104 (1991) (commenting on the Convention drafter's concern to identify forms of harm reflective of a breach by a state of its obligations of protection).
73. See 1 Atle Grahl-Madsen, *The State of Refugees in International Law* 189 (1966).
74. 1951 Convention, art. I(A)(2).
75. United Nations High Commissioner for Refugees, Handbook on Procedures and Criteria for Determining Refugee Status under the 1951 Convention and the 1967 Protocol Relating to the Status of Refugees, para. 65 (Geneva 1992).
76. See generally Stephanie Farrior, 'State Responsibility for Human Rights Abuses by Non-State Actors', 92 *Am. Society of Int'l L. Proc.* 209 (1998); Deborah Anker *et al.*, 'Women Whose Governments Are Unable or Unwilling to Provide Reasonable Protection from Domestic Violence May Qualify as Refugees under United States Asylum Law', 11 *Geo. Immigr. L. J.* 709 (1997).
77. Stephanie Farrior, 'State Responsibility for Human Rights Abuses by Non-State Actors', 92 *Am. Society of Int'l L. Proc.* 299, 301 (1998).
78. 1951 Convention, art. 31.
79. For a review of procedures in Belgium, Germany, Italy, the Netherlands, Spain and the United Kingdom, see Aika van der Kleij, *Provisions for Victims of Trafficking in Bonded Sexual Labour, i.e. Prostitution – in 6 European Countries* (Blinn, Novib and Humanitas eds., 2002), *available at* http://www.humanitas.nl/project/Blinn_Final_Report.pdf.
80. § 10 FrG BGBl 75/1997 (Law for Foreigners). For further information regarding victim assistance in Austria, see C.C. Jones Pauly, *Report on anti-trafficking laws in six European countries (Austria, Belgium, Czech Republic, Federal Republic of Germany, Italy Poland) and compliance with the International Convention Against Trafficking* 84–109 (1999).
81. Danish Aliens Act, art. 33. For more on Denmark, see *Prevention and Fight Against Trafficking: Institutional Developments in Europe – Denmark Report* (European Migration Centre ed., 2003). This report was published by the European Migration Centre as part of its project on trafficking. This and other EU country reports are available on its website, *at* http://www.emz-berlin.de (click on projects to access the webpage on the trafficking research project).
82. *Dep't of State, Trafficking in Persons Report: Country Narrative – France* 65–6 (June 2003).
83. Ch. B17, Aliens Circular.
84. Ibid.
85. Instructions to the Foreigners Department office, the prosecuting authorities, the police and the social law inspection and social inspection services concerning assistance to victims of human trafficking (13 January1997), *Moniteur Belge* (7 July 1997).
86. See E. Neisner and C.C. Jones-Pauly, *Trafficking in Women in Europe* 169–204 (Leine Verlag 2001).

87. See Mano Candappa, *Prevention and Fight Against Trafficking: Institutional Developments in Europe – UK Report* (European Migration Centre 2003), available at http://www.emz-berlin.de (click on projects to access the webpage of the trafficking research project).

88. 8 C.F.R. §§ 214.11(b)(1), 214.11(b)(3)(i), 214.11(b)(4) (2004).

89. Article 18, Decreto Legislativo, 25/07/1998, No. 286, §§ 1, 2, 4, 5, Gazz. Uff. 08/18/1998, No. 191.

90. For a report on the analysis of laws and procedures relating to trafficking in Italy, see *STOP Programme, European Commission, Article 18 Protection of Victims of Trafficking and Fight Against Crime (Italy and European Scenarios) Research Report* (On the Road ed., 2002).

91. Council Directive on the residence permit issued to third-country nationals who are victims of trafficking in human beings or who have been the subject of an action to facilitate illegal immigration, who cooperate with the competent authorities (2004/81/EC), *Official Journal of the European Union*, Vol. 47 (4 August 2004).

92. Council Directive on the residence permit issued to third-country nationals who are victims of trafficking in human beings or who have been the subject of an action to facilitate illegal immigration, who cooperate with the competent authorities (2004/81/EC), articles 5, 6.

93. Ibid., art. 7.

94. Ibid., art. 8.

95. *Revised draft Council of Europe Convention on Action Against Trafficking in Human Beings*, Council of Europe Ad Hoc Committee on Action Against Trafficking in Human Beings, INFO 4 (5 July 2004).

96. See Amnesty International and Anti-Slavery International, *Council of Europe: Drafting a European Convention Against Trafficking: Make it a Transparent Process* (June 1, 2004), at http://web.amnesty.org/library.

97. Amnesty International and Anti-Slavery International, *Enhancing the Protection of the Rights of Trafficked Persons: Amnesty International and Anti-Slavery International's Recommendations to Strengthen Provisions in the July 2004 Draft European Council Against Trafficking in Human Beings* (27 September 2004), at http://www.antislavery.org.

98. Interview with Carlos Botran Prieto, Chief Commissioner of the Central Brigade for Immigration Networks, in Madrid, Spain (29 October 2003) (on file with author).

99. For a discussion on the benefits of providing immigration status to protect victims and promote law enforcement, see Dina F. Haynes, 'Used, Abused, Arrested and Deported: The Case for Extending Benefits to Protect Victims of Trafficking and Secure Prosecution of Traffickers', 26 *Hum. Rts. Q.* 2 (2004).

100. Global Alliance Against Traffic in Women, *Human Rights Standards for the Treatment of Trafficked Persons* (Foundation Against Trafficking in Women and the International Human Rights Law Group ed., January 1999).

101. Model Law to Combat Trafficking in Persons, State Dep't News Release (12 March 2003).

102. For a discussion of immigration issues and prostitution in EU Member States, see Daniella Danna, *Trafficking and Prostitution of Foreigners in the Context of the EU Countries' Policy about Prostitution* (April 2003), available at http://www.danieladanna.it/.

103. See Colectivo Ioe, *Mujer, Inmigracion y Trabajo* 728 n.418, available at http://www.imsersomigracion.upco.es/.

104. See Anna Marie Gallagher, *Country Report Spain: Trafficking and Smuggling of Women* (3 November 2003), available at Network for European Women's Rights, http://www.newr.bham.ac.uk.

105. The European Court of Justice has issued a decision holding that prostitution is an 'economic activity'. Consequently, Polish and Czech nationals can work as self-employed sex workers in the EU on the same basis as nationals. Case C-269/99, *Aldona Malgorzata Jany v. Staatssecretaris van Justitie* (E.C.J. 2001).

106. International Organisation for Migration, *Trafficking in Women to Italy for Sexual Exploitation* (June 1996), available at http://www.iom.int.

10
Trafficking in Women: A Cosmopolitan Approach to Long-term Prevention

Christien L. van den Anker

Introduction

Despite the contested nature of the concept, combating trafficking in human beings is an area of growing interest and activity. International organisations, governments and non-governmental organisations (NGOs) are all busy devising strategies to combat it. A diverse array of responses has been put in place since 2000: a new UN protocol, bringing in the first internationally agreed definition of trafficking, national policies (varying from the Swedish model of criminalisation of clients of sex workers to the Italian model of granting victims of trafficking a visa whether or not they testify against their traffickers in court), international monitoring, assistance for victims and local efforts for reintegration are among them. Some of these new measures are now in the process of being evaluated.

All this activity takes place in the context of nation-states aiming to control immigration and especially to reduce the number of illegal immigrants. This agenda, however, is proving to be counterproductive in combating trafficking; tightening border controls and eligibility criteria for legal migration force more people into illegal migration (Doomernik, in van den Anker, 2004).

As alternatives to the anti-migration approach, NGOs have proposed victim-centred approaches based on human rights. Most recently the Expert Group of the EU has proposed a holistic, integrated approach (Report, 2004). These alternatives differ in that they recognise the realities of the global economy and the pressures to migrate. They address a wider set of root causes of trafficking than the anti-migration approach. Another common strand between the alternative approaches is that they recognise the need to address prevention measures, both long- and short-term. However, what is meant by prevention is different for different organisations.

In this chapter I evaluate these various approaches to the prevention of trafficking by assessing their conception of prevention and their analysis (or lack of it) of the root causes of trafficking. I propose a third approach, cosmopolitanism, and outline how it addresses the most complex set of root causes and the best integrated proposals for long-term prevention.

The reality of trafficking, current policies and NGO responses

Due to its illegal nature, reliable statistics on the numbers of people trafficked are hard to find. Estimates are often based on the expectation that the reality will be worse than the cases NGOs and law enforcemen agencies come across. However, lobbying groups also have cause n to give low estimates, as their aim is to solicit action by the public an policymakers. Despite the lack of reliable figures on the number of people involved, information exists on trafficking routes and some of the circumstances of the women involved. The IOM's recent findings show that the experiences of trafficked people differ widely according to their region of origin. In south-eastern Europe most trafficking occurs into sex work and most victims are women aged between 18 and 24. One group that is especially vulnerable is young single mothers. The countries of origin are mainly Moldova, Romania (especially the area near the border with Moldova) and the Ukraine. Recruiters promise jobs abroad and even though most of the women have worked before, they are looking for better prospects than their previous wages of less than $50 per month. In Albania, another country of origin for many trafficked women, the story women are given often involves an offer of marriage and the promise of a new life abroad.[1]

Currently, there are three main actors initiating responses to trafficking: international organisations, national governments and NGOs. In some countries grass-roots organisations of sex workers, migrant domestic workers, migrant workers more generally or occasionally victims of trafficking have a voice in the debate. In the Netherlands two women trafficked into prostitution set up the campaign group for victims of trafficking in women for prostitution, Atalanta (Opzij, January 2004).

The international response in the context of the UN has been to draft additional international protocols in the context of the prevention of crime. The Protocol to Prevent, Suppress and Punish Trafficking in Persons, Especially Women and Children, supplements the UN Convention on Transnational Organised Crime in 2000, which provides the first definition of trafficking in international law (Ould, in van den Anker, 2004). However, several problems with the protocol have been identified, for example, Anderson and O'Connell Davidson (2002; and in this volume) point out the risk that the concept of trafficking will deflect attention from the exploitation of the individual and encourage the creation of moral hierarchies, as well as practical and legal barriers between victims. This would allow policymakers to obscure the effects of their policies on the rights of migrants.

The so-called Palermo Protocol came into force on 25 December 2003; the United Nations provided an additional document that emphasises the need for a human rights-based interpretation of the Protocol. In addition, the European Union has set up a group of experts, whose report argues for a holistic, integrated approach to trafficking (Report of the Experts Group, 2004).

On a national level, governments have responded to pressures from NGOs to combat trafficking by introducing measures to restrict migration. Exceptions are the government of Sweden, which has adopted a law to make the use of prostitutes illegal, and the governments of the Netherlands, Belgium and Italy, which all have measures in place for some form of visa for victims of trafficking. Italy is the only country where a visa is not dependent on the victim giving evidence in court. The criminalisation approach has been criticised for implementing the agenda of the moralistic right-wing campaigns against prostitution. However, the Swedish government makes the case for its legislation on the basis of an argument for the protection of the rights of women. Equality between men and women means that women's bodies should not be offered for sale. In some countries (especially the Netherlands and Belgium) campaigns for the rights of victims of trafficking have resulted in victims being allowed a period of respite before having to decide whether they will proceed with a case against their traffickers (Dormaels, Moens and Praet, in van den Anker, 2004) However, these rights are still conditional on cooperation with the police.

National NGOs have developed victim support services in many countries and the IOM supports victims of trafficking worldwide. Many NGOs see victim support and lobbying policymakers as their main goals. Some NGOs campaign for the abolition of prostitution *per se*, equating the concept of trafficking with trafficking into prostitution. Victim support is an area where many campaigners still see a vast area for improvement: the requirement of evidence is seen as putting too much pressure on women and the protection of witnesses is haphazard in most countries (Pearson, 2002). In her report, Pearson argues for a human rights approach to trafficking. This includes an emphasis on the rights of victims to protection, compensation and reintegration, a focus on labour rights and legal prosecution of traffickers. The rights-based perspective provides an opportunity to put the needs of the victims of trafficking central and leads away from narrow immigration perspectives.

However, a rights-based approach will need to address some of the problematic areas that have been pointed out with regard to the human rights doctrine more generally. For example, rights can conflict and some approaches prioritise certain categories of rights over others. A successful rights-based approach to trafficking needs to view all human rights as interconnected. It also needs to make a clear distinction between rights on the level of human rights as moral norms, international human rights law and national rights either as part of a constitution or of regular laws. Although the human rights discourse has problems of its own (it has been accused of portraying male, liberal, Western biases) the vocabulary of human rights is the most widely used moral and legal framework of reference for campaigns at this moment in time. Whereas governments may gladly make use of academic critiques of the human rights doctrine, the lack of ultimate foundations for human rights does not prevent local groups from claiming their rights and using international law to their advantage (Wilson, 1997).

One of the main problems with present approaches to combating trafficking is the lack of attention paid to the need for prevention. Even the rights-based approach does not address this urgent issue explicitly enough. The version of the rights-based approach campaigned for by NGOs should be explicitly aimed at the long-term prevention of trafficking. In addition to a human rights approach, strategies to combat trafficking need to engage with the wider picture of creating justice in a world where a high level of interdependence makes the structural factors more important in influencing local and personal circumstances and choices than previously. Although a human rights approach would help victims of trafficking enormously, in order to strengthen the case for additional measures focused on the prevention of trafficking a wider cosmopolitan perspective should be adopted. This would have two immediate benefits: long-term prevention would be taken more seriously and the widest set of root causes would be taken into account. Before I show the implications of such a perspective I first set out the current situation with respect to the long-term prevention of trafficking.

The prevention of trafficking: state of the art

NGOs working with victims of trafficking and law enforcement bodies are increasingly reaching the conclusion that the present measures to combat trafficking are not working. According to Helga Konrad, head of the OSCE Stability Task Force in South Eastern Europe, half of the victims of trafficking in that region are re-trafficked after having been deported (see this volume, Chapter 7). The case study of Sylvia, a Nigerian woman trafficked to Italy and deported back to Nigeria, shows that this is a real problem in West Africa too.

> Many women face reprisals from traffickers if they are returned to Nigeria, but the police do nothing to provide protection, nor do they take steps to prevent the women from being re-trafficked. Due to the on-going threats from the agent, Sylvia felt she had to find a way of repaying the debt. In order to protect her family, she agreed to be re-trafficked into Europe, it was her only chance of earning the money the agent demanded. (Anti-Slavery International's Stop Human Traffic Campaign, URL)

At present, prevention is mainly understood to mean short-term prevention campaigns, focusing on awareness-raising among young women especially at risk of trafficking. Existing reintegration programmes for women who have been repatriated are piecemeal and lack investment. In order to develop concerted efforts for the long-term prevention of trafficking, international organisations and governments need to address the structural factors or root causes of migration in general and of trafficking in particular. So far, NGOs have campaigned for the prevention of trafficking by reference to the wider context of women's rights. Lack of gender equality is one of the main root causes of trafficking in women. For example, Kvinnoforum/Foundation of Women's Forum calls for a

> multifaceted approach where also NGOs and government organisations co-operate. Trafficking cannot be understood unless seen in a wider context of women's rights, equal opportunities, women's education and empowerment, women's health, traditional gender roles, poverty of women and the gendered labour market.

The specific recommendations of Kvinnoforum fall into two categories: the long-term prevention work on gender equality (including sexual harassment and unequal access to the labour market) and the shorter-term work of informing young women about the risks of going abroad as well as promoting their self-esteem and training police, border guards, school teachers and youth organisations in how to promote the safety of young women.[2] Although the long-term prevention of trafficking is addressed by this NGO, it is viewed in terms of gender equality only and there are no specific recommendations on the long-term strategy.

Another NGO promoting the prevention of trafficking is La Strada, which lists prevention as its first goal and assistance for victims as its second. La Strada's work includes:

- providing a broad range of assistance for trafficked persons;
- maintaining a 'hot-line' for emergency telephone assistance;
- researching the problem of violence against women;
- providing expertise on legislation;
- conducting educational programmes for youths on the problem of women's rights,
- prevention of trafficking in women and other kinds of violence and exploitation;
- cooperation with mass media, and distributing information about the issues.[3]

Here again prevention is focused mainly on education and the distribution of information about trafficking. A factor that is not mentioned widely in the NGO documents on prevention of trafficking is the economic situation of the countries of origin in general and the women who are being trafficked or are vulnerable to decide to go along with recruiters in particular.

The European Women's Lobby (EWL) holds that prevention of trafficking is best done by addressing the demand side of prostitution. The EWL's contribution to the Brussels conference in 2002 stated that:

> [t]rafficking in women and girls as well as prostitution are expressions of the prevailing domination of men over women .... The EWL strongly believes that strategies aiming at preventing trafficking should address the root causes of trafficking. These are to be found partly in the persistence of gender inequalities and the feminisation of poverty and the consequent limitations in life-choices for women, but also in the expansion of the demand, especially in the sex industry of the receiving countries, and particularly in the European Union. ... One of the most important root causes of prostitution and

other forms of sexual exploitation of women is the persistence of patriarchal structures and ideologies in our societies, and in particular the unequal share of power and resources in society. ... In order for any trafficking prevention strategies to be effective, policy-makers must be prepared to take a stand against the sexual exploitation of women, including prostitution, and tackle the demand side of the industry, i.e. the clients of sexual services.[4]

The EWL clearly does address the issue of poverty, yet solely through the lens of gender inequality; it emphasises the feminisation of poverty as one of the root causes of trafficking. It also focuses solely on the trafficking of women and girls into prostitution, claiming that this involves the greatest number of people; although this may be true for one particular region, namely trafficking from Eastern Europe and Russia, this is not true for other regions from where people are being trafficked into Europe. The latest figures from IOM show that large numbers of men and women are being trafficked into other economic sectors and industries. In order to claim importance for trafficking in women and girls into the sex industry it is unnecessary to make the wider claim that this involves the largest numbers. The EWL lists several priorities for policies aimed at the prevention of trafficking. They argue for measures fighting poverty and contributing to women's empowerment, legislation against prostitution, criminalising men buying sexual services, while promoting alternatives for women in prostitution.

In its recommendations, EWL does not follow up its concern for poverty as a root cause, as all measures proposed are to do with the prevention of trafficking into the sex industry and therefore on the abolishment of the sex industry altogether.

Finally, some NGOs argue for the prevention of trafficking through support for the reintegration of victims of trafficking in their country of origin. The IOM, for example, views reintegration as a measure to prevent trafficking as it helps victims of trafficking to resettle in their country of origin with some support to build a livelihood.[5]

International organisations are also addressing the prevention of trafficking. For example, in Resolution 1997/19, the Commission on Human Rights 'requests the Sub-Commission on Prevention of Discrimination and Protection of Minorities to encourage its Working Group on Contemporary Forms of Slavery to continue to address the issue of the traffic in women and girls under its Programme of Action for the Prevention of the Traffic in Persons and the Exploitation of the Prostitution of Others'.[6] According to some UN representatives, however, prevention of trafficking has not been given as much attention as is necessary in the work of the UN (personal communication, Siena, 22 November 2003).

The European Parliament agreed in 1997 during the first reading of the report on trafficking in women for sexual exploitation that:

> With regard to prevention [of trafficking], Parliament considered that all the Member States' embassies in third countries should provide information on the dangers of recruitment into the entertainment business targeted at women. Accompanying measures should also be planned for women from third countries who were victims of sexual exploitation in the Community and who returned to their country of origin. Coordinated information campaigns were required to inform women about the mechanisms and networks established in relation to trafficking in women.[7]

At this time, the EC focused almost solely on short-term prevention through support for victims of trafficking into prostitution and on information campaigns. The phrase 'who have returned to their country of origin' masks the fact that in most cases this would not have been a free choice but the result of deportation as an illegal immigrant.

However, the EC, under the influence of NGO campaigns, moved towards paying more attention to long-term prevention. The Brussels Declaration of 2002, for example, put prevention before combating trafficking in the title of the conference it was discussed at. The Declaration states that:

> Furthermore, root causes of trafficking, not least including unemployment, poverty, gender inequalities, including the status of girls, social and cultural attitudes, and the demand for sexual services, cheap labour and other forms of exploitation must continue to be at the forefront of the long-term efforts to fight human trafficking effectively. A global approach to trafficking must address all forms of exploitation, including sexual exploitation, labour exploitation, in particular child labour, and begging.[8]

This shows a commitment to addressing a wider variety of root causes than gender equalities. Poverty and the demand side for cheap labour are mentioned, both of which are of great importance in addition to gender inequalities. The Annex to the Brussels Declaration on Prevention of Trafficking shows that the conference took prevention seriously by dedicating a whole chapter to it. However, the Declaration does not make specific practical suggestions on how to address these root causes, other than recommending an integrated approach to migration. It also lacks reference to racism, xenophobia and other related intolerances such as disrespect of the rights of indigenous peoples. These forms of discrimination are another major cause of trafficking (ASI URL). Finally, no mention is made of conflict as a root cause of migration, including illegal migration, nor is the presence of peacekeeping forces mentioned as contributing factors to the market for trafficked women in the sex industry.[9]

The SAARC Convention goes one step further by including a reference to development in its article on prevention of trafficking. In its Article VII on Measures to Prevent Trafficking in Women and Children, the state parties to the Convention first make a commitment to make available funding for the prosecution of traffickers, promise to train their law enforcement officers and judiciary and to set up a Regional Task Force to facilitate implementation of the Convention. They state that it is allowed to set up bilateral mechanisms to do so effectively and they agree to exchange information. Innovative parts of the Convention are the promise to take the necessary measures for the supervision of employment agencies in order to prevent trafficking in women and children under the guise of recruitment. And they commit to 'endeavour to focus preventive and development efforts on areas which are known to be source areas for trafficking'. Finally, the state parties to the Convention promise to promote awareness of the problem of trafficking in women and children and its underlying causes including the projection of negative images of women.[10]

This Convention is innovative in its specific focus on prevention. It also includes a wider conception of prevention than the usual call for awareness-raising; prevention here includes cooperation between countries and law enforcement agencies, the supervision of employment agencies and developmental efforts in vulnerable areas, in addition to the promotion of awareness. Although this is the first explicit agreement to focus developmental efforts on vulnerable areas in the context of the prevention of trafficking, the proposal could be read as if the focus is solely on the developmental efforts of governments in regions of their own countries. Yet, as I will argue in the final section of this chapter, from a cosmopolitan perspective this should also be done internationally.

The most innovative policymaking on long-term prevention of trafficking in human beings is part of a new initiative by the OSCE. The OSCE in its Action Plan to combat trafficking in human beings shows concern that the root causes of trafficking remain insufficiently tackled,

in particular causes such as poverty, weak social and economic structures, lack of employment opportunities and equal opportunities in
general, violence against women and children, discrimination based on
sex, race and ethnicity, corruption, unresolved conflicts, post-conflict
situations, illegal migration and the demand for sexual exploitation
and inexpensive socially unprotected and often illegal labour.[11]

In its Action Plan the OSCE therefore calls for measures by states in all
areas important to prevention mentioned by other organisations; however, the Plan contains at least one element that goes beyond other calls
for action: it recommends social and economic policies aimed at
addressing the root causes of trafficking in both countries of origin and
countries of destination.[12] These recommendations fit in with the argument made here for the need for long-term prevention. However, once
more, specific measures are recommended to governments to take
within their own jurisdiction, for example, to raise social protection or
to enhance job opportunities for women. In a cosmopolitan approach
countries have responsibilities beyond their own borders, for example in
cases where governments may need support to be able to implement
social protection measures.

Most recently the Expert Group has called for a 'holistically and
integrated' approach which includes long term prevention. The report
states that:

[Prevention] strategies need to be based on a broad, multidisciplinary
knowledge of trafficking in human beings, its causes and counter
trafficking best practices. At the same time they have to be gender
sensitive and integrate a human rights perspective. ... Root causes,
research, awareness raising, training and administrative control will
be the main subjects for discussion in this chapter. (Report of Experts
Group, 2004: 83)

In this list of subjects, the Group initially does not seem to meet, let
alone move beyond, the OSCE proposals. However, when outlining the
main focus of prevention strategies, the Group talks about 'alleviating
circumstances that make people vulnerable to trafficking' like discrimination, marginalisation and social exclusion. They recommend promoting well-being through sustainable development with a particular focus
on women, minorities and children. The security approach to trafficking

should link to human security and therefore bring in human rights. The Group also calls for appropriate rights and financial support for victims of trafficking in countries of destination, in order to reduce the risk of re-trafficking. Finally, prevention needs to look into demand side factors (Report, 2004: 83).

Despite its initial modesty in listing subjects for prevention strategies the report lists a wide set of root causes, including gender and ethnic discrimination, poverty and lack of development, particular trends in the global labour market and conflict. However, in its recommendations the report does not move beyond the OSCE's call for sustainable development although it contains some more specific recommendations. Although the report mentions conflict as a root causes, it does not call for efforts by governments in this area.

In conclusion, the current proposals for long-term prevention, even those based on a human rights-based or integrated approach, generally do not address a wide set of root causes, and where they do they do not take the perspective that recommendations to prevent trafficking in the long term would involve concrete proposals to governments to address these root causes. Despite recommendations getting increasingly detailed and now more often linked to sustainable development, issues of a just global economy and peaceful international relations are left out. In the next section I argue that it is possible to adopt an approach that does address all root causes in its strategy for long-term prevention of trafficking, namely a cosmopolitan approach to global justice.

Cosmopolitanism and root causes of trafficking

As seen from the evidence above, the prevention of trafficking is a growing policy area. NGOs and international organisations have developed programmes and initiatives; and governments can do more to complement these efforts. The choice of prevention measures depends on the recognition of root causes. What would a cosmopolitan perspective contribute?

As indicated above, a cosmopolitan approach views the scope of justice as global. This is sometimes expressed in terms of global citizenship (see, for example, van den Anker, in Williams and Dower, 2002) and sometimes in terms of the lack of moral relevance of borders between nation-states (Bader, 1997). In the context of trafficking the main difference with existing approaches would be the widest perspective on root causes and the most elaborate long-term prevention programme.

An objection would be that a cosmopolitan approach moves too far away from the specifics of the trafficking issue; however, as shown by several authors, a productive balance can be found between the specifics of an important issue such as trafficking and the abstract principles of cosmopolitanism (see van den Anker, 2004; Konrad, this volume). Also, from the cases discussed at NGO meetings, it becomes clear that structural factors like globalisation and changing labour markets, as well as European enlargement, play an important role in the practice of trafficking and therefore need to be addressed in research and recommendations for policymaking.

A cosmopolitan approach to root causes would address the issue of trafficking as a global problem since it is at least partly caused by structural factors in the global political economy and therefore the responsibility of policymakers and citizens in all countries of the world benefiting from the present global inequality. As Stiglitz (2002) has argued: 'Global capitalism can be reshaped to realise its potential for the common good.' I would add, moreover, that the present global economic system needs to be reshaped for the common good and this implies duties beyond borders on governments, NGOs and citizens everywhere.

Another set of structural factors is related to the worldwide existence of patriarchy and the violation of women's human rights. A gendered lens on the effects of globalisation is therefore required. One of the questions asked by feminist analyses is why so many degrading life experiences of women have not been understood as human rights issues. Most women's experiences of human rights violations are gendered and many forms of discrimination or abuse occur because the victim is female. Women whose rights are violated for reasons other than gender often also experience a particular form of abuse based on gender, such as sexual assault. Assessing the situation for women in Europe requires looking at how women's situations have been altered as well as how women are effecting change. This aspect of women's agency is crucial for any work on women's rights as human rights (Bunch, 1995). Gender must also be analysed in relation to other factors such as nationality, race and class in order to discern multiple forms of human rights abuse women suffer. Inter-sectionality, or double discrimination, is a factor that can be recognised well in a cosmopolitan approach, as root causes recognised are not limited to one particular form of discrimination. Sapana Pradhan-Malla mentions examples of double discrimination in the areas of armed conflict, human trafficking, health care practices, the criminal justice system, the labour market, and displacement (Pradhan-Malla, 2001).

Another outcome of the complex set of processes we call globalisation is the increased multiculturalism of most nation-states through migration. Almost as the other side of the coin, globalisation has provoked processes of localisation in the increased identification with ethnic, religious and national ties below the level of the nation-state (Scholte, 2000). Ethnic wars are viewed by some as the opposite force of the universalising tendencies of globalisation. Although self-determination is incorporated as a right of peoples in the Universal Declaration of Human Rights, in cases of violent nationalism it becomes a threat to the human rights of minorities. The conflicts and transitions witnessed in the final part of the twentieth century have created the circumstances for trafficking in human beings to grow exponentially.

A further important part of the cosmopolitan agenda is the call for the establishment and development of democratic forms of global governance. David Held argues that since there is less and less overlap between decision-making units and those affected by decisions, wider circles of governance are needed (Held, 2002). Moreover, global justice requires cosmopolitan democracy and cosmopolitan democracy would lead to better implementation of global justice: a more equal distribution of resources and freedom of movement (van den Anker, 2004). Such arguments are increasingly relevant to the implementation of specific human rights, such as in the case of trafficking and more generally freedom from slavery.

Cosmopolitan prevention measures

In general, measures to counteract the root causes of trafficking, such as poverty and gender discrimination, will also have many other beneficial effects. It would make a big difference if the UN, the EU and the individual governments would adopt a more cosmopolitan stance and work towards persistent and co-ordinated programmes to prevent trafficking. Designing policies on the basis of the principle of equal respect for all, taking into account the structural factors that shape and limit people's choices, would make a real difference for the prevention of trafficking.

Some of the implications for policymaking would be that actors would work from the perspective of women's rights as human rights towards a rights-based approach to trafficking; showing that human rights violations, such as domestic violence, but also lack of social entitlements and lack of democratic governance contribute to trafficking.

They would discuss trafficking in the context of rights for all. This means including all women living in Europe and not only European women. This is highly relevant in the context of the global care chain, where domestic work and care tasks, in both private and public settings, are increasingly carried out by migrant women. Migrant labour is increasingly demanded in other industries and services, too. They would look beyond migrants' rights or labour rights, since both of these perspectives exclude some others. Where some receive better labour protection, others, like part-timers or non-unionised labour, may get a rougher deal as a result.

Support for victims should still be part of NGOs' role. Yet, they should go beyond this; they should also be collaborating with other NGOs and academics and developing analysis. The role of NGOs is to change the world by making these links. Fortunately, some movement in this direction is already taking place. For example, recently, a former sex workers leader responded to my proposal that she thought that sex workers need to move beyond looking into how to abandon trafficking into alternatives, such as the causes of migration, liaise with organisations on migration, domestic migrant workers, and so on.

Finally, a successful approach to combating trafficking needs to look into local factors influencing actors in the trafficking process. Cultural perceptions as well as national policies contribute to the set of alternatives open to actors and will need to be taken into account in any recommendations for policy making and NGO activity in combating trafficking. The issue of trafficking and of contemporary slavery more generally, cannot be remedied successfully by reference to universal moral and legal norms alone, as freedom from slavery and protection from trafficking are already incorporated into international law and, in the case of slavery, even part of customary law, binding for all nation-states in the world. The problem is therefore one of implementation and not justification.

On a large scale a cosmopolitan approach would contribute to conflict resolution, the reduction of poverty and inequality, protection of the environment and more generally human rights protection. Measures such as global taxation, debt reduction and a fair global trade system and more open borders would contribute to the long-term prevention of trafficking by addressing its root causes. Striving for democratisation, the protection of women's rights, accountable global governance, an active global civil society and global citizenship may seem a long way away from such a concrete problem as trafficking, but their realisation would help in preventing not only trafficking but also other injustices. This involves taking a view on the structural change of the current system of global capitalism, considering the proposals for open borders, to avoid the criminalisation of migration, thinking about the case for cosmopolitan democracy and aiming to build peace through win-win solutions instead of through armed conflict. It also means thinking actively about how to create distributive justice globally. In this respect, the Tobin tax (Dowling, in van den Anker, 2004) and other global taxation (Pogge, 1998; 2002) need to be discussed for their transformative impact, human rights implementation needs to be taken more seriously, and we need to reassess the development framework for transition countries and the rest of the majority world (Dower, in van den Anker, 2004).

A cosmopolitan approach would also contribute to the smaller-scale efforts of combating trafficking. Better regulation of travel agents (especially in Latin America where a lot of trafficking happens through these agencies), the provision of job opportunities and vocational skills training, the negotiation of living wages for families who would otherwise need to send their children out to work with the risk of them being trafficked or who would otherwise sell their children, support for reintegration packaged and permits to stay instead of deportation would all help present victims of trafficking as well as potential victims.

Conclusion

NGOs and international organisations recognise the need for policies on the prevention of trafficking in addition to combating trafficking through criminal justice proceedings against perpetrators and through supporting victims. The different approaches to prevention that have been put forward can be divided into two categories: short- and long-term prevention. The first includes awareness-raising of potential migrants, training of law enforcement officers and victim support in countries of destination and reintegration programmes for returned victims in order to prevent re-trafficking. The second includes the many calls for the recognition of gender inequality as one of the root causes of migration in general and of trafficking in particular. It also includes a few calls for a comprehensive approach to migration and for specific measures for development in poverty stricken areas. Most recently, the OSCE has proposed pursuing long-term prevention of trafficking by addressing social and economic factors in detailed recommendations (OSCE, 2003).

In this chapter I have argued that policymakers need to work towards long-term prevention in addition to the short-term measures. Yet, instead of focusing on only one of the root causes such as gender inequality, a more productive way forward would be to take a comprehensive, cosmopolitan approach which holds that the scope of justice is global and therefore all human beings are owed equal respect. The implications of a cosmopolitan approach to trafficking will shift the emphasis from combating trafficking through restricting migration and other forms of short-term prevention towards long-term prevention and an analysis of the complex set of major root causes such as the role of globalisation in increasing poverty, gender discrimination, racism and the discrimination of indigenous peoples and armed conflict, including the resulting presence of peacekeeping troops.

Many of these factors contribute to the causes of the recent increase in migration in general and of illegal migration in particular. Taking a cosmopolitan approach to trafficking will also help by strengthening the international protection of human rights which will play a role in the prevention of trafficking as well as in the attitude taken to victims of trafficking. Human rights violations contribute to the pressure to migrate and the protection of migrants' rights, especially rights to work and health and safety at work will make a real difference to the vulnerability of people to the potential power of traffickers over them. Furthermore, treating victims of trafficking as people whose human rights have been violated means the government of the country of destination has a duty to provide support rather than a right to deport them as illegal migrants. My version of a cosmopolitan approach would include respect for human rights, yet would also go beyond the human rights doctrine.

Although this suggestion may be met with the objection that a cosmopolitan approach is aiming for too much change at once, recent exchanges with NGOs and relevant UN officers underline the importance of addressing the long-term structural factors contributing to trafficking. Although there is some reference made in the international community to the need to address root causes of trafficking, long-term prevention programmes have not been developed and even short-term prevention projects are in their infancy. Moreover, short-term prevention programmes are not very effective. This chapter therefore proposes that all actors working to prevent trafficking in their policies, programmes and projects take cosmopolitanism seriously and start to address the short- and long-term prevention of trafficking as a concerted effort.

Finally, the reflection on the long-term prevention of trafficking through adopting a cosmopolitan approach is also helpful to the development of the cosmopolitan approach in international political theory. The pressure on cosmopolitanism is to provide more guidance to practical issues, institutional reform and policy-making. The example of trafficking requires us to think about where cosmopolitanism can be helpful and whether or not different versions of cosmopolitanism would lead to different sets of recommendations.

Notes

1. IOM presentation at NEWR workshop in Siena, November 2003.
2. Nina Strandberg and Carolina J Wennerholm, Stockholm, November 1999, Kvinnoforum/Foundation of Women's Forum. See also La Strada (1996) 'One Year la Strada, Results of the First Central and East European Program on Prevention of Traffic in Women', a report from the one year project (September 1995–September 1996) focusing on Poland, the Czech Republic and the Netherlands. Supported by the Dutch Foundation against Trafficking in Women (STV), the Young Women's Christian Association of Poland (YWCA), the Polish feminist Association (PSF) and the Central European Consulting Centre for Women's Projects Pro Fem.
3. La Strada publicity leaflet.
4. EWL http://www.womenlobby.org/document.asp?DocID=492 [Accessed 5 December 2003].
5. IOM London (http://www.iomlondon.org/docs/Oct%2002.pdf).
6. See E/CN.4/Sub.2/1995/28/Add.1.
7. http://wwwdb.europarl.eu.int/oeil/oeil_ViewDNL.ProcedureView? lang=2&procid=2546
8. Brussels Declaration on Preventing and Combating Trafficking in Human Beings.
    The European Conference on Preventing and Combating Trafficking in Human Beings – Global Challenge for the 21st Century – brought together, on 18–20 September 2002, the EU Member States, Candidate Countries, neighbouring countries such as Russia, the Ukraine, the NIS as well as US, Canada, China, regions, international organisations (IOs), inter-governmental organisations (IGOs), non governmental organisations (NGOs) and the institutions of the European Union. More than 1000 representatives of the above mentioned sectors participated.
9. On the role of peacekeeping forces in the market for trafficked women and girls see Firmo Fontan, in van den Anker (2004: 91–106).
10. States of the South Asian Association for Regional Cooperation (SAARC), Draft Convention on Preventing and Combating Trafficking in Women and Children for Prostitution: http://www.apcprocess.net/Publications/saarc_ draft_convention.htm#Article%20VIII%20-%20Measures% 20to%20Prevent%20Trafficking%20in%20Women%20and%20Children).
11. OSCE Decision no. 557 (24 July 2003): 1.
12. OSCE Decision no. 557 (24 July 2003): 8.

References

Anderson, B. and O'Connell Davidson, J. (2002) *Trafficking – A Demand-Led Problem?* Stockholm: Ministry of Foreign Affairs, SIDA and Save the Children Sweden.

Anti-Slavery International's Stop Human Traffic Campaign. Available at: http://
www.stophumantraffic.org/.

Anker, C. van den (2002) 'Global Justice, Global Institutions and Global
Citizenship', in N. Dower and J. Williams, *Global Citizenship*, Edinburgh:
Edinburgh University Press, pp. 158–68.

Anker, C. van den (2004) 'Contemporary Slavery, Global Justice and
Globalisation', in C. van den Anker (ed.), *The Political Economy of New Slavery*,
Basingstoke: Palgrave, pp. 15–36.

Anker, C. van den (2007) *Global Social Justice: A Cosmopolitan Theory*, Basingstoke:
Palgrave, forthcoming.

Anderson, B. (2004) 'Migrant Domestic Workers in Europe', in C. van den Anker
(ed.), *The Political Economy of New Slavery*, Basingstoke: Palgrave, pp. 107–17.

Bader, V. (ed.) (1997) *Citizenship and Exclusion*, Basingstoke: Macmillan.

Bunch, C. (1995) 'Transforming Human Rights from a Feminist Perspective', in
J. Peters and A. Wolper, *Women's Rights, Human Rights*, New York: Routledge.

Dormaels, A., Moens, B. and Praet, N. (2004) 'Anti-Trafficking Policies and
Support for Victims in Belgium and the European Union', in C. van den Anker
(ed.), *The Political Economy of New Slavery*, Basingstoke: Palgrave.

Dower, N. (2004) 'The Global Framework for Development: Instrumentality or
Contested Ethical Space?' in C. van den Anker (ed.), *The Political Economy of
New Slavery*, Basingstoke: Palgrave.

Dowling, E. (2004) 'Strategies for Change: The Tobin Tax', in C. van den Anker
(ed.), *The Political Economy of New Slavery*, Basingstoke: Palgrave, pp. 201–16.

Einhorn, B. (1996) 'Gender and Citizenship in East Central Europe after the End
of State Socialist Policies for Women's "Emancipation"', in B. Elnhorn,
M. Kaldor and Z. Kavan (eds.), *Citizenship and Democratic Control in
Contemporary Europe*, Cheltenham: Edward Elgar.

Firmo-Fontan, V. (2004) 'Post-conflict Increases in Human Trafficking: From the
Balkans to Afghanistan', in C. van den Anker (ed.), *The Political Economy of New
Slavery*, Basingstoke: Palgrave, pp. 91–106.

Held, D. (ed.) (2002) *Governing Globalisation. Power, Authority and Global
Governance*, Oxford: Polity.

Luckhoo, F. (2003) *Trafficking in the World Today: A Briefing*, London: CHANGE.

Manokha, I. (2004) 'Modern Slavery and Fair Trade Products: Buy One and Set
Someone Free', in C. van den Anker (ed.), *The Political Economy of New Slavery*,
Basingstoke: Palgrave, pp. 217–34.

Opzij (2004) 'Wij zijn geen zielige vrouwen meer' [We are no longer victims], 1: 82.

OSCE Decision no. 557 (24 July 2003).

Pearson, E. (2002) *Human Traffic, Human Rights, Redefining Victim Protection*,
London: Anti-Slavery International.

Pogge, T. (1998) 'A Global Resources Dividend', in David Crocker and T. Linden,
The Ethics of Consumption, Oxford: Rowman and Littlefield.

Pogge, T. (2002) *World Poverty and Human Rights: Cosmopolitan Responsibilities and
Reforms*, Cambridge: Polity.

Pradhan-Malla, S. (2001) 'Gender and Racism', in S. Feldman, *Discrimination and
Human Rights: The Case of Racism*, Oxford: Oxford University Press.

Rawls, J. (1999) *A Theory of Justice* (rev. edn.), Oxford: Oxford University Press.

Report of the Expert Group on Trafficking in Human Beings (2004) Brussels:
European Community.

Scholte, J. A. (2000) *Globalisation. A Critical Introduction*, Basingstoke: Palgrave.
Sen, A. (1999) *Development as Freedom*, Oxford: Oxford University Press.
Stiglitz, J. (2002) *Globalisation and its Discontents*, London: Allen Lane.
Van Bueren, G. (2004) 'Slavery as Piracy – A Legal Case for Reparations for Historical Slavery', in C. van den Anker (ed.), *The Political Economy of New Slavery*, Basingstoke: Palgrave, pp. 235–47.
Wilson, R. (ed.) (1997) *Human Rights, Culture and Context: Anthropological Perspectives*, London: Pluto.

11
The Globalisation, Migration and Trafficking Nexus: European Outcomes

Jeroen Doomernik

Introduction

Trafficking is often equated with the sexual exploitation of women (and sometimes children), and discussion surrounding the subject at times ends up in arguments about the (im)morality of prostitution, especially when the position is taken that prostitution by definition is exploitative in nature. In this contribution, our point of departure is not prostitution as such; rather, we want to explore to what extent vulnerability of certain people is produced or increased by the globalisation process. We shall demonstrate that among those people, females are particularly vulnerable and not at all just when they are sex workers. The ILO estimates that where women and girls make up 98 per cent of people in forced commercial sexual exploitation, 56 per cent of people in forced economic exploitation are women (ILO, 2005: 15).

It is undisputed by most observers that the globalisation process has a poorly charted reverse side when it comes to the international mobility of people. We shall briefly go over the main arguments in that respect. Subsequently, we shall address in more detail how and to what extent globalisation makes migrants vulnerable to various types of exploitation. Sexual exploitation is prominent among those, but is not by far the only way in which a migrant can find him/herself in slave-like conditions.

The United Nations in its Protocol to Prevent, Suppress and Punish Trafficking in Persons (a Protocol to the Convention against Transnational Organised Crime of 2000) defines trafficking in the following terms:

'Trafficking in persons' shall mean the recruitment, transportation, transfer, harboring or receipt of persons, by means of the threat or use of force or other forms of coercion, of abduction, of fraud, of deception,

of the abuse of power or of a position of vulnerability or of the giving
or receiving of payments or benefits to achieve the consent of a person having control over another person, for the purpose of exploitation. Exploitation shall include, at a minimum, the exploitation of
the prostitution of others or other forms of sexual exploitation,
forced labor or services, slavery or practices similar to slavery, servitude or the removal of organs ... (Article 3 of the Protocol)

It should be noted that this definition does not necessarily imply that a
victim is transported or has migrated across an international border.
Moreover, it is self-evident that 'exploitation' is not easily defined,
whereas it stands central to the UN's definition (see Van Liempt, this
volume). We have referred to the moral position in which prostitution
cannot be anything but of an exploitative nature (see Dickenson, this
volume). An argument along Marxist lines proposing all exchange of
labour for money to be exploitative in nature would likewise be defend-
able. It would appear, however, not to have been the UN's intention to
embrace such a line of reasoning, otherwise the phrase 'exploitation of
prostitution' would be tautological. In all other respects, however, the
definition suits the purpose of this chapter and so may be in order. To
pursue our exercise we should be willing to settle for a common-sense
approach to what constitutes exploitation and what does not, accepting
that between clear cases at each extreme there is a grey area.

Globalisation

One could argue that globalisation can be traced back to Christopher
Columbus' discovery of the Americas and the colonial occupation that
followed, or to the seventeenth-century United Dutch East Indian
Company which can be considered as the first 'global' company. As
Stone (2003) argues, globalisation is not necessarily something new in
kind but rather in degree. Without going into the most apt definition of
what globalisation entails today, what appears to be uncontroversial is
that it goes hand in hand with, or perhaps even is more or less the same
as, increasing mobility. Capital faces few boundaries and can be trans-
ferred from one end of the globe to the other almost instantaneously.
The same applies to information: few inhabited places are without television or radio; the Internet has rapidly become more than just a toy for
a few computer-literates and enables the free exchange of opinions and
information virtually unfettered by censorship.[1] The capitalist mode of
production has hardly any rival left and its products are no longer

bound to geographical constraints. Formally speaking a US company, Nike, produces its shoes in South East Asia; Japanese and German cars are made in Britain; many Fuji films stem from the Netherlands; and one should not forget the global presence of Pepsi or Coca Cola. The fact that business has become global not only creates increasing streams of products, it also necessitates the mobility of managers, all kinds of specialists, and of those persons who actually transport these people as well as the products. In addition, for many highly skilled workers it has become a fact of life that their occupation implies a fair amount of travel: to conferences, business meetings, exchange programmes and such. In the aeroplanes they fly, the rows at the back are crowded with tourists who likewise take frequent trips to faraway (and warm) places for granted. These are all *direct* – and usually applauded – consequences of globalisation.

However, there are also a number of *indirect* consequences that are not necessarily recognised. Restricting ourselves to mobility, this was true in Columbus' times, when 'trading' meant that indigenous peoples were exposed to deadly viruses brought from Europe and subsequently were superseded by European settlers. That the slave trade meant creating entirely new societal realities in countries of origin and of destination in the Americas in all likelihood entered no one's mind at the time. The same can be said about the coolie trade, which followed slavery's abolition, which in name was free labour migration but in practice amounted to bonded labour preventing many from returning home. What to all intends and purposes was supposed to be temporary in effect led to the establishment of Chinese and other Asian communities in numerous non-Asian countries. We should also recognise that much post-war immigration from Latin America, Asia and Africa to France, the Netherlands or the United Kingdom, for example, could only take place because at an earlier stage these states had colonised other continents. Many similar such unforeseen effects of globalisation are with us today.

For one, globalisation seems to have done little to induce global economic convergence, i.e. to reduce the discrepancies between per capita incomes in the highly industrialised world and those in the developing world. In most instances the gap between the two has increased rather than decreased. At the same time several processes can be observed to be taking place in many poorer regions of the world: while improved medical care has greatly reduced the mortality rate, especially among children, taken with high fertility rates this produces extremely 'young' populations and rapid population growth. Where subsistence farming in rural areas only a few decades ago could sustain large parts of the population, this is no longer the case partly because of the population growth, and partly because traditional modes of production have been replaced by cash crops. The latter, furthermore, means vulnerability to fluctuations in world market prices for such products as coffee, rice and drugs. It also often means depletion of natural resources (e.g. fertile lands and water). Compounded with this are incomplete processes of state formation in many parts of the post-colonial world (Westin, 1999). In these circumstances political unrest easily erupts or can even lead to the ethnic strife the world has witnessed during the past decade.

As one outcome of these processes most Third World countries are faced with rapid urbanisation in the form of young men and women hoping to find employment and housing not available to them in rural areas. Already, most of the world's largest cities are located in the developing rather than in the industrialised regions. Even though these cities form the economic nucleus of countries, they fail to offer meaningful employment or suitable housing to most newcomers. Rapidly growing shantytowns are the most visible sign, as are growing informal economies and increased female labour market participation. The latter is related to the lagging employment opportunities in agriculture – traditionally an economic sector in which female labour played an important yet almost invisible role – to ever-increasing populations (male and female), and, closely related, economic diversification as household survival strategies. Examples of such diversification are migration to the city or abroad *and* increased reliance on the waged labour of the female members of the household in as far as these are not needed for the household's day-to-day reproduction. In this light it is not surprising to see that the proportion of females among the world's migrants (including refugees) has been increasing steadily (Lim, 1998; Zlotnik, 2003). Migration to the industrialised nations is further fuelled by the lack of opportunities for many, resulting from the economic and political transition in the former Soviet Union and its satellite states during the early 1990s. The proportion of females among these migrants is also high but this is less unexpected because the labour market participation rate for women in those countries was already almost on a par with that of men when the transition set in.

Regular versus irregular migration

Not only is there an increase in emigration potential in many of the less developed countries, globalisation also impacts on the demand for certain types of labour, at home and abroad. This demand is not only differentiated according to skill levels but is also gender-specific (Moghadam, 2000). As we will see, female migrants are more likely to end up in situations in which they are vulnerable to exploitation than men.

Classic labour migration is made up by men who move abroad (or at any rate away from their trusted environment) to earn higher wages than those available domestically. Often such movements are cyclical in nature either because they are directly related to the seasons (crops that need harvesting) or to fluctuations in the demand for certain products. Migration can also be temporary without being tied to the seasons and span several uninterrupted years because a certain goal is set (like saving enough to set up a business, building a house) and the migrant intends to return once it has been reached. The latter type of temporality easily turns into more or less permanent migration (the intention to return can last a lifetime) as saving is often more difficult than originally expected. Living expenses in the country of temporary resettlement in such cases were often left out of the equation. Large outflows of temporary migrants can, moreover, change the conditions locally to such an extent that return migration is not easy. Examples include where families become dependent on the remittances from abroad or such remittances cause local inflation, undermining the prospect of successful investment of savings. The extension of the residence abroad following from these processes sets in motion a process of chain migration of persons joining this 'first generation' of labour migrants, constituted at first by spouses and children and later also others. It is usually at this stage that receiving governments impose immigration restrictions as secondary migration is not necessarily economically welcome. This was markedly the case in West European states that pursued 'guest-worker' policies (e.g. Germany and the Netherlands). If such migration is allowed, it usually is because human rights regimes exert their influence, like those enshrined in the European Convention on Human Rights. There are limits, however, to the extent to which states are willing to grant rights on the basis of such international legal instruments.[2] In effect, soon the potential or actual candidates for (temporary) migration to such countries surpass the numbers states are willing to allow in. On the one hand, many prospective migrants will be restrained by the lack of opportunity to move legally to another country. Others may have such compelling reasons to move that they do so without formal permission.

Among the migrants with strong reasons to move are asylum seekers and refugees. Whereas massive labour migration to Europe is currently first and foremost to the Mediterranean countries (especially Italy and Spain), further north uninvited migrants often ask for asylum.[3] During the 1990s asylum seekers have been in the news on an almost permanent basis and in almost all West European countries. Applications for asylum in the EU were highest in 1992 (notably in Germany) when they reached 675,000 and lowest in 1997 when they totalled 250,000. Since then the figures have fluctuated (see Figure 11.1). In 2003 applications came close to 300,000.

Generally speaking, the response to this varying yet always sizeable number was and is characterised by a sense of urgency and panic – not so much because of the scale of the humanitarian problem these asylum requests imply but by the feeling of being out of control. When migrants invoke the international obligations states have towards certain categories of non-nationals, first and foremost among them refugees, in the hope of gaining legal entry and residence in a country this inherently is at odds with a state's claims to sovereignty over its borders and territory. For it is not on the basis of domestic considerations that these foreigners should be admitted, but on the basis of universally

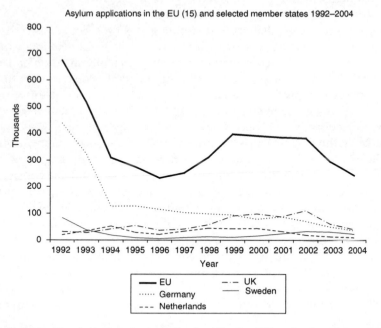

Figure 11.1 Number of asylum applications in the EU and selected countries 1992–2003

Source: UNHCR statistics (www.unhcr.ch)

valid criteria which the receiving state should apply to all, regardless of the number of people involved. Especially the latter aspect tends to make officials nervous and has led to attempts to keep potential asylum applicants from arriving in the first place. Welfare states moreover face the problem that admitting newcomers who are (at first) not able to provide for themselves creates 'free rider' problems.

Governments, first among them the German, took two distinct measures: 'stemming the flow' (an analogy frequently invoked by government officials and taken up in the media) and making legal procedures more efficient. The first response consisted of stronger border controls, more visa requirements and the 'shifting out' (Guiraudon, 2001) of control functions to private partners, notably airline companies and other carriers by imposing sanctions for bringing in migrants without proper documentation and/or as stowaways. Together, these measures are meant to reinforce what some observers call 'Fortress Europe'. The second type of response again can be subdivided into two distinct policy instruments: on the one hand, the designation of certain countries as safe, either as countries of origin or as third countries, and on the other, by simplifying the adjudication process. The former measure serves to classify asylum application as unfounded (when the individual stems from a 'safe country') or inadmissible (when the applicant has passed through a safe third country where he already would have been able to apply for asylum). This step, which was first set by the German government, had an immediate effect on the number of asylum applications in Germany: they fell dramatically from 438,000 in 1992 to 127,000 in 1994) It also had clear effects elsewhere: in neighbouring countries the numbers of applications showed a steep increase. These countries thus saw little alternative but to adopt Germany's measures.

In 1997 the Dublin Convention came into force, which aimed to prevent states shifting the burden onto each other by clear rules as to which signatory state was responsible for any particular asylum application. This has resulted in a system whereby asylum seekers are returned to the member state where they first set foot if they apply in second country that is party to the Dublin Convention (which today is integral part of EU law and referred to as the Dublin regulations). In so far as this may mean that an asylum seeker does not necessarily apply for and find asylum in the country he may have preferred, this is not an ideal outcome of these defensive measures but it does not cause great concern when the issue of protection as such is at stake. This is different when no due process is guaranteed during the asylum procedure. Although states are likely to deny any such allegations, there are clear signs that some of them (the Netherlands is a case in point) are on the verge of violating human rights principles or have already crossed that line.[4] The author interviewed a female asylum seeker from Sierra Leone (who had fled after a prolonged period of being a sex-slave to a rebel group) who had been dismissed from the asylum adjudication process within 48 working hours on the grounds that her account of how she had reached the Netherlands was incredible.[5] Rejection thus took place on technical grounds without the substance of the claim being examined. Her case is not unique: it is the explicit goal of the Dutch government to reject as many asylum requests as possible at the earliest possible stage. Of course, the Dutch case cannot completely be taken as *pars pro* European *toto* as policies between countries do vary. Yet current policies are possible only because they fit in with the general trend towards asylum policies that are formulated, interpreted and implemented as sparingly as possible.

The effects of a declining willingness to accommodate uprooted migrants in Europe are twofold: it becomes more difficult to reach Europe and cross its borders due to increased investments in Fortress Europe, and by having uncompromising asylum policies those who have penetrated the EU's borders are left to fend for themselves as undocumented migrants. We shall return to the consequences below.

Much less noted is migration of the highly skilled. Their mobility is part of the front side of the globalisation process. It is generally recognised that highly skilled workers are vital to the growth of western economies and most governments actively encourage such migrants to settle (or at any rate do not actively try to keep them from doing so) (De Lange *et al.*, 2003). These migrants usually settle in the major cities and not least in those Sassen (1991, 1996) calls 'global cities': the financial hubs of the modern world, such as New York, Tokyo, London, Paris and Amsterdam. Much less recognised or at least acknowledged is the demand for low-skilled labour that goes hand in hand with this growing presence of an urban elite of highly paid and highly time-poor people; e.g. dog walking, shopping, cleaning, (child) care, personal assistance, catering and cooking. Sassen's global cities may be typical cases yet it seems safe to assume that they are not unique in that such polar labour demands can be found in many if not all urban areas – i.e. the demand for highly skilled, and thus well-paid and secure employment on the one hand, and unskilled, low-paid, insecure and flexible work on the other.

Highly organised welfare states especially have a problematic relationship with demands for unskilled labour as it can be met only by unregulated, unorganised labour. People with a claim to social security and unemployment benefits – the natural labour reserve in such states – can hardly be mobilised to fulfil the three D's (dirty, dangerous and difficult) jobs in a regular fashion but at the same time the goal to integrate these people into the labour market is of considerable political importance. In effect, states may turn a blind eye to the employment of people who (also) claim benefits, irregular migrants and rejected asylum seekers. They all find a role for themselves in the grey zones of the modern industrialised state. For obvious reasons (see Wylie, this volume) precise numbers are unknown but we can safely assume that the numbers of irregular residents in *all* European urban centres are sizeable[6] and growing; depending though on the ability and willingness of governments to regularise undocumented workers in a number of Mediterranean countries – something which we have seen is difficult for welfare states. This does not necessarily make migrants less vulnerable to exploitation by employers and others.[7] It should be added that there is a difference in the extent to which such migrants are visible or come to the attention of the authorities in order to be regularised. Especially live-in care workers are at risk of remaining unprotected if they are confined within the walls of the home they serve. Due to the nature of the work and the gender-biased expectations of many employers as to who is most suitable to perform these duties, these domestics are more often females, whose vulnerability to (sexual) abuse is particularly large.

Vulnerability and exploitation

Trafficking can start at home; it can also result from being in an irregular position after migration has taken place. In so far as trafficking means being kidnapped, taken across borders by force (e.g. hidden in a vehicle) or being deceived about the true purpose of the migration and subsequent being enslaved, the risks the victim is exposed to are easily imagined. This, not surprisingly, is what people fear and loath most, and think about first when trafficking comes to mind. Because these are common notions, we should perhaps limit ourselves to underline the fact that women especially are the victims of such *prima facie* cases of trafficking and try to explore less obvious instances of slave like relationships resulting from or related to international migration.

First of all, we should be aware of cases where migrants have no alternative but to use the 'services' of traffickers. Women who seek employment abroad – for instance, but not necessarily as prostitutes – may well be aware of the nature of the relationship they are entering into and take an unfair share of the profits as unavoidable part of the deal. From such a situation, however, can also arise one in which a female migrant is exploited beyond her expectations. She has to work longer hours; perform acts she would not normally engage in; is held prisoner; is battered or otherwise abused; or is not rewarded with even a minimal share of the profits she generates.

Second, there are those migrants who wittingly enter into debt bondage with smugglers who can pass them from their country of origin and/or into a desired country of destination; either because they have to flee persecution or because they are seeking a better life. Examples of the latter are well documented by Chin (1999) in his study of Fujian Chinese who are smuggled into Manhattan to work in sweatshops.

Slavery-like relationships can also come into being (long) after the migration as such has taken place. It should have become clear that those migrants who are in an irregular situation as a result are often also labelled illegal migrants, and depend for their survival on interactions with those who are regular residents of immigrant origin and on natives. These persons may well be willing, either because they are close relatives or friends, or because they simply are decent people. Yet, such relationships of dependency – especially if not between spouses or close relatives – are unlikely to last indefinitely. In such instances the moment comes when reciprocity to some extent is called for. Staring (2001) shows how, among the Turkish community of Rotterdam, solidarity is extended to irregular compatriots but the pressure on those migrants to compensate for this solidarity gradually mounts or forces them to seek support elsewhere. As a rule this means that the migrant looks for employment, usually again through his co-ethnics, but given his irregular position often ends up working long hours for little pay. Not uncommon are sweatshop-like working conditions. To the migrants this may not necessarily seem unreasonable if this is the means to an end (e.g. saving in order to return home). Chin (1999) found that the migrants from Fujian are even willing to repay debts as high as $80,000, something they knew was expected of them before embarking. So even instances which common sense would define as extremely exploitative can be acceptable to migrants who know what they are letting themselves in for, and expect hardship to last for an agreed period of time. That the migrant is prepared to engage in such a deal in all likelihood is only possible precisely because exploitation takes place within the confines of an ethnic network. For this sets natural boundaries to the exploitation. After all, if the exploiters are known, they need to be able to pretend there is a certain legitimacy to their enterprises lest no new clients come forward, or more 'benevolent' competition takes over. Fulfilling expectations is expected from both sides, however, and probably is more easily enforceable within ethnic networks. In late February 2004, for instance, two Chinese students were found murdered in Oslo, presumably because they had failed to pay their debts. This crime apparently was such a breach of an informal contract that four other Chinese in a similar position sought (and were granted) police protection (*Migration News*, March 2004: 8).

Even if ethnic familiarity not always and by definition protects migrants from unexpected abuse, unrelenting and merciless exploitation is much more likely to occur when victim and trafficker have little in common. In such more anonymous contexts, situations can much more easily arise like those alluded to earlier where a sex worker finds herself in circumstances much worse than she had bargained for. Migrants who are uprooted as a consequence of the globalisation process by and large stem from different countries from those migrants who can count on older, established, ethnic networks in many countries of destination: the Turks, the North Africans, migrants settled after the end of the colonial era in countries like France, Britain or the Netherlands. Currently, unsolicited migrants come from almost all underdeveloped countries and we can expect to meet them in virtually all cities in the industrialised world. This enormous diversification in migration patterns of the last decade or so can mainly be attributed to the changing nature of the intermediary structures that connect countries of origin to those of destination (Doomernik, 2004; Doomernik and Kyle, 2004; Van Amersfoort and Doomernik, 1998). Where these previously lent considerable predictability to migration flows, this is no longer the case. This is the result of the growing involvement of travel agents (or human smugglers) in the movement of unsolicited migrants. On the basis of a whole range of considerations – among which possible preferences for a certain destination of their clients is only one – they decide where a migrant ends up. Added to that come interventions of the receiving states aimed at curbing such immigration which tend to dislocate migrants in yet another way: they may interfere before the final destination selected by the agent is reached. Examples are migrants who end up in the 'wrong' country as a result of the Dublin principle outlined earlier, or who are stranded outside Fortress Europe in such cities as Kiev, Bucharest or Istanbul for an indefinite period.

In those instances in which a migrant ends up living irregularly in a foreign city without the potential support of a well-established ethnic network, exploitation looms around every corner. Accommodation is likely to mean sharing a room (or even a bed) with strangers who are in a similar situation. The buildings used for these purposes may well be below standard in terms of basic hygiene and fire safety. Rents will follow their own free market logic of high demand among uncomplaining clients and low supply. When it comes to employment the same logic applies. Without trusted contacts an undocumented migrant depends on agents who will negotiate between the demands for labour in the shadowy parts of the Western dual economy and the supply of exploitative labour. These agents can reap the benefits of selling labour on the basis of prices approaching those negotiated on the regular market, whereas the wages paid are based on the competition for jobs between people without rights. If the migrant can negotiate wages with an employer directly his or her position may be stronger. Yet we also know of cases in which employers refuse to pay (part of) the agreed wages on the basis of some excuse and threaten to inform on the migrant in case he pursues his claims for full payment.

Migrants in an irregular position may also find housing or employment without the help of an agent, for instance through chance meetings with other migrants who have relevant contacts. The extent of the networks they can tap into in this way tends to be very limited. In general people know best others who are similar in terms of class, ethnicity, legal position and neighbourhood. Those without rights thus tend to be acquainted with others who are living on the margins of society. In addition, they may establish useful contacts through advertisements in local newspapers, on notes distributed through private letterboxes, shop windows and on advertisement boards in supermarkets offering cleaning work, sexual services or odd jobs. This may enable them to stay alive and afloat, but is unlikely to yield a stable basis on which to build a future. Yet these people are not likely to return to their country of origin. Not even forceful removal will be very effective as long as a migrant has not been able at least partly to fulfil the goals which inspired the move abroad. The extent to which third parties are involved in this migration process – be it smugglers or traffickers – has a highly significant impact on the outcome. Needing smugglers requires investments, running into traffickers or otherwise being exposed to exploitative circumstances by definition means losing out economically. Both have a detrimental effect by frustrating the achievement of the migrants' goals and thus potentially create a growing army of destitute people reproducing their own poverty and exploitation.

Trafficking?

We started this chapter with a general notion of trafficking being the exploitation of a person's (usually a migrant's) labour. On the one hand, this helped us to identify many instances of human rights abuse, or at any rate situations in which a migrant's human rights are threatened that would otherwise remain insufficiently noted. On the other hand, putting all the (possible) exploitative practices under the single, catch-all definition of *trafficking* can make us insensitive to the many diverse forms the phenomenon can take and the degree of exploitation it entails. Exploitation may mean not getting paid without recourse to the law, but also includes instances where exploitation goes as far as being without regard for human dignity or even human life. However, one could argue that it is unethical and thus fundamentally inadmissible to differentiate between one human rights abuse and another – there can be no hierarchy in suffering. On the other hand, we find those, like Frederick (1998), who do attempt to do these nuances justice. He has coined the terms *hard* trafficking and *soft* trafficking. Soft trafficking is reserved for instances where exploitation takes place as part of a family or household survival strategy. Parents may agree to their daughters being taken to a big city to be prostituted. For our purpose perhaps we might extend the meaning of soft trafficking to those forms of exploitation that take place within the context of an ethnic community. The term hard trafficking is reserved to those instances where anonymous perpetrators violate the dignity and human rights of (usually) females and children (usually) employed in prostitution. This brings us back to older (pre-Protocol) definitions. Dutch penal law, for instance, until recently spoke of trafficking only if it concerned exploitation for prostitution. In the past, combating precisely this has had priority with law enforcement authorities and arguably it should have as it seems to address the most burning issues. However, we should consider the possibility that even then, the crime is not what it seems. Consider the following:

The Hague's Hollands Spoor railway station, Winter 2000. The author takes a taxi to arrive well in time to present a lecture on migration and security. He engages the driver, a scruffy, middle-aged man, in a conversation on the new rules issued by the government on licence plates for the taxi branch to prevent fraud. For some reason this prompts the driver to remark on a highly profitable deal he has made to drive three female customers to Ukraine.

A.: *But that's a very long trip. Why don't these ladies fly?*
D.: *Because they have too much luggage. I'll fix a trailer to the back of my car and that way it'll all fit in nicely.*
A.: *But this is a very expensive car you're driving. Aren't you afraid it will be nicked in that part of the world?*

D.: *Nope. I go there quite regularly. In fact, I have a girlfriend in Poland whose father is high up in the police force. Once I have crossed the border, he gets me Polish licence plates. No bother. And I have another girlfriend, she's from Slovakia. Her family lives in a small village where everybody knows everybody else. I can't remember the name of the place. Can you decipher it? [hands the passport of young woman to his passenger]. I only have that passport because I needed to get something at the post-office.* [At this point, the taxi has to stop at traffic lights, next to a small van with the insignia of the Dutch Justice Department.]

A.: *What kind of van could that possibly be? Looks like a cool box on wheels.*

D.: *Ah, that's heading for the prison at Scheveningen. My mate could be in there. He faces a three-year imprisonment.*

A.: *He must have been up to no good then!*

D.: *In this country you can kill someone sooner than evade taxation. He has these two Ukrainian girls working for him, and someone has convinced them that if they file charges against my mate for trafficking they will get a residence permit. But that's all complete nonsense. These girls have contracts but they've torn them up and now pretend things were done wrongly. I know:I myself have two girls working for me. I go to Ukraine, we make a proper contract, she works six days a week for two years, one month a year she gets off, I pay for her housing and medical care and we split what she earns 50–50. That's fair, isn't it? The babushka sits next to her at the table and I slip her some money too, and that's it.*

But these two girls – you just wait and see, I'll get them to retract their statement.

What this example demonstrates quite clearly is that this taxi driver-cum-pimp has no idea, or at any rate no sense, of acting outside the law by importing foreign prostitutes and having them work for him. He does implicitly concede that he does not pay taxes and levies for them but to him (and many other 'law-abiding' citizens) that is no more than a petty offence, not something that should be punishable with several years' imprisonment. This goes to show that laws and regulations are effective only in preventing undesirable events if the people concerned know the laws, and, even more importantly, recognise them as legitimate and relevant.

Of course, we have no means of knowing whether this unwitting interviewee was telling the truth about this case. On the other hand, it would seem safe to assume that such voluntary arrangements exist, for it makes practical sense.

Having said that, instances have been reported where girls from Western Africa have arrived in Europe (e.g. through the Dutch asylum procedure) who ended up being sold from brothel to brothel and country to country. They appear to have known that they would be working as prostitutes but not that they were to lead a life of complete dependency on their 'owners'.

One could argue that more police intervention and state regulation could be a remedy against trafficking, but some caution is justified. In the Netherlands prostitution has recently been legalised and recognised as a regular profession. The advantage for Dutch prostitutes is that they now have the full protection of the law against pimps and others, in return for which they pay taxes and licences. The legalisation, however, also made it necessary for brothel owners to check whether their employees are legal residents and have a valid work permit. Large numbers of prostitutes did not meet these criteria and therefore could no longer 'normally' (where the practice formerly was more or less tolerated) work. It is generally believed that these prostitutes have not given up their work but have moved into the much less visible escort service branch or work in closed and hidden brothels. This would appear to make them considerably more vulnerable to extortion by their pimps and abuse by clients, bringing them into trafficking-like situations – a somewhat paradoxical outcome of the legalisation process.

In conclusion

We have seen that certain categories of people are clearly more vulnerable to exploitation and at risk of ending up in slavery-like working conditions than others: women, migrants and – above all – female migrants. Industrialised and post-industrial economies in particular have a considerable demand for cheap, flexible, compliant workers. Irregular migrants fit these demands perfectly. The sectors in which these demands are much in evidence are gender-biased and as far as demand for female labour is concerned it is first and foremost located in the personal service sector – sex work or domestic services in and around households. If these services cannot be provided on a legal basis, the workers run the risk of being virtually invisible and unprotected from abuse. Whether the demand side can be meaningfully addressed is difficult to answer. At the very minimum the rights of migrants should be strengthened, e.g. by granting them residence and work permits, thus bringing them under the protection of the law.

In some European countries undocumented migrants have a better chance of regularising their situation than in others. The north-western European welfare states tend to pursue much more rigid, not to say binary, policies than the Mediterranean countries. The latter traditionally expect their government not to be omnipotent and omnipresent and many spheres of their societies, in effect, are accepted as being informally organised. But this tends to go against the grain of the welfare states. With the arrival of growing numbers of unsolicited migrants these have tended to close their doors – externally, but arguably even more significantly internally. The reasoning is that either you are in and enjoy full citizenship rights, or you are out and have no rights at all. This principle can only hope to be effective in discouraging migrants from arriving if this binary logic is complemented with no possibility *ever* of regularisation.

Even though we have argued that regularisation does not necessarily mean the end of exploitation, here lies the only option open to governments (of welfare states and *laissez faire* states alike) if they recognise it as in their interest to protect migrants from falling prey to unscrupulous exploiters, and thus putting people in a vicious circle which may spiral down to situations we might label as *hard* trafficking.

As far as *hard* trafficking is concerned, it would be stating the obvious to say that it requires repressive responses. The caveat to that would be that instances might easily arise that do correspond to the *legal* definition of a criminal act, but do not necessarily pose a serious problem in terms of *sociological* reality. The necessary attention to law enforcement should also not obscure the facts that cause trafficking to occur: the perpetrators 'only' exploit the vulnerability resulting from far-reaching and long-term processes that require their own patient responses. These are to be found in the domains of economic growth, development policies and due attention to basic human security (see also van den Anker, this volume).

Notes

1. Although there are some states that do try to restrict access to certain parts of the Internet.
2. Yet only where such regimes are not applied (or at any rate not deemed applicable to non-nationals), secondary migration can and often is effectively made impossible. Examples are found in labour-importing countries in the Middle East (Saudi Arabia and Jordan, for example) (van Amersfoort and Doomernik, 1998).
3. It is not easy to establish whether people in need of protection prefer to move to north-western Europe because it offers better refugee protection regimes, or people apply for asylum because – unlike in southern Europe where irregular

labour migrants can hope to be regularised – there are few other routes to a residence permit.

4. See, for instance, Human Rights Watch's comments on current Dutch refugee policies at http://www.hrw.org/reports/2003/netherlands0403/ [Accessed 22 June 2004]. The United Kingdom too can be seriously criticised: http://www.hrw.org/press/2003/09/uk092203.htm (also 22 June 2004).

5. Her story was that she had arrived at Rotterdam harbour as a stowaway, a story very commonly told by asylum seekers from western Africa but one which does not fit in with the authorities' general assessment of how asylum seekers usually arrive.

6. Jandl (2004), for instance, finds indications for an additional 1–1.5 per cent undocumented residents in addition to the regular population in a number of European countries.

7. In fact, reports in *Migration News* provide illustrative examples. The April 2004 issue reports a Spanish court refusing to protect a Colombian female migrant on the grounds that irregularities in working conditions are normal practice in Spain, for migrants and nationals alike. The March issue of that year documents the exploitation of Portuguese workers in the Netherlands (and earlier in the UK). Significantly, Portuguese workers, as citizens of an EU member state, are legally present.

References

Amersfoort, H. van and Doomernik, J. (eds) (1998) *International Migration. Processes and Interventions*, Amsterdam: Het Spinhuis.

Chin, K. (1999) *Smuggled Chinese: Clandestine Immigration to the United States*, Philadelphia: Temple University Press.

Doomernik, J. (2004) 'Migration and Security: The Wrong End of the Stick?' in C. van den Anker (ed.), *The Political Economy of New Slavery*, Basingstoke: Palgrave, pp. 37–52.

Doomernik, J. and Kyle, D. J. (guest eds.) (2004) 'Introduction', *Journal of International Migration and Integration* (special issue on Organised Migrant Smuggling and State Control: Conceptual and Policy Challenges), 5(3).

Frederick, J. (1998) 'Deconstructing Gita', *HIMAL: The South Asia Magazine*, 11(10), October.

Guiraudon, V. (2001) 'De-Nationalizing Control. Analyzing State Responses to Constraints on Migration Control', in V. Guiraudon and C. Joppke (eds.), *Controlling a New Migration World*, London and New York: Routledge.

ILO (2005) *A Global Alliance against Forced Labour*. Global Report under the Follow-up to the ILO Declaration on Fundamental principles and Rights at Work, Geneva: ILO.

Jandl, M. (2004) 'The Estimation of Illegal Migration in Europe', *Studi Emigrazione/Migration Studies*, XLI(153): 141–55.

Lim, L. L. (1998) 'The Processes Generating the Migration of Women', paper for the UN Technical Symposium on International Migration and Development, The Hague, 29 June–3 July.

Lange, T. de, Verbeek, S., Cholewinski, R. and Doomernik, J. (2003) *Arbeidsmigratie naar Nederland. Regulering en demografische en economische aspecten in internationaal vergelijk*, Den Haag: Adviescommissie Vreemdelingenzaken.

Moghadam, V. M. (2000) 'Economic Restructuring and the Gender Contract', in M. H. Marchand and A. Sisson Runyan (eds.), *Gender and Global Restructuring. Sightings, Sites and Resistances*, London and New York: Routledge, pp. 99–128.

Sassen, S. (1991) *The Global City: New York, London, Tokyo*, Princeton, NJ: Princeton University Press.

Sassen, S. (1996) *Losing Control? Sovereignty in an Age of Globalisation*, New York: Colombia University Press.

Staring, R. (2001) *Reizen onder Regie. Het migratieproces van illegale Turken in Nederland*, Amsterdam: Het Spinhuis.

Stone, J. (2003) 'Globalization and the Future of International Migration', in J. Doomernik and H. Knippenberg (eds.) *Migration and Immigrants: Between Policy and Reality*, Amsterdam: Aksant, pp. 121–33.

Weston, C. (1999) 'Regional Analysis of Refugee Movements: Origins and Response', in A. Ager (ed.) *Refugees: Perspectives on the Experience of Forced Migration*, London: Cassell, pp. 24–45.

Zlotnik, H. (2003) 'The Global Dimensions of Female Migration', *Migration Information Source* (web-based documentation centre provided by the Migration Policy Institute, Washington, DC).

12

Trafficking for Exploitation Outside the Sex Industry

Heleen de Jonge van Ellemeet and Monika Smit

Introduction

Although slavery has long been officially abolished in all countries, it still exists today. People are being transported across borders or within countries with the intention of exploiting them. These practices are currently most often referred to as trafficking in human beings (THB). Where THB was initially associated especially or exclusively with women and with exploitation in the sex industry, a wider interpretation is increasingly gaining ground. Males are also known to be exploited in the sex industry, while men, women and children are being exploited in other economic areas as well. Rightly, therefore, the definition of THB in the UN Trafficking Protocol[1] covers trafficking for the purpose of exploitation in both the sex industry and other work situations, and additionally trafficking for the removal of body parts for transplantation.

In the Netherlands, the national criminal legislation on THB was broadened on 1 January 2005. This in turn implied a broadening of the area on which the reports of the Dutch National Rapporteur on THB and her bureau (BNRM), which have the task of collecting information on THB and reporting to the Dutch government, including recommendations on the fight against THB, should focus.[2]

In order to explore this newly acknowledged realm of THB, this chapter focuses on exploitation in work situations outside the sex industry ('other forms of exploitation'), particularly in the Netherlands. But first we touch on two possibly confusing matters in defining and tackling THB.

Two possibly confusing matters in defining and tackling THB

Although significant, it is not always easy to make a distinction between trafficking on the one hand, and human smuggling and prostitution on the other. Here we discuss each in turn.

Trafficking and smuggling

There is a tendency to regard THB as a form of illegal immigration and to confuse it with human smuggling. Although both phenomena can be regarded as undesirable consequences of globalisation, and although both traffickers and smugglers of human beings exploit people's desire to improve their lives by building a better future for themselves elsewhere, there are also fundamental differences (see also ILO, 2005; Shelley, 2003). Smuggling concerns assisting people to enter or stay in another country illegally. It involves, first and fore-most, compromising a state's territorial integrity. It may be that a smuggled person is subsequently exploited, in order to pay for the journey, for instance, but this need not necessarily be the case. Furthermore, the transport and accommodation organised for the smuggled person may be so dangerous or degrading that he or she could be regarded as a victim whose human rights have been violated, but again this need not necessarily be the case. Whenever the 'voluntary' agreement between a human smuggler and the party smuggled is the result of deception, or involves high debts, and leads (directly or indirectly) to forced labour, the smuggling case becomes a trafficking case. THB is in itself and by definition a serious violation of the funda-mental rights and personal integrity of the person being trafficked. It often involves cross-border activities, but this is not an essential fea-ture. The essence of THB is exploitation, the abuse of people in the pur-suit of profit, by way of violence, threats, deception or the abuse of the victim's vulnerable position, as a result of which his or her freedom to choose is considerably restricted. It is a form of modern slavery. The protocols supplementing the UN Convention against Transnational Organised Crime also make this distinction between human smug-gling and human trafficking. Whereas the Smuggling Protocol[3] refers to the smuggling of migrants, the Trafficking Protocol refers to the traf-ficking of victims. And in the most recent proposal for a European Union Council Directive dealing with trafficking and smuggling, a similar distinction is made.

Trafficking and prostitution

The fight against THB for sexual exploitation is often confused with the battle that some wage against prostitution. They regard not only THB but all prostitution as a form of violence (generally against women) and as a form of slavery that needs to be combated or even criminalised. In this (abolitionist or prohibitionist) view, the phenomenon of prostitution is lumped together with the one of THB (Agustín, 2001). Countries or authors who do not seek a solution to the problem of THB by prohibiting the buying and selling of sexual services are criticised, often using suggestive or incorrect information (BNRM, 2005).

However, there are disadvantages associated with a repressive approach to prostitution in the fight against trafficking. Opponents of such an approach take the view that it is precisely the criminalisation that plays into the hands of criminal and exploitative networks in the sex industry (see, for example, Sörensen, 2003). They feel that prostitution continues regardless of criminalisation, while at the same time sex workers are being stigmatised, criminalised or – because their clients could be prosecuted – marginalised. Moreover, they have to solicit their clients in secret, which makes their work more dangerous (e.g. Boonen, 2000L 47; Östergren, 2003).[4]

The reverse of the prohibitionist or abolitionist approach is the labourist approach. Labourists take the view that not all (migrant) prostitutes are victims of THB (see e.g. Butcher, 2003; Gülçür and Ilkkaracan, 2002). They regard prostitution as work and a prostitute not as a victim, at least not by definition (see also Boonen, 2000; Verhoeven, 2003), but as a person competent to act for herself. According to labourists, the essence of THB and forced prostitution is that, within the context of a labour situation, a person's freedom to choose is violated. The fact that it concerns prostitution is less relevant. Labourists seek solutions to THB in improvements in the conditions under which prostitutes live and work, and a strengthening of their legal position (Haveman, 1998; Loff *et al.*, 2003), for example by regulating the sex industry.

Whatever position one takes in the debate, it is important not to devote too much energy to the debate itself, all the more since the study by a Norwegian working group on the legal regulation of the purchase of sexual services, which compared the Swedish (abolitionist) with the Dutch (regulative) approach, showed that neither solved the problem of THB, while both had (albeit different) negative side effects (Working Group on the Legal Regulation of the Purchase of Sexual Services, 2004

[English abstract]). It would be more fruitful to join forces to tackle THB, the issue on which international agreement has already been achieved in drawing up the UN Trafficking Protocol, and which involves coercion, forced labour or the exploitation of minors, not only in the sex industry, but elsewhere.

With regard to exploitation in other economic sectors, the partly ideological and moral debate on prostitution described above does not play a role. However, there are other issues involved, as we shall see in the following sections.

Do 'other forms of exploitation' occur in the Netherlands?

The main reason for the new trafficking Article in the Dutch Penal Code (Article 273a)[5] was to amend national law in line with international treaties, such as the UN Trafficking Protocol and the EU Framework Decision on combating trafficking in human beings,[6] rather than from a sense of urgency based on actual (local) experiences with 'other forms of exploitation'. There is in fact limited insight into what might be going on in this respect, but on the basis of information from neighbouring countries, we at BNRM suspected that 'other forms of exploitation' occur in the Netherlands too.

Experiences in neighbouring countries

A report from the Belgian Centre for Equal Opportunities and the Fight against Racism (1998), for example, goes into exploitation of foreign football players and of domestic servants in diplomats' families. From the annual reports of this Centre we know furthermore that, for some time now, a substantial proportion of all trafficking victims in Belgium are victims of exploitation outside the sex industry. Figures mentioned range from 25 per cent to 50 per cent (Centrum voor Gelijkheid van Kansen en Racismebestrijding, 1999; 2000; 2002). High percentages, but the reports also mention definition problems: when is something trafficking, when is it moonlighting or smuggling?

A report from a French parliamentary commission (2001) deals with exploitative employment of foreign workers in clandestine confection and leather workshops and in restaurants, forced begging by minors and domestic slavery.

The findings in these reports were among the reasons for BNRM to prompt the Dutch government to expedite the new THB law and to study the occurrence of 'other forms of exploitation' in the Netherlands (Dutch National Rapporteur, 2002).

Since then, more publications have come out, indicating situations of labour exploitation in other Western European countries. Anderson and Rogaly (2005), for example, who studied forced labour in the UK, found abuses in a wide range of labour situations, such as cheap takeaways, expensive restaurants, mushroom picking, bakeries, private homes, fishing vessels, all-night stores, the food managing and packaging industry, construction, (contract) cleaning and (residential) care. In a 2005 ILO study on trafficking for labour and sexual exploitation in Germany, malpractices were observed in domestic services, construction, the hotels and catering industry (abuse of seasonal workers), the fun fair/entertainment sector, the international transport business and the distribution of advertisements (Cyrus, 2005).

Research in the Netherlands

A literature review that was indeed commissioned, as recommended by BNRM, and carried out by Van der Leun and Vervoorn (2004), shows that there is a lot of illegal employment in the Netherlands and that illegal employment is on the increase. Although the authors found little tangible evidence for slavery-like situations, they considered the risk of excesses to be growing, because of the involvement of *mala fide* employment agencies – which reduces the distance between criminal circuit and undocumented worker – and because of a seemingly growing number of illegal workers in private homes. According to Bucquoye *et al.* (2003), in Europe the demand for services in private homes will grow, due to changing family structures, limited availability of affordable day care for children and because of the ageing population. Although illegal domestic workers who live with the families that employ them may be relatively well protected from discovery of their illegal status by the authorities (Willemsen, 2005), the limited visibility, social isolation and multiple dependency that can easily develop in such a situation make these workers especially vulnerable to exploitation.

Van der Leun and Vervoorn concluded that excesses can be found if you look for them. Paraphrasing this conclusion, we are convinced you will *not* see them if you do *not* look for them. After all, the same goes for exploitation in the sex industry.

Building on the outcome of the aforementioned literature study, BNRM decided to extend the knowledge about 'other forms of exploitation' in the Netherlands by collecting recent[7] casuistry on the topic. Starting at the beginning of 2005, very short questionnaires were sent to a large number of possible respondents (social workers, legal advisers/ lawyers, police, labour inspectors and pressure/support groups for specific minorities). Because of the novelty of the subject, a rather broad working definition of 'other forms of exploitation' was used: flagrant wrongs in a labour situation outside the sex industry, in which a victim is forced to work. Some of the many possible indicators mentioned were: force (physical or otherwise), bad working conditions (for example, unreasonable hours, low pay), lack of freedom (for example, being deprived of one's passport) and multiple dependency (for example, debt bondage, or being dependent not only for employment, but also for food, transport or shelter). Respondents who indicate that they encountered possibly exploitative situations, are being interviewed extensively, either by phone or face to face. More organisations (such as branch/ employers' organisations and trade unions) will be approached in the near future.

Preliminary results

So far, we have received a great variety of signals of very bad circumstances and lack of freedom in labour situations. They concern jobs in cleaning, restaurants, factories, meat processing, agriculture, construction and other industries. Victims are most often individuals who reside and/or work in the Netherlands illegally, or who have a dependent status in the form of a permit to reside with a partner.[8] Individuals with illegal or a dependent status, especially those who do not speak a Western European language, are particularly vulnerable, as is apparent in the following examples.

In 2003, the labour inspectorate and the police specialised in illegal migration jointly inspect a Chinese restaurant. They find S., a 23-year-old Chinese waitress working on a false ID. S. works there for a few euros a day, as well as a place to sleep (a room above the restaurant). She is taken to the police station for further questioning, but does not want to make any additional statement. She seems afraid and police officers discover that her body is covered in small scars. Some of the fresh scars on her back are possibly caused by cigarette burns. They suspect that the employer also abuses his illegal waitress privately. However, due to the lack of any incriminating statement, this does not lead to an investigation.

In 2003 L., well educated, 30 and pregnant, migrates to the Netherlands in order to move in with O., whom she has met in her home town in Morocco. She is granted a temporary residence permit on the basis of her relationship. L. has been led to believe that O.'s financial situation is comfortable, but upon arrival L. discovers that he does not have a regular job and the couple shares a small room with two others. Using psychological pressure and violence, O. forces L. to do all the housework and to work in a factory as well. Although the working conditions in the factory are normal, L. becomes a victim of economic exploitation in the sense that she is forced to work and does not have access to her own income: O. spends the money and leaves L. materially neglected. On top of all this, O. abuses L. by videotaping their sexual intercourse without her consent. L. is under the impression that he shows these videos to others, possibly for a fee.[9] Due to the abuse, the workload, the worries and the progressing pregnancy, L. is exhausted. The birth of a son does not change the relationship: O. does not even provide enough food for the baby, while L. has no control of her income. When L. can no longer stand the situation, she takes her child and flees to a women's shelter, where she is offered, among other things, legal assistance to arrange an independent residence permit.

Some of the cases that were reported to BNRM, such as those mentioned above, are undoubtedly examples of THB. Others clearly indicate abuse of the vulnerable position of individuals, but do not constitute situations that can be described as THB, and still others are in between cases. The boundary between illegal employment and exploitation in the sense of THB is not always clear, and exploitation does not only occur in employer–employee relationships, as the next case illustrates.

C., a foreign male (from an EU country), has a (dependent) residence permit on the basis of his marriage to a (Dutch) woman. In 2002 his wife dies and he loses his legal status. C. and his then six-year-old son tramp about for a while, before ending up living in a shed owned by a rack renter. During the procedure for a new residence permit, they do not qualify for public housing. Apart from rent, the rack renter also demands domestic services of his 'tenant', and confiscates his credit card as means of coercion. Eventually, the landlord throws C. and his son out. Shortly thereafter C. gets a new residence permit, and he and his son find suitable housing.

Although we have not yet finished our study, we can conclude that 'other forms of exploitation' in the sense of THB do indeed occur in the Netherlands. Perhaps not on a very large scale, but the cases that have come up so far are not restricted to one or two specific economic areas. Comparable notes were heard at a meeting BNRM organised with the Dutch Ministry of Justice in March 2005, with the aim of informing (possible) partners in the fight against THB of the broadening of the definition, but also to encourage and stimulate them to tackle 'other forms of exploitation' and to talk about responsibilities and task allocation among themselves. Police, special investigation services and social workers attended the meeting. Many say they have encountered exploitation outside the sex industry. At the same time it was obvious that, due to lack of capacity to tackle exploitation *within* the sex industry, not everybody was 'ready to go' as far as tackling 'other forms of exploitation', or taking care of the victims involved. Clearly, not everybody warms easily to the case of undocumented migrants who end up being exploited in a work situation. Similar reluctance was voiced during the final conference of the Network for European Women's Rights, in Birmingham.[10] It seems that a change of attitude is needed.

What needs to be done?

In spite of the reluctance among some, we are of the opinion that 'other forms of exploitation' need to be tackled and that police and social workers, as well as the general public, must be alert to its signals, not only because we will not see it otherwise, but also because those practices have to be stopped, as they can have very serious consequences. This is clearly true in a case involving a Moroccan girl.

> *A., from Morocco, is ten years old when, in 2000, her mother entrusts her to a Moroccan family that lives in the Netherlands. A. is brought into the country illegally. There she lives in a small apartment together with the large family. She has to do all the housework, take care of the children (some of whom are older than she is), and be available 24 hours a day. A. is not being paid, she is being abused, she is not allowed to go out and she does not go to school. After a couple of years she escapes, the police find her on the streets and put her up in a general shelter. From there she moves on to protected living.*

The family not only exploited the girl, but violated several basic rights by not giving her the opportunity to make friends or to play, and by shutting the door to education, thus severely damaging her development.

This girl finally escaped, but only after a long period of abuse. Yet how many victims do not manage that, and how many comparable situations go on unnoticed? The question remains how we stop such practices and how we catch the people profiting from them (for example, recruiters, businesses that use cheap illegal labour, individuals who provide false identity documents, individuals who offer poor accommodation for exorbitant rents, and families that exploit an au pair or domestic worker).

Recognising the victims

It is crucial to recognise the victims, to know which signals to look for and to act on them. In this respect it is worth mentioning that, in the Netherlands, the list of criteria used by the police to recognise victims of exploitation in the sex industry is currently being adapted to be used to recognise victims of 'other forms of exploitation' as well.

A complicating factor is that people in exploitative work situations may not regard themselves as victims, and they can be rather reticent and uncommunicative about their experiences, as is known to be the case with many trafficking victims who end up in the sex industry. The reasons for their reserve are the often illegal residence or working status, which makes them afraid of deportation, should their status become known. The often not so rosy perspective in the country of origin makes deportation an unappealing alternative, especially when there are debts to be paid. Furthermore, victims of 'other forms of exploitation' may have to deal with threats, fear of repercussions, and with a sense of shame about what has happened to them, and about the fact that they failed abroad. These feelings are apparent in some of the interviews in a recent Dutch study on the possibilities of returning to the country of origin after alien detention.[11] One respondent states: 'The longer I stay in Europe, the more the home front expects from me. We want to return to our country of origin one day, but not empty handed. I would be burning with shame and rather die than go back empty handed'. Another respondent says: 'How can I justify the fact that I spent 15 years in Europe without returning with something?' And a third: 'I really cannot turn up empty handed' (van Kalmthout *et al.*, 2005: 11, 56, 92). Exactly because the victims of exploitation may be unwilling to bring their case forward, Anderson and Rogaly (2005) recommend basing investigations into forced labour situations – to the extent that is possible – on intelligence-led investigations, taking account of complaints from trade unions and other agencies, instead of relying on the testimony of victims. In the Netherlands, 'intelligence-led investigations' is a popular topic, and an approach that is being tested at the moment, but the expectation of many is that the testimonies of victims will still play a decisive role in successful prosecutions of perpetrators.

An extra complication in recognising the victims is that part of the exploitation takes place in hidden sectors, such as the informal economy and behind private family doors (as was the case with the Moroccan girl above), while these families are sometimes protected by diplomatic immunity. Still, in cases that take place in private homes, somebody (relatives, friends, neighbours) must have an idea of what is going on. So how do we get them to act?

Public information and education campaign

The question is, are the signs of exploitation being recognised, is it known that exploitative conduct can be punishable as THB, and where can one report abuses? A public information and education campaign by the government is recommended to raise awareness of the phenomenon. In the first report BNRM made such an appeal to the Dutch government with respect to exploitation within the sex industry. The fact that in the Netherlands sexual services from consenting adults can be bought freely and without breaking any law does not absolve clients from the responsibility of buying such services only in the regulated sector, or from the responsibility to be vigilant even then. At the moment, an information and education campaign targeting (possible) clients of the sex industry is in preparation.

Such a campaign regarding THB for exploitation outside the sex industry is also needed. This is in fact what the UN Commission on the Status of Women calls for in her resolution on *Eliminating Demand for Trafficked Women and Girls for All Forms of Exploitation*: 'to raise public awareness of the issue of trafficking in persons'.[12] It is important to state that exploitation can and will not be tolerated in our society. It has to be prevented where possible, and when it does occur, it must be identified and dealt with.

Concluding remarks

We plead for attention to trafficking for 'other forms of exploitation', without slackening in our efforts to tackle exploitation in the sex industry. The cases presented in this chapter illustrate that a variety of factors can lead to a situation in which a victim – male or female, adult or minor – provides work or services under the threat of some sort of penalty, be it physical harm, threats to denounce his or her illegal status to the authorities, or other forms of abuse or intimidation. In other words: it is not necessary for a victim to be held in captivity in order to speak of grossly exploitative work situations. While extremely poor or hazardous working conditions do not constitute exploitation as such in the sense of THB, in combination with restriction of the victim's personal freedom, for instance due to debt bondage, they can represent a severe violation of human rights. A recent ruling of the European Court of Human Rights[13] shows that states that signed the Universal Declaration of Human Rights do have the obligation to protect inhabitants from being held in slavery or servitude. In line with earlier jurisprudence, the Court judged that states, by virtue of Article 1 of the Universal Declaration of Human Rights, are under an obligation to take measures in their national laws that offer concrete and effective protection against violation of the rights warranted in Article 4 of that Declaration[14] to anyone in their jurisdiction. This applies not only to violations that result from acts by a state or state bodies, but also to violations inflicted by private individuals.

Still, the concept of exploitation in work situations outside the sex industry is not clear. In the Netherlands as well as in many other countries we do not know the exact dividing line between illegal employment and trafficking for exploitation outside the sex industry. In due course, additional jurisprudence (national and supra-national) will we hope bring more clarity. However, we do not have to wait for that. As BNRM recommended in its third report on THB, we need to strive for agreement on the scope of the term 'other forms of exploitation' on an international, or at any rate European, level. This may give prosecutors and judges a handle on future cases, as well as facilitate international cooperation in (police investigations of, and in possible extraditions in) trafficking cases.

In conclusion, a remark about the people who are at stake: the victims. In the current political climate, undocumented migrants can expect little compassion in the Netherlands or in the rest of Europe. Great efforts are made to tackle illegality. In the Netherlands, for example, we have a governmental memorandum on undocumented migrants (Illegalennota, 2004), as well as a steering group on the approach of illegality, and a nationwide network of intervention teams that tackles moonlighting, social security and tax fraud, as well as employment of undocumented migrants. In such a repressive climate, it is crucial that the authorities involved recognise, regard and treat victims of THB first and foremost as victims of a crime, including when the exploitation took place outside the sex industry. This approach is legitimised, at least on paper: Illegalennota concerns the approach of illegality as well as the tackling of exploitation of undocumented migrants and states that special attention should be paid to victims of trafficking among people who are being encountered without a (valid) residence permit. In this respect it is also worth mentioning that, in the Netherlands, the so-called B9 regulation, which offers alien victims of THB a temporary residence permit for the duration of any criminal investigation and prosecution (similar provisions exist in Belgium and Germany) now also applies to victims who were exploited outside the sex industry. They too are entitled to shelter, medical care and legal aid. However, what these arrangements will look like in practice remains to be seen since most currently existing services are tailored to the needs of females who fall victim to exploitation in the sex industry. For instance, the shelters currently used to accommodate victims (mostly shelters for battered women) may be adequate for female victims of domestic slavery, but they are not suited for males who have been exploited in, for example, restaurants or agriculture.

Notes

1. The Protocol to Prevent, Suppress and Punish Trafficking in Persons, especially Women and Children, which is linked to the UN Convention against Transnational Organised Crime and came into effect in December 2003.
2. The Rapporteur holds an independent position. Various methods are used to collect information for the reports, including literature study, the studying of laws, treaties and jurisprudence, interviews with key figures, organising meetings, participation at symposia, conferences and expert meetings and secondary analysis of information collected by others. The authors of this chapter both work for BNRM.
3. This UN Protocol against the Smuggling of Migrants, by Land, Sea or Air came into force in January 2004.
4. At a presentation of the risks of the Swedish policy that criminalises customers of sexual services, at the meeting *Weven met een zijden draadje*, Rotterdam, 20 November 2003.
5. Punishable under this Article are certain activities (recruiting, transporting, accommodating someone), using specific means (force, violence, deception, misuse of a vulnrable position) with the intention to exploit that person (in the sex industry, forced labour, or slavery-like practices), profiting (economically) from sexual acts of minors, and certain activities aimed at removal of healthy organs for transplantation.
6. The purpose of this EU Framework decision is to bring the member states more in line as far as legislation and regulations with regard to THB are concerned. The Framework decision came into force in August 2002.
7. As from 2000.
8. From cases not described in this contribution, another group at risk appears to be less able, unassertive women who face all kinds of social and psychological problems.
9. In cases of labour exploitation within private homes, sexual abuse or exploitation are often involved as well.
10. The conference took place on 30 June-1 July 2005, and was organised by the Centre for the Study of Global Ethics of the University of Birmingham (for reports see www.newr.bham.ac.uk).

11. These findings are relevant because a common feature among most irregular migrants in alien detention and victims of THB is that they went abroad to improve their (economic) situation. Besides, although not all undocumented foreigners who end up in alien detention have experienced exploitative labour, we know that some have.
12. March 2005.
13. It concerns the case of Siliadin against France (decree 73316/01, Strassbourg, 26 July 2005).
14. No one shall be held in slavery or servitude; slavery and the slave trade shall be prohibited in all their forms.

References

Agustín, L. M. (2001) 'Sex Workers and Violence against Women: Utopic Visions or Battle of the Sexes?' *Development, Society for International Development*, 44(3).
Anderson, B. and Rogaly, B. (2005) *Forced Labour and Migration to the UK*, Londen: Trade Union Congress.
Boonen, K. (2000) 'Prostitutie: legaliseren of strafbaar stellen? Een crimineel-politiek-filosofische beschouwing', in R. Haveman, Th.A. de Roos, A.L.J. v. Strien and F.P. Ölçer (eds.), *Seks, zeden en strafrecht*, Deventer: Gouda Quint, pp. 31–55.
Bucquoye, A., Cruysberghs, W. and Vermeulen, G. (2003) *Internationaal huispersoneel in België. Een exploratief-kwalitatief onderzoek*, Brussel: Koning Boudewijnstichting.
Butcher, K. (2003) 'Confusion between Prostitution and Sex Trafficking', *The Lancet*, 361: 1983.
Centrum voor Gelijkheid van Kansen en Racismebestrijding (1999) *Strijd tegen de mensenhandel – Tussen beleid en middelen: de diepe kloof? Jaarverslag 1999*, Brussel: Federale Voorlichtingsdienst.
Centrum voor Gelijkheid van Kansen en Racismebestrijding (2000) *Strijd tegen de mensenhandel – Beeldvorming van de mensenhandel en analyse van de rechtspraak. Jaarverslag 2000*, Brussel: Federale Voorlichtingsdienst.
Centrum voor Gelijkheid van Kansen en Racismebestrijding (2002) *Strijd tegen mensenhandel – Pleidooi voor een integrale benadering. Analyse wetgeving en rechtspraak. Jaarverslag 2002*, Brussel: CGKR.
Cyrus, N. (2005) *Trafficking for Labour and Sexual Exploitation in Germany*, Geneva: International Labour Organisation
Dutch National Rapporteur (2002) *Trafficking in Human Beings – First Report of the Dutch National Rapporteur*, The Hague: Dutch Rapporteur on Trafficking in Human Beings.
Dutch National Rapporteur (2005) *Trafficking in Human Beings – Third Report of the Dutch National Rapporteur*, The Hague: Dutch Rapporteur on Trafficking in Human Beings.
Gülçür, L. and Ilkkaracan, P (2002) 'The "Natasha" Experience: Migrant Sex Workers from the Former Soviet Union and Eastern Europe in Turkey', *Women's Studies International Forum*, 25(4): 411–21.
Haveman, R. (1998). *Voorwaarden voor strafbaarstelling van vrouwenhandel*, Leiden: Willem Pompe Instituut.

Illegalennota (2004) *Aanvullende maatregelen voor het tegengaan van illegaliteit en de aanpak van uitbuiters in Nederland*, Den Haag: Ministerie van Justitie.

International Labour Organisation (2005) *Human Trafficking and Forced Labour Exploitation. Guidance for Legislation and Law Enforcement*, Geneva: ILO.

Loff, B., Overs, C. and Longo, P. (2003) 'Can Health Programmes Lead to Mistreatment of Sexworkers?' *The Lancet*, 361: 1982–3.

Shelley, L. (2003) 'The Trade in People in and from the Former Soviet Union', *Crime, Law and Social Change*, 40: 239–41.

Sörensen, P. (2003) *New Perspectives and Policies on Protection of Victims*, Antwerp: P. Sörensen.

Van Kalmthout, A. M. (2005) *Terugkeermogelijkheden van vreemdelingen in vreemdelingenbewaring. Deel 3 – Het vergeten gelaat van de vreemdeling*, Nijmegen: Wolf Legal Publishers.

Van der Leun, J. P. and Vervoorn, L. (2004) *Slavernij-achtige uitbuiting in Nederland. Een inventariserende literatuurstudie in het kader van de uitbreiding van de strafbaarstelling van mensenhandel*, Den Haag: Boom Juridische Uitgevers.

Verhoeven, M. (2003) *'Me libere'. Een nuancering van het begrip vrouwenhandel*. Utrecht: Universiteit van Utrecht.

Willemsen, E. (2005) *Human Trafficking for Domestic Labour. A Study of the Situation in the United Kingdom, Spain and Belgium*, Amsterdam: University of Amsterdam.

Working Group on the Legal Regulation of the Purchase of Sexual Services (2004) *Purchasing Sexual Services in Sweden and the Netherlands. Legal Regulation and Experiences. A Report by a Working Group on the Legal Regulation of the Purchase of Sexual Services*, Norway: Ministry of Justice and the Police.

Index